A
History of the
Town of
Livingston, Alabama

A History
of the Town of
Livingston, Alabama

by Robert D. Spratt, M. D.

edited by Nathaniel Reed

Livingston Press
The University of West Alabama

ISBN 0-942979-40-0, paperback
ISBN 0-942979-39-7, library edition

Library of Congress Cataloguing in Publication # 96-80443

Copyright © 1997 by

Printed on acid-free paper.
Revised edition

Manufactured in the United States of America.

Text Layout and Design by Joe Taylor
Indexing by Beth Grant
Typing and proofreading by Beth Grant, Lee Holland-Moore, Margaret McGough

*The opinions set forth in this work are not necessarily those of
The University of West Alabama or its Board of Trustees.*

**This book has been made possible through a generous grant from
The Sumter County Historical Society.**

To obtain a complete list of our books, please contact:

**Livingston Press
Station 22
The University of West Alabama
Livingston, AL 35470**

Table of Contents

Introduction

In 1995, the Publications Committee and the Board of Directors of the Sumter County Historical Society authorized the republication of Robert D. Spratt's *A History of the Town of Livingston, Alabama*. Demand for the work still existed although all copies of the 1974 printing had been distributed and it had been essentially out of print for several years. Further, the Committee recommended that the *History* be edited before reprinting to make it more "readable." This present edition is the result of those directives.

It was in the 1920's, after his retirement from the United States Public Health Service, that Dr. Spratt put together his volume on the history of Livingston. He apparently worked on it a number of years and then, in 1928, presented a typescript copy to the Livingston Public Library. Later he added to this copy a section labeled "Corrections, Additions, Etc.," which obviously contained information that came to his attention after he had completed the original book. In a few instances, also, he seems to have taken this copy and typed in some later updates within the text, and over the years he also penciled in numerous marginal notes in the Library copy. These added materials rarely correct facts in the original but, instead, usually supplement the information in the original typescript, such as adding full names to replace initials, clarifying a family relationship, or adding a date previously unknown.

At some point, this Library copy was bound in leather, and it was only in this format—and primarily by this one copy—that the public had access to the Spratt *History* until 1974, when the Sumter County Historical Society, under the leadership of Publishing Committee Chair Marcus McConnell, published the work by offset printing. This publication was meticulously faithful to the Library typescript, following it carefully, not only in wording but also in such mechanical matters as paragraphing, abbreviation, punctuation, etc. It reproduced in full Spratt's "Corrections, Additions, Etc.," and it also included many of the marginal annotations. The only new materials were the "Foreword" written by McConnell and a letter relating to the Horn family which the Historical Society had recently received from a Ralph Stilwell of Los Angeles.

With the decision in 1995 to republish the work and to make it more accessible to the general reader of the 1990's, the question arose: What could legitimately be done to achieve this objective? An answer evolved over a period of time as I worked through the text and as I sought the advice of members of the Publications Committee, the Director of the Livingston Press of the University of West Alabama, and others.

Initially, several ways to enhance the readability seemed obvious. First, each item in Spratt's "Corrections, Additions, Etc." and in his marginal notations could be worked into the text at the appropriate place. In fact, many of the marginal notations had already been included in the 1974 printing. A second obvious way to enhance readability was to eliminate non-standard abbreviations, especially the abbreviations for proper names. Indeed, the standardization of all mechanical matters—spelling, punctuation, capitalization, and such—could improve the readability. These changes were easily agreed upon, but going beyond these obvious decisions was more complicated.

The reader should understand that Robert D. Spratt was by profession a physician, not a writer, and his prose is that of an amateur—direct and simple with few qualifying clauses or other complexities of syntax. Since I felt it important to retain a sense of the original author's voice insofar as possible, I early determined not to rewrite Dr. Spratt's sentences except when overriding considerations compelled a new wording. For example, the insertion into the text of material he had added later often required some rewording of sentences. A few sentences have been rewritten to ensure clarity, as in the section on "The Streets" in Chapter 4. (This section has also been moved from an earlier location to a position where it is more relevant to the discussion of the various buildings.) In other instances, two or more extremely short sentences have been combined. Even so, in all these situations, I have tried to keep as much of the original language as possible, and elsewhere I have generally retained Spratt's words, including his use of terms and constructions peculiar to the region.

On the other hand, I agreed with the suggestion of Dr. Joe Taylor, Director of Livingston Press, that readability would be enhanced by combining many of the short paragraphs which characterize the original typescript and eliminating many of Spratt's parentheses, which seemed to serve no purpose except to interrupt the flow of the text. I had originally planned to use parentheses to identify material which had been inserted after the original date of 1928, but this proved too cumbersome and seemed only to impede the reader's progress.

Because of the unique plan of the book—presenting the history of the town through the buildings on each street—the Publications Committee suggested that some of the buildings be identified in relation to the present town so that the contemporary reader could more easily locate the places referred to. This I have done occasionally—often enough, I hope, to serve this purpose. This added information is easily distinguishable because it is in brackets.

Several items, such as the letter received in 1974 relating to the Horn family, have been placed at the back as appendices, since they, while relevant, seemed only to interrupt the narrative when included within the text. A brief note regarding each appendix has been inserted, however, at the appropriate point in the text. In addition, the book has been given formal chapter headings, following the original divisions provided by the author, and a Table of Contents and an Index have been included to enhance accessibility.

The Publications Committee had a further concern that was somewhat complex. This work was originally written in the 1920's by a white professional man in a Black Belt county of Alabama, and it inevitably reflects the ethnic bias of that milieu. Although Dr. Spratt frequently expressed respect and admiration for individual African-Americans, his original book, nevertheless, contained a few instances of anecdotes, generalizations, and language which African-Americans today, as well as most whites, would consider offensive.

The Committee felt that such references should have no place in an edition whose main purpose was to provide a readable volume for the general public. For this reason, a few passages perceived as offensive in this way have been removed, and occasionally in other instances, language has been emended. I should point out, however, that a conscious decision was made to retain the two terms the author uses almost always to refer to African-Americans—*Negroes* and *Colored People*. Although one or both of these might be considered "politically incorrect" by some persons in the 1990's, they were the polite terms in the usage of both White and Black in the 1920's and, indeed, are still widely accepted today. In the same way, I have retained the term *Indians* in reference to Native Americans.

Basically, the text for this edition is that of the 1974 printing—with the changes explained above—but I have collated it with the typescript copy in the Ruby Pickens Tartt Library. As a result, I was able to correct several errors in the 1974 edition and, also, to include some additional material from the marginal annotations.

Having explained at length what I have done in trying to achieve a more readable edition of Spratt's *History,* I feel compelled to assure the reader that there are certain things I have *not* done. Foremost, I have not made factual changes in the text or modified in any way the opinions expressed by the author, except within the guidelines stated above. Further, except for the items in brackets—mostly the notes correlating 1928 locations with contemporary sites—I have added no material that is not in the Library copy.

I hope the general reader will find this edition of Spratt's *History* readable. At the same time, I believe that, with the addition of a comprehensive index, it will be a useful source for the historian and the genealogist. We must note, however, that this new version *cannot* replace the 1974 edition. By reproducing Dr. Spratt's original text verbatim, that edition still constitutes an important historical and sociological document.

It remains for me to thank the many people who have helped to make this volume possible. These include Dr. Richard Holland, President, and the Board of Directors of the Sumter County Historical Society, for providing funds; my fellow members on the Publications Committee—Dr. David Taylor (Chair), J.K. Arrington, Tina Jones, and Thomas F. Seale—for supplying advice and encouragement; Dr. Joe Taylor, Director of the Livingston Press, and the staff members and volunteers—Lee Holland-Moore, Beth Grant and Margaret

McGough—for showing such patience as we worked through several versions and for producing the computer-generated index; and Dr. Don Hines and other University of West Alabama officials, for allowing facilities and personnel to be used in the production of this book. To David Taylor, chair, special gratitude is due, also, for supervising the illustrations. In addition, I must thank those other persons whom I consulted and whose input was useful in one way or another. Among these—probably along with others whom I cannot recall at the moment—were Margie Hutcheson, Mary Jones, Billye McElroy, Flora Ormond, Louis Smith, Mary Tartt, Alice Taylor, B.B. Williamson and, of course, the late Marcus McConnell. For the errors and shortcomings, however, full blame must fall on me—and on Dr. Spratt.

Nathaniel Reed

A
History of the
Town of
Livingston, Alabama

FOREWORD

The Sumter County Historical Society is grateful to the family of the late Robert D. Spratt, M.D., for granting it the privilege of printing and publishing his *History Of Livingston, Alabama.* The Society undertook this project to memorialize the late Robert D. Spratt—doctor, scholar, historian, and humanitarian—and to commemorate the 200th anniversary of the founding of this Nation by making available to the public this historic work.

The author of this history, Robert D. Spratt, was the eldest son of J.P. Spratt and Mattie Beggs Spratt. He was born in Livingston, Alabama, in 1879 and died here in 1950. Most of his long and useful life was spent in and around the town of Livingston. He did his undergraduate work at the University of Alabama, where he received his A.B. degree, and he received his M.D. from Tulane University. Upon graduation from medical school, Dr. Spratt entered the United States Public Health Service and served for a number of years. One of his longest stations was at Ellis Island, New York City, where he examined immigrants entering the port there.

Upon retirement from the U.S. Public Health Service, he returned to Livingston, where he took up life as a country gentleman and engaged in the practice of medicine. He was a skilled and learned practitioner who enjoyed an enviable reputation in his chosen field. He had a large charitable practice and was known for his generosity and humanitarian endeavors. Dr. Spratt was a man of noble character and versatile nature. He was an accomplished musician and was endowed with a keen and searching intellect. He had many fields of interest, one of the chief of which was the study of Indians, their habits and customs. He was an authority on this and other subjects of local interest.

He had a keen wit and was an entertaining and enlightening conversationalist. He was kind, generous and charitable, but had a fiery temper which, though well-governed, on occasion was known to erupt with devastating fury.

At the outbreak of World War II, although a man of advanced years, Dr. Spratt volunteered his services to the County and became the County Health Officer. He served in this capacity throughout the war period in order that younger men might be available for the defense of their country.

On the following pages is a history of the town of Livingston as written by Dr. Spratt and put in the Livingston Public Library in [1928]. It is here published in its original form so that the reader may perceive and appreciate the unique style of the author. There are certain additions which have been added to the book as per the author's request at the end of the book. No change has been made in the additions which have been made, but as the reader peruses the book, where he notes an asterisk, if he will turn to pages 181-195, he will find a reference and additional data on the subject at hand. [In this edition, these materials have been incorporated in the text.]

The manner in which the story unfolds is most unique in that Dr. Spratt takes up the houses which stood in the town of Livingston and tells of the

1

families who occupied them throughout the years. He also takes up the farms and tracts of land lying adjacent to the town and tells of the families who occupied these areas. The story as told contains a vast store of information about the town, its happenings and its people.

At this date, some forty-five years since the typed copy of this work was placed in the Livingston Public Library and one hundred forty-four years since the town was settled, many of the homes and buildings described in the work have been destroyed by fire, torn down, or removed, but posterity will be indebted to Dr. Spratt for this labor of love which he performed in putting down what he knew and what he could learn of the people of the town where his family had lived for many years. Some think he lived in the Golden Era of our town; others do not think the Golden Era has yet been reached; but, nonetheless, this work which Dr. Spratt has left for those with interest in what has gone before will stand as a beacon light honoring his memory and showing the way for lesser lights to follow.

Marcus E. McConnell, Jr., Chairman
Sumter County Historical Society Publishing Committee
July, 1974

Chapter 1

Indians, Pioneers, and the Development of a West Alabama Town

Indians

So far as the white man is concerned, the history of this region begins with the signing of the Treaty of Dancing Rabbit Creek on September 27, 1830. Up to that time, what is now Sumter County, Alabama, was a part of the land belonging to the Choctaw Nation of Indians. How long these Indians had lived here and owned these lands is something no one knows.

A brief mention of these people may not be out of place here. The Choctaw are classed as belonging to the Choctaw group of the southern branch of the great Muskhogean family. They were much the largest tribe of this group but were not so warlike as the Chickasaw, who also belong to the Choctaw group and spoke practically the same language.

The Choctaw seem to have been the upholders of the older culture once spread over the southern country, as opposed to the Creeks, who had formed their confederacy and introduced many changes. The Choctaws were numerous, for Indians, and were able to contend with the Creeks on equal terms. In early days the Choctaw controlled most of the country lying between the Mississippi and the watershed between the Alabama and Tombigbee Rivers. This extended from the Chickasaw country on the north to the Gulf on the south. On account of boundary disputes they had bloody wars with the Creeks, but, as a rule, they were not aggressive people. They were strong and enduring and loved their homeland so that they would dare any danger in its defense.

The better class Choctaw and Chickasaw seem to have had a common tradition of an origin in the far west where they were beset by more powerful enemies. They left, taking along the bones of their ancestors, and were guided by a sacred pole that leaned in the direction they were to journey. The pole ceased to lean in what is now Winston County, Mississippi. They built a great mound over the ancestral bones and remained in that region.

According to the *Hand Book of American Indians*, the Choctaw, as a race, are of medium height and are a trifle thick-set. They are active and fond of out-of-door games.

They were allies of the French, and some of the early English traders did not like them, but as a general thing, their relations with the white races have been pleasant. They were and still are inclined to be friendly, hospitable and honest. In warfare they are noted for their ability to conceal their trails in an enemy country and for the skill with which they mimicked the calls of birds, etc. They had many conflicts with the Creeks and with trans-Mississippi tribes. In the time of our Creek War they gave active aid to the white settlers.

Most of these people went to what is now the state of Oklahoma (Oka, *people*; Humma, *red*). A few remained near the sacred mound, and there are now about fifteen hundred living in the State of Mississippi.

They were divided into three Ulhti, or Fire Council Districts: the Western, the Northeastern, and the Southeastern. Each of these had a head chief with his corps of assistants.

Every person in the whole Nation belonged to one or the other of the two great Ikea, or "Marriage Clans"—a man of one clan had to choose his wife from the other clan.

One reason that they so successfully avoided a war with the white men seems to be that their head chiefs were wise and sensible men.

In the orthography ordinarily used among these people, *V* is used to represent a sound like *u* in cup. Thus, Vpa, *to eat,* pronounced as Up-pah.

Hl is the aspirated *l.* (As in Po-hlo-mo-li)

Ai is pronounced *i* in fine

I is pronounced *ee* in seen

E is pronounced *a* in fate

A, i, o and *u* may be strongly nasalized. When this is to be indicated, a line is made under the vowel. Thus: Paki, *grape,* pronounced Pong-kee.

Noted Men among the Choctaw were:

Puckshennubbee (Apakshvnvoi—*He Strives To Kill*) and his successors, Robert Cole and Greenwood Leflore, all of them at various times Head Men of the Western District.

Homoastubbee (Hummvchitvbi—*He Reddens and Kills*) and his son Amoshulitvbi (*He Has Courage and Kills*), heads of the Northeastern District. The noted "Red Shoes" was a Northeastern District head Chief of an earlier day. "Little Leader" of Narkeeta was a noted sub-chief of this district. The latter opposed the Treaty of Dancing Rabbit Creek and refused to go west. He died at Narkeeta in 1847.

Pushimataha (Apushi im ataha, or vihtaha—*Sapling Prepared for Them*), Nitakechi (*Early Part of the Day*), and Oklahoma (*Red People*) were noted head men of the Southeastern District.

Dancing Rabbit Creek is in the southwestern part of Noxubee County, Mississippi. It is formed from the junction of Big Rabbit and Little Rabbit, and the old treaty ground now marked by a monument lies between them.

The following names of watercourses, etc., in Sumter County are of Choctaw origin.

Common Spelling	Choctaw	Meaning
Alamucha	*Aluma asha*	"Hiding places are there"
Bodka	*Hopvtka*	"Wide places noted for overflows"

4

Coatopa	*Koi hotupa*	"Wounded panther"
Chikki ansse	*Sheki a nusi*	"Buzzard roost"
(-ance is a misprint)		
Cotohaga	*Kvti a hika*	"Honey locust stands there"
Fenacha	*Feni asha*	"Squirrel place"
Hallalla	*Halonlvbi (Hllonlawi)*	"Bullfrog
Hitopsiluka	*A tanchi chilukka*	"Cornshelling place"
Holeeta	*Holihta*	"Fort, fence, pen"
Kinterbish	*Kinta ibish*	"Beaver nose"
Looksookolo	*Lukchuk kvllo*	"Tenacious mud"
Miyuka	*Maiyuka*	"Everywhere the same" (crooked)
Noxubee	*Naksobi*	"A tangy smell," not necessarily a bad odor which would be *Kosoma* or *Shua*. I venture to say that a weedy odor is responsible for the name.
Panola	*Ponola*	"Cotton"
Ponca bayou	*Paki abaiya*	"Grapes (summer grapes) along side of it"
Ponti	*Panti*	"Cattails"
Quilby	*Koi ai vlbi*	"Panther killed there"
Saktaloosa	*Sakti lusa*	"Black Bluff"
Sanhouchie	*Issi anusi*	"Deer sleep there"
Sucarnatchie	*Suko i hvcha*	"Muscadines, their river"
Soctum	*Sakti humma*	"Red Bank"
Shumulla	*Shumbvla*	"Cottonwood"
Tallayhaly	*Tvli hieli*	"Standing rocks"
Teoc	*Tiac*	"Pine tree"
Timmilichi	*Tvmolichi*	"He causes to scatter"
Tifalilli	*Iti fvlla illi*	"Dead scaly bark tree"
Tombigbee	*Itombi ikbi*	"Box maker"
Toomsuba	*Tusubi*	"Blue hawk"

Some of the meanings have to be partly guessed at, and some of the names have been so hashed up in spelling, etc., that not even a guess would be worthwhile.

There were ancient river crossings at Black Bluff, at Epes, and at Moscow. The main Indian settlements in Sumter County were along Quilby, Bodka, and Factory Creeks.

Some eminent scholars have derived the name of our State, ALABAMA, from the Choctaw language. It is well known that a tribe of Alabama Indians once lived near the present Montgomery, but what the name of this tribe really meant has been a matter of dispute. Frequently the name that one tribe gave another became the name by which this tribe has gone down in the white man's writings. For instance, the Catawbas of the Carolinas called themselves *Iswa,* but we know them as Catawbas, derived from the Choctaw word *Katapa,* meaning *divided.* Some authorities, including the late H.S. Halbert and the Reverend Allen Wright (the latter was a Choctaw Indian), decided that Alabama was derived from the Choctaw words, *ulba vmo,* meaning in that language *vegetation gatherers.*

Development of a Town

Alabama was a territory in 1817 and became a State in 1819. When more land was added by the Treaty of Dancing Rabbit Creek in 1830, one of the new counties so obtained was named Sumter for General Thomas Sumter of South Carolina, known in the War of the Revolution as the "Gamecock." The boundaries of this new county were determined in 1832.

A lawyer of Philadelphia, Mississippi, a Mr. Odis Moore, recently showed me a list of the white people who lived in this region before the Treaty of Dancing Rabbit and has promised to send me a copy. These people were here by consent of the Choctaw, but were commonly known as "squatters." One of them, named Jesse Cooper, was living on what is now the site of Livingston. There were also other people named Cooper living near here at the time—Captain John among others.

Some white settlers pushed in before the Indians left, but most of them came later. These settlers were mainly from North Carolina. Some were from South Carolina, some were from Georgia, some were from Tennessee, some were from Virginia and there was a sprinkling of Northerners. Drinking water was scarce in this region, and some families settled about a spring located near the present residence of W.S. Nichols in Livingston. This spring is still used, and the street running by it is known as Spring Street.

Act of Congress of May 24, 1824, granted each county a quarter-section of land for the establishment of seats of justice. So, in 1833, a commission was appointed to organize Sumter County and select a county seat. These men were William Anderson, John C. Whitsett, Andrew Ramsay, Charles J. Puckett, William O. Winston, Warham Easley, and Edward B. Colgin. After much debate they selected the northeast quarter of Section 33, Township 19, Range 2 West for the county seat and named it Livingston in honor of Edward Livingston, a prominent American jurist and statesman of that day. The first county officers were W.B. Anderson, Judge; Daniel Womack, Clerk; George W. Harper, Sheriff; and A.G. Anderson, Tax Collector.

Of the organizers, John C. Whitsett is mentioned in Garrett's *Public Men of Alabama.* He was one of the first settlers of Gainesville. Charles J. Puckett is said to have been a doctor who lived at old Payneville. Andrew Ramsay was an uncle of the late J. Reid Ramsay. Warham Easley had a store in

Livingston and lived east of town on Cedar Creek. Until recent times there were people of the name of Colgin in Gainesville. William O. Winston was a brother of Augustus Winston and of Captain James M. Winston. He was the father of the late Charles Winston of Bodka.

Thomas Sumter, for whom Sumter County, Alabama, was named, was a native of Virginia who moved to South Carolina. He was a colonial brigadier general and a member of the State Convention, the Congress, and the Senate. He died in 1832, aged 97. He was known as the "Gamecock" of the Revolution.

Edward Livingston was of the noted New York family of Livingston, said to be descended from that Sir Alexander DeLivingston who was one of the guardians of the young King James II of Scotland. Edward graduated at what is now Princeton and entered the practice of law and soon went to Congress. He was intimately associated with Aaron Burr, Alexander Hamilton, James Kent, James Monroe, and various other noted men of the time. In 1804 he removed to Louisiana and had an honorable career in that state. Among other things, he simplified the extremely complicated legal code of Louisiana. He became a congressman from Louisiana and then went to the U.S. Senate. Jackson made him Secretary of State and then Minister to France. He was born at Clermont in New York State on May 26, 1764, and died in New York State on May 23, 1836. It is said that he was a large-hearted and scholarly jurist, and about the only modern improvements not provided for in his code are juvenile courts, indeterminate sentences and paroles.

In 1834 a commission was appointed to survey, lay off and sell lots in the town of Livingston. (The first surveyor's map and certificate of which we can find any record is that of Wilson G. Myers of 1839 when Price Williams was Clerk). Those appointed for this service were John Horn, Warham Easley, John P. McIntosh, Jefferson C. McAlpine, John C. Whitsett, A.B. Thomas, Benjamin F. Bullock, William Anderson, and James Savage.

John Horn was a great uncle of John L. and Alex G. Horn of the present day. He lived near what is still called Horn's Bridge, and Albert Sledge afterward lived at this same place. John Horn's wife was Asenath Sims. Jacob Horn came from England, originally from Holland. His wife was Millicent Thomas. Among the children of this couple were William, John, Henry, Jere, Harrison, Josiah and several daughters. These lived in North Carolina. William settled in Choctaw County, Alabama, and left descendants. His son, William T. Horn, was the father of Mrs. Joel C. DuBose, Mrs. Fletcher Williams, and Mrs. Florence Haynie. John Horn (1776-1841) was the builder of Horn's Bridge. His wife was Asenath Sims, said to be related to the family of John Sims of Ramsey. Among the children of John Horn and his wife were Mrs. Wade R. Thomas, Sr., Mrs. B.F. Bullock, Mrs. Albert Sledge and the first wife of Harris W. Killian. A number of this family are buried at an old burying ground near Horn's Bridge, a short distance upstream from the bridge. Henry Horn's people left this region after a short stay. Jere Horn and Harrison married Grice sisters, related to the family which once lived at the Grice place in the Emelle region. After Harrison died, Jere, who was a widower, married Harrison's widow. Jere Horn was the father of Alex G. Horn, a noted newspaper man of the early days. Harrison has been mentioned as the father of Isaac W. Horn.

There was a Jacob Horn living at old Gaston who was related to these, but the exact degree of relationship was not known even by the late Isaac W. Horn. Among the children of this Jacob Horn were Robert Horn, John H. Horn, Mrs. Martha Brockway (wife of Dr. Augustus E. Brockway) and another daughter who married first a Wylie and later on Dr. J.N. Gilmore, having a daughter by each marriage (her Gilmore daughter married Robert Blakeney). William Robert Horn served as a Confederate soldier and left two sons, Robert and Walter Horn, who live in Mobile. John H. Horn was serving in the Confederacy and was captured at Island No. 10 and died a prisoner of war in 1862.

Information is wanted by the authorities at the University of Alabama as to one John H. Horn who matriculated in 1864 from Coatopa. I have been so far unable to place him. Mrs. Dr. A.E. Brockway's brother, judging from old letters, etc., that I have seen, was evidently an educated man, but we have it on good authority that he died in 1862. Henry Horn (who married Mary Sims, a sister of Asenath) had a son John, but this man was probably too old to have been at college in 1864; in 1864 the *grandsons* of Henry's brother John were serving as Confederate soldiers. Then we have John the bridge builder, who died in 1841, and John L. Horn who graduated from the University in 1886 or thereabouts. The oldest people asked about the matter in recent years had no recollection of any family of Horns living near Coatopa excepting the family of Isaac W., which has been mentioned. Anyone having any idea as to who this man could have been please make note.

[Appendix A contains a letter relating to the Horn family, which was received just prior to the 1974 publication of this work.]

Of the other members of the surveying commission, Jefferson C. McAlpine was in the State Legislature along in those days and was an early owner of the Planters Hotel. Benjamin F. Bullock is said to have been the grandfather of Frank Bullock. He married a daughter of John Horn of Horn's Bridge. James Savage was a native of Ireland who lived in Livingston and seems to have succeeded Womack as Clerk. Savage died in 1837 and is the only one of these buried in the Livingston Cemetery, so far as known to the writer. James Savage lived at the Nat Kennard place and is said to have built the house in which Mrs. Kennard lives.

Many of the wealthy planters who came in about that time assisted in laying off the town, and most of the lots were sold off during the year.

Judge Sion L. Perry of Tuscaloosa organized the first court. His daughter married John C. Cusack, son of Thomas Cusack, an early settler who came from South Carolina.

The first settlement was about the spring and along Spring Street to the "Big Gulley" on the north and along what was later called West Main to the river. Another settlement grew up about the present A.G.S. depot and the two settlements grew together.

Most of the first houses were of logs with mud and stick chimneys. Some had floors of puncheons, and some had dirt floors. Some of these old log houses were weatherboarded when it was possible to get lumber and are still in use. Until 1837, it was almost impossible to get lumber unless it was "whip-sawed" out by hand, a most tedious process. The period 1834-1837 was the "Flush Times" made famous by Joseph G. Baldwin. Among the old log houses still in use are the Edwin L. Mitchell home, the W.G. Little home, the W.H. Lawrence home, and the Nat Kennard home.

A sort of inn was kept by one Rains on the W.G. Little corner (Spring and West Main). It was told that his wife once entered the house and found a large wild cat standing over her baby. She seized a stick of wood and the beast ran. There were two saloons on the Dr. Brockway lot. Stores and dwellings continued to be built and goods were hauled in from Moscow on the Tombigbee River. Lewis Parrent, who came from Tennessee in 1834, said one of these early stores was kept by an old Indian named Moshulitubbee—having the same name apparently as the noted chief who signed the Dancing Rabbit Treaty.

The first frame store was that of James Abrahams, located where Abrahams Hall afterward stood. The first brick store was that of J. C. Cusack, located about where the store of G.H. Grant now stands. The first frame dwelling is said to have been built by Willis Crenshaw. Much of the original material remains in this house, and it is now the home of L.B. Spratt. Two frame hotels were built in very early times. These were the Planters Hotel and the Choctaw Tavern.

The first courthouse was of logs with open cracks and stood about the intersection of Spring and West Main Streets. This place was used for all sorts of meetings. The various churches organized here, etc., etc. Another courthouse—of brick—was built in the Square, but its foundations gave way and it was demolished. A third courthouse, a frame building, was erected in the square in 1839 and was used until it burned on November 5, 1901.

The present courthouse had its cornerstone laid on July 9, 1902. There was a public barbecue. Dr. Cunningham, a former Lieutenant Governor, and Major J. G. Harris, a former State Superintendent of Education, took prominent parts in the ceremony. The Masons had charge of the cornerstone laying and there was quite a large crowd of them. The young people had a dance at the Old Cedar Grove Academy Hall that night. In all probability this was the last dance ever held in that building. A number of papers, etc., were placed in the cornerstone.

A jail once stood south of the W.G. Little house. Then there was a jail about where Mr. T.V. White now lives. Then there was a jail just to the east of the present jail. About 1885 a brick jail was erected on the southwest corner of Lafayette and Madison. About 1914 a new jail was built on the northeast corner of the same intersection and is still used.

In connection with the frame courthouse that burned in 1901, there were several smaller offices in the square. One of these, the Probate Office of former days, is now used as a Library. A Clerk's Office stood near the Bored Well and was burned, supposedly by Steve Renfroe to destroy certain papers in a case against him. There was a Treasurer's Office near the site of the Confederate monument.

The "Bored Well" was begun in 1854 and completed in 1857. It was really bored, not drilled. An old blind gray mule pulled the auger around day after day. Dr. R.D. Webb and Mr. M.C. Houston kept a record of the various strata encountered in the boring. The salty water so obtained was a great disappointment at first. In time Mr. Houston found that it benefitted his chronic indigestion and by degrees others began using it. At first the water ran out. Then a pit was dug and the water ran more freely while steps went down into the pit. About 1904 the late G.B. Fellows installed a hand pump and in 1928 an electric pump was put in.

A wooden pavilion with a sort of Chinese-temple roof stood over the well. This was removed in 1924 and the present substantial brick structure was erected.

Analysis of this water shows 295 grains of sodium chloride (common salt) to the gallon. There are also gases and small amounts of the following: silicates, iron, magnesium, calcium, potassium, strontium, and a trace of sodium bromide.

Just south of the old pavilion was a tallish hexagonal structure originally built for use as a bandstand and later on used by D.H. Trott as a Mayor's Office. This building was moved to several situations and was finally torn down.

It seems that in the early 1870s a foreign musician named Pfeoffenschlager came along and organized a brass band of fourteen pieces. He afterward went to Warsaw and is said to have married the widow of Lewis M. Stone of Pickens County. The band played at picnics, etc., and on one occasion took a steamboat trip to Mobile in the Mardi Gras season. This musician was also shown as Professor F.A. Pfaffenschlager. He died in 1882. Among the members of this band were F.H. Jones, J.O. Scruggs, W.K. Smith, Robert Wetmore, James B. Cobbs, Albert Bedell, W.J.(Jabe) Praytor, D.H. Trott, Jr., D.T. Battle, Jim McConnico, John A. Johnston, and L.D. Norville.

Among the lawyers of the very early days were Samuel B. Boyd, Tully Cornick, Peter Doty, James Hair, Amos H. Green, Murray Smith, William M.

Inge, Samuel W. Inge, Lemuel F. Whitehead, Robert H. Smith, John Little Smith, Samuel Chapman, Joseph G. Baldwin, E.M. Vary, James T. Hill and T.B. Wetmore.

Murray Smith, an early lawyer, is said to have married a daughter of Robert Desha and it is said that Smith's daughter of this marriage married first W.K. Vanderbilt and then O.H.P. Belmont and this lady's Vanderbilt daughter married the Duke of Marlborough. Whether this was the Robert Desha who once lived here I do not know. Accounts of this that I have read are somewhat confusing.

Among the doctors of early days were R.H. Dalton, J.L. McCants, William Harris Coleman, E.T. Garrett, M.B. Posey, Joseph A. Smith, R.T. Gibbs, H.F. Arrington, A.M. Garber, and R.L. Hunter. Dr. McCants, a native of South Carolina, died April 25, 1837, aged 33.

The first newspaper seems to have been *The Voice of Sumter*, first issued on March 1, 1836, with W.B. Ochiltree and T.K. Thomas, Publishers and Proprietors. Mr. Ochiltree is said to have been the first owner of the Choctaw Tavern. He moved to Gaston and then went to Texas.

There was a dam across Sukanachi down below town. It was in connection with a mill. The mill and dam were owned by Colonel James Rhodes and were operated for him, so it is said, by one Chiles, grandfather of W.S. Chiles. In 1835, there was much sickness for which the dammed up water was blamed, and on February 20, 1836, the dam was cut, much to the irritation and annoyance of Colonel Rhodes.

Early comers forded Sukanachi. About 1837, a bridge was put up near the old tanyard, and about 1861, the late Captain W. A. C. Jones built a covered bridge a short distance below the old bridge. Somewhere about the same time I.D. Hoit built the Hoit Bridge some distance above the old bridge.

In 1924, the covered bridge was removed and put up over Alamuchee, while Hoit's Bridge was removed and put up over Bodka. The places of both bridges being taken up, a new bridge was erected still farther down the stream. [The covered bridge is now on the campus of the University of West Alabama.]

About a hundred and fifty yards down stream from the site of Hoit's Bridge was a good swimming place that was used for some eighty years. It has been ruined for swimming purposes by pollution of the water above and this is an unnecessary evil that should be corrected, and probably will be, by a new sewage project.

The old cannon in the Square was left at Moscow by Union forces during the Civil War. It is said that W. D. Battle, Jr., and Zane Hoit later brought it to Livingston, where it was occasionally fired to celebrate some unusual event. Now and then the boys would fire it off at unreasonable hours. I think the last to shoot the old gun was Joe Boggs Jenkins. Then the town authorities plugged it up so it could not be fired.

The "D.U.D.'s" tradition seems to be a survival of some old English or Scottish New Year's celebration. The custom seems to have originated with the settlement of the town. The maskers were originally known as "Indomitables" and they were well organized. There was a parade on horseback about noon and a march that night which ended with a supper at one of the hotels. In earlier times the D.U.D.'s marched at night on New Year's Eve and the next day held a horseback parade. During the Mexican War the horseback parade went to Gainesville and greatly alarmed the Gainesville people, who took them to be Mexicans. This interesting old custom is gradually passing away. The name "Indomitable" is about forgotten, as it was supplemented by the more easily understood but much less elegant, "D.U.D.," standing for Damned Ugly Devils.

In 1836, there appear to have been two military companies, one of infantry and one of light artillery. The latter company was commanded by Captain Cleveland Robbs with M. Muckleroy as Orderly Sergeant.

Early editions of *The Voice of Sumter* are full of the political and other issues of that day, the sayings and doings of Martin Van Buren, the trouble between Texas and Mexico, the Seminole War, etc. One of these papers mentions that Mims Jemison of Tuscaloosa, Brother of John S. Jemison of Livingston, was killed in battle with the Seminoles.

In the time just after the Civil War there was a purely social organization of unmarried men known as the D.V.V.'s (Dum Vivamus Vivamus). Among the members were James R. Garber, B.L. Garber, Joseph B. Garber, John Lewis Brown, P. Bestor Brown, Reuben T. Thornton, James P. Spratt, J.G. Lake, Thomas B. Stone, E.W. Smith, A.G. Smith, J.C. Richardson, Thomas D. Cobbs, E.W. Hooks, T.E. Lockard, W.J. Praytor, and D.H. Trott, Jr.

In the 1870's and 80's, the younger men indulged constantly in all sorts of athletic contests, such as wrestling matches, walking races, running races, tournaments and ball games. There was a famous twenty-mile walking race around the courthouse square won by J.S. Johnston. About 1886 a gun club was organized. The members practiced at glass balls and clay pigeons and on Thanksgiving had a big hunt which was followed by a game supper. The man who broke the most targets at a practice shoot was entitled to wear a gold medal, and among those who wore this were D.U. Patton, Douglass McMillan, H.E. Little, and W. K. Smith. The one who broke the fewest wore a medal of leather, and this was usually worn by Harry Fellows. In those days quail were plentiful. The first boxing contest ever held here was held in June, 1929, under the auspices of the American Legion.

The Confederate monument in the Square was unveiled on June 17, 1909, by the following veterans: L.A. Cockrell, W.D. Battle, Jr., A.I. Grove, W.T. McKnight, S.H. Sprott, and J.P. Spratt.

The Salmagundi Club of the 1880's, a social organization, included the following members: Miss Lucy Ashe, Miss Lily Hibben, Miss Minnie Hibben, Miss Jennie Barker, Miss Lizzie Caldwell, Miss Mary Baldwin, Miss Saiven Parker, Messrs. James L. Parker, R.P. Wetmore, S.F. Mellen, J.L. Mellen, J.H. Little, John McQueen, Frank Herr, and Emil Brown.

Chapter 2

Schools and Cultural Organizations

Schools

According to notes left by Judge Perry, the first school was taught by a Miss Carey, a graduate of the LaGrange School. R.M. Howard, Charles A. Wyeth, R.H. Smith and J.J. McCants taught what appears to have been a boys' school one after the other. Mr. Smith became a noted lawyer. A school for girls seems to have been conducted by a Mr. Duncan. Then it was conducted by the Misses C.E. and M. Duncan, then by the Reverend L.B. Wright and then by Miss A.E. Thompson. At the same time, a Miss M.A. Allison, native of Wales, had a school for girls, Pine Hill Academy, located about 3½ miles south of town near Cooper's Spring. Cooper's Spring is on land now owned by Elijah Daley. It is said one Colonel John Cooper lived out near the Spring in very early times and owned much land.

In 1835, a movement was begun to get a good school for the girls. At a meeting held July 4, 1836, these trustees were elected: Judge Samuel Chapman, Dr. J.L. McCants, Seaborn Mims, William P. Beers, Willis Crenshaw, A.S. Arrington and R.F. Houston. In 1840, we find the Livingston Female Academy conducted by one A.A. Kembrell. [This institution was the forerunner of the Livingston Normal School, now (1996) the University of West Alabama.] Concerning this school, it is well to quote largely from Miss Hettie Jones' history of the Normal School. It seems that Miss Lizzie Houston graduated from this school in 1843, and her diploma was signed by A.A. Kembrell, Mrs. A.A. Kembrell, and Dr. George A. Ketchum, who was later a noted medical man of Mobile.

In 1847, Mr. Walker and a Mrs. McShaw (or McShan) taught. In 1848, Mr. & Mrs. James T. Bradford came and remained some years. They are buried in the Livingston cemetery. Mrs. Bradford was named Jerusha. They were from Plainfield, Connecticut. The writer's father remembered the academy as it was in Dr. Bradford's time. The main building stood on the site of Jones Hall and there was a music room somewhat in front. The old main building was added to and used until it burned about Christmas time 1894. An open air pavilion was built about on the site of the old music room about 1887 and was used for some twenty years as a place to hold commencement exercises, etc.

After the Bradfords, C.E. Brame, I.H. Tichnor, Miss Johnson, Colonel T.B. Wetmore and Mr. Brame again all taught from time to time. C.E. Brame was a merchant and was also a preacher. Mr. Tichnor was Rector of the St. James Episcopal Church. Miss Johnston was a native of Canada and was a sister of "Bighead" Johnston, who taught at the boys' school. Colonel Wetmore will be mentioned later.

1856-1858 Mr. George Dews taught. 1858-1863 Mr. O. Rockwell taught. Mrs. Rockwell was a Miss Fletcher and was a sister of Daniel Webster's wife. Mrs. Rockwell's brother, Dr. Fletcher, lived in Livingston and was a Southern sympathizer during the Civil War. Dr. Fletcher died in one of the small "office" rooms still standing that were once a part of the Choctaw Tavern. It is said that Dr. Fletcher taught our people to make their own matches when the supply of these was shut off by the blockade of the Southern ports. It is said Dr. Fletcher was buried here and his body removed some time after the Civil War.

In 1864, the Reverend Elisha Phillips and Mrs. Dodson taught at the Academy. Then Professor Henry J. Carter took charge. In June 1868 he granted diplomas to Miss Cora Lockard, Miss Mattie Beggs and Miss Hortense Thornton. Miss Beggs was the writer's mother and her diploma was signed by H.J. Carter, Abbie A. Carter and Miss Nellie C. Gibbs. The Trustees also signed. They were M.C. Houston, J.L. Scruggs, R.D. Webb, W.M. Stone, P.G. Nash, and Thomas Cobbs. Miss Lockard taught a private school some time and married John J. Altman. Miss Thornton, who died in 1927, taught for many years in the public schools of Birmingham, Alabama.

During and just preceding the Civil War, some of the teachers were Northerners with abolitionist sympathies. Joseph G. Baldwin, in his *Flush Times,* relates how there was a very disagreeable old maid of this type teaching here and how "Samuel Hele, Esq." (no other than the Samuel Hale who will be mentioned later on) was induced to tell her so many prodigious yarns about the savage nature of the people here that she packed her trunk and left on the next stagecoach. According to Colonel A.M. Garber, this took place about 1847, but who the lady was we have no idea. No doubt she took these tales home with her and told them to all and sundry and so helped bring on this unfortunate war. This may have taken place in Dr. Bradford's time.

From 1870 to 1878, the following taught: Miss Lizzie Houston, Miss Nellie C. Gibbs, Mrs. Mary C. Short, Mrs. I.C. Brown, Miss Mattie Beggs, Judge Daniel James and Miss Mary James.

Dr. Carlos G. Smith took charge of the school in 1878. He was a noted educator and had been president of the University of Alabama. Miss Julia S. Tutwiler came as his assistant in 1881. Through the efforts of Dr. Smith, and of Miss Tutwiler and the Trustees, the School became a Normal School, and the first Normal School diplomas were delivered in 1886.

Dr. Smith resigned and Captain James W.A. Wright came here and became co-principal with Miss Tutwiler. In 1890, Captain Wright resigned and took charge of the school for boys. Miss Julia then conducted the Normal School until she retired as President Emeritus in 1910. Since Miss Julia retired, this school has been conducted by Dr. G.W. Brock.

The Tutwilers were a noted family. Professor Henry Tutwiler came from Virginia and taught in several places. He finally established a famous school for boys at Green Springs, near the present Moundville. His wife and Dr. Carlos G. Smith's wife were sisters. He had a number of children, among them some who served in the Confederate Army. One of his daughters married Captain J.W.A. Wright; another married Colonel T.C. McCorvey of the University of Alabama; another was the mother of our townsman Dr. E.A. Young; another married Paoli, son of Dr. Carlos G. Smith. Miss Julia S. Tutwiler was another daughter of Professor Henry Tutwiler. She never married but did her share in advancing the cause of civilization.

Captain J.W.A. Wright was a remarkably interesting man. He taught at Green Springs, at Greensboro, at Livingston and at Talladega. He may have taught in other places. He lived in California in the early days of that state and it is likely that he knew more about the early Spanish explorations in this country than any other man of his day. He served as a Captain in the Confederate Army. He was captured, escaped to Canada, went to Bermuda and returned on a blockade runner, entering at Wilmington, North Carolina. The children of Captain and Mrs. Wright were Dr. Ruffin A. Wright of Mobile, Julius T. Wright of Mobile and Henry T. Wright, who reached high rank as a Naval officer.

Along in the 1850's, there was a school for boys behind the old Methodist Church that stood near the cemetery. One Johnston, a Canadian, conducted this school for some time. The eastern part of the cemetery was not used for cemetery purposes then, and it was full of pine trees and the boys played there. When the railroad came, it passed almost through the school building, so the school was removed to what is now the Dr. Brockway corner, where there was a large two-story building. Newton J. Hamill, assisted by Jesse Garrett, taught at this place, and afterward Professor David Rast, who married a daughter of W.K. Ustick, taught at the same place. Hamill was born in 1836 and died in 1867. His two sons, Greer and Fred P. Hamill, went to Texas.

The writer's father was going to school here to Hamill in October 1857. One day he and another boy were sent for a bucket of water, and they were within thirty yards of the Hainsworth and Scales duel. Hainsworth fell in the doorway of a store that stood on the W.H. Coleman & Company corner, and Scales lay in the street just south of the present Bank of Sumter. Mr. Hainsworth was killed and Mr. Scales was desperately wounded.

Hamill afterward taught on the northwest corner of Washington and Madison Streets and then on the southwest corner of the same in a sort of office that once stood in "Major" Battle's yard. Then he taught in an old building that once stood about on the site of J.H. Lee's house. A Mr. Kelley, an Irishman, taught a school for boys at a house that stood in the pine grove near the present Earl Godfrey home.

Soon after the Civil War, there was a school on the "Bob Tankersley Hill" near the Hopkins Place. This was known as Pine Ridge Academy and was

15

taught by J.C. Richardson, J.W. Dubose, a Mr. Holzclaw, a Mr. McGowan, C. L.Winkler, Professor Robert B. Callaway, and Robert J. Smith. Then Professor Callaway taught at a house that once stood where Judge Jarman's house burned. Then the late Dr. G. Fred Mellen taught at the same place.

A new schoolhouse was built on the southeast corner of Spring and Madison Streets and Dr. Seth S. Mellen took charge of this school, which was for some years known as Cedar Grove Academy (there were once many cedar trees on the school lot). This was a military school and many boys attended. Among those who assisted Dr. Mellen were Mrs. Mellen, G. Fred Mellen, Andrew Jackson, Joel C. Dubose and W. Collins. Then for two years, Joel C. Dubose had this school. He was assisted one year by Mr. Collins, and the next year by Dr. Ruffin A. Wright. Dr. Seth S. Mellen opened Cedar Grove Academy in 1883.

In the year 1888-1889 Colonel A.M. Garber and W. Henry Seymour were principals of this school. In 1889-1890 W.H. Seymour had the school and was assisted by a Mr. Rain, Thomas A. Curry, and Pen Tate. At times the aged Dr. Seth S. Mellen would assist him, also a Presbyterian pastor of the time named R.B. McAlpine. In 1890 Captain J.W.A. Wright had the school and kept it until the end of the school year of 1893. Among those assisting Captain Wright were Julius T. Wright, Allen D. Carden, R. B. Hall, William Weir and Henry T. Wright. Then L.A. Cockrell became principal and was succeeded by R.B. Callaway, who remained some years. Then J.M. Dill, and possibly others, had this school until the co-educational system went into effect about 1900. It remained a military school until Captain Wright left, and the boys drilled with old style Springfield rifles.

In addition to the schools mentioned, various small "mixed" [i.e., boys and girls together] schools were taught from the earliest times. Among those who conducted such were Mrs. Truehart, Miss Lizzie Houston, Mrs. Mary C. Short, Miss Nellie C. Gibbs, Miss Norville Dinkins, Miss Cora Lockard, Miss Mattie Beggs, Mrs. Virginia Ustick Carré, Miss Nini Smith, Miss Bettie Richardson, and possibly others.

Dr. Seth S. Mellen was a noted educator. He was born at Pelham, Massachusetts, and married a Miss Susan Bush. They had four children, G. Fred Mellen, Charles H. Mellen, William Mellen and Henry L. Mellen. Charles H. taught at Sumterville and died. William also died prematurely. G. Fred Mellen resided at Knoxville, Tennessee, and was a noted teacher himself. Henry L. Mellen married Miss Annie Grace Tartt and lived in Livingston. Dr. Seth S. Mellen taught at Mt. Sterling in Choctaw County and then taught with the late Alonzo Hill in Tuscaloosa. Then he came to Livingston and spent the rest of his life.

Andrew Jackson, mentioned as one of the teachers, was a brother of John and James B. Jackson, also an uncle of "Pete" and Brockway. He married a daughter of Oliver Wylie and became a prominent lawyer of Ft. Worth, Texas.

There were once three rather noted men named DuBose living in the state of Alabama. These were John Witherspoon Dubose, John Wesley Dubose and Joel Campbell Dubose. John Wesley taught at the Pine Ridge Academy here, and Joel C. taught at the Cedar Grove Academy some years afterward. The wife of Joel C. Dubose was a Miss Horn, a sister of Mrs. Florence Haynie and Mrs. Fletcher Williams.

Organizations

In the 1890's, some ladies organized the Twentieth Century Club, the object of which was to read and discuss books, etc. Among the members were Miss Hettie Jones, Mrs. Stephen Smith, Miss Hattie Bradshaw, Miss Mattie Sprott, Mrs. James P. Spratt, Miss Bessie Tartt, Mrs. John H. Norville, Mrs. H.L. Mellen, Mrs. James A. Mitchell, Mrs. W.K. Pickens, Mrs. James L. Parker, and Mrs. Quarles.

As some of these married and moved away and others became enfeebled by ill health, this club ceased to function, but about that time Miss Nellie C. Gibbs came back here to teach in the Normal School, and she had a Saturday Morning Reading Class among some of the younger women of that day. She and some of the members of this class, along with some members of the older clubs and others, organized the Primrose Club at the residence of Judge W.R. DeLoach. This club has lasted to the present day and has been responsible for many good works in the town. It recently celebrated its twenty-fifth anniversary.

Among the early members of the Primrose Club were Mrs. M.B. Quarles, Mrs. Stephen Smith, Mrs. J.P. Spratt, Miss Hettie Jones, Mrs. Fred H. Jones, Miss Nellie Gibbs, Mrs. W.W. Patton, Miss Margaret Sprott, Miss Lizzie Scruggs, Miss Nellie DeLoach, Miss Florence DeLoach, Miss Julia S. Tutwiler, Mrs. R.B. Callaway, Mrs. James L. Parker, Mrs. Branch, Mrs. Bachman, Mrs. Travis, and Mrs. W.P. Tartt. The old Probate Office in the Square was obtained for use as a Library and the Book Committee consisted of Mr. [Mrs.?] W.K. Pickens, Mrs. J.P. Spratt, Miss Nellie C. Gibbs and Mrs. Fred H. Jones.

In 1905 the membership of the Library Association was Miss Julia Tutwiler, Miss Nellie C. Gibbs, Mrs. Stephen Smith, Mrs. Eva Arrington, Mrs. Fannie Branch, Mrs. R.B. Callaway, Miss Sallie Coleman, Mrs. Florence Ennis, Miss Maud Gowdey, Miss Ruby Hightower, Mrs. Harn, Miss Hettie Jones, Mrs. Fred H. Jones, Miss Willie Feagin, Mrs. Ruby P. Tartt, Mrs. James L. Parker, Miss Leonard Meriwether, Miss Anna Patton, Mrs. J.P. Spratt, Mrs. Carrie L. Brockway, Miss Tempie Scruggs, Miss Gertrude Tartt, Miss Ruby Moore, Miss Bessie Gulley, Mrs. Daisy Everitt, and Mrs. Jessie Tartt.

Librarians have been Miss Ruby Moore, Miss Ella P. Smith, Miss Minnie Simmons, Miss Hettie Jones, Miss Olive Mitchell, Mrs. Robert McMahon, Mrs. Esther S. Drever, and Mrs. Pratt Tartt.

Presidents of the Primrose Club have been Mrs. M.B. Quarles, Mrs. Stephen Smith, Mrs. R.B. Callaway, Mrs. James L. Parker, Mrs. C.W. McMahon, Mrs. Fred H. Jones, Mrs. R.L. Stephenson, Mrs. H. L. Mellen, Mrs. T. F. Seale, and Miss Hettie Jones.

The following ladies are or have been members of the Colonial Dames of America: Mrs. Fred H. Jones, Mrs. C.W. McMahon, Mrs. James L. Parker, Mrs. W.H. Ziegler, Mrs. L.A. Ward, and Miss Lilah McMahon.

A charter establishing the Bigbee Valley Chapter of the Daughters of the American Revolution was granted May 15, 1913. The charter members were Mary Stansel Brockway (Mrs. D.S.), Lula Chapman, Lilybeck Chapman Cobb, Bessie Gulley (Mrs. H.V. Hudson), Nina Bohn Hall (Mrs. Laporte), Mary Hutchinson Jones (Mrs. Fred), Bessie Bradshaw Little, Mary E. McConnell (Mrs. Dr. R.P. Morrow), Gage Winston McMahon (Mrs. C.W.), Mabel Clare Randall Wrenn (now Mrs. Thomas), Lily Ashe Parker (Mrs. James L.), Alice Bolton Patton, Anna Chapman Patton, Julia Olive Praytor, Lula Bradshaw Rogers, Mary B. Smith, Mattie Rountree Stephenson (Mrs. R.T.), Margaret Turner Travis, and Olive Winston White.

The local chapter of the United Daughters of the Confederacy was organized in 1900. It is said that some of the records were destroyed in a fire. The earliest applications for membership are dated July 15, 1900. Among the first members were Mrs. Reuben Chapman, Mrs. W.D. Battle, Jr., Mrs. M.E. Whitehead, Mrs. C.J. Brockway, Miss E.C. Gibbs, Miss J.S. Tutwiler, Miss Charlotte T. Gibbs, Mrs. James P. Spratt, Mrs. Emily R. Lawrence, and Miss Florence DeLoach.

Chapter 3

CHURCHES

Presbyterian

About August 11, 1833, the Presbyterians organized at the old log courthouse. The Reverend Jacob Richards preached a sermon. The following were enrolled: Zacariah Graham, Flora Graham, Angus McNeal, Susannah McNeal, Ann Brewer, Margaret H. Lockard, Amanda F. Brewer, Catherine C. Carson, and Sarah Bates. Ann Brewer was the wife of William Brewer of Holita, and Mrs. Lockard and Amanda Brewer were her daughters, while Sarah Bates was her relative.

In 1834 Squire James Hair came and became prominent in affairs of this church, and soon afterward Mr. M.C. Houston came. Mr. Houston donated the lot on which the church was built [on the northwest corner of the intersection of Washington and North Streets]. He and Mr. Hair took their slaves to the forest and got out the timbers and the lumber for the church. This church was completed in 1838. According to L.A. Cockrell, it was finished a little sooner than the Methodist Church, which was then being built. The ladies of the two churches gave a "fair" by means of which money was obtained to buy the bells still used in these churches. The Presbyterian church was altered in 1900, but a part of the old structure is used as a Sunday School room.

The first recorded baptism is that of Mary L. Watts in 1834.

Among those who have served as elders are Zacariah Graham, Angus Graham, C.P. VanHouten, James Hair, M.C. Houston, R.F. Houston, I.D. Hoit, E. Walker, William Beggs, M.C. Kinnard, R.D. Webb, S.H. Sprott, T.B. Stone, T.B. Smith, D.S. Brockway, James L. Parker, James A. Mitchell, T.V. White, C.C. Boyd, Thomas M. Nelson, and W.A.C. Jones.

In early days, the Church Session was severe with those who offended against church discipline. The offender was tried as by court martial and might be cautioned or lectured from the pulpit, or he might, in extreme cases, be excommunicated. It is recorded that a member was so tried for telling a "smutty" story, and when he denied doing so, he was then tried for telling a lie.

In 1861 a Northern man, a Reverend John S. Beekman, was pastor and was reported by some newspaper of the time as being disloyal to the South. A committee was sent to him to get a written statement as to his position. This was done and the matter was dropped. This committee consisted of A.W. Dillard, R.D. Spratt, James Hair, R.D. Webb, and W.A.C. Jones.

Pastors from the earliest times have been J.M. Carruthers, Isaac Hadden, Alexander Smith, W.S. Peck, G.W. Boggs, R. Nall, B.F. Peters, B. Wayne, S.J. Bingham, John S. Beekman, Edwin Cater, A.F. Silliman, C.M. Hutton,

W.B. Bingham, J.W. Phillips, J.S. Frierson, R.H. Raymond, Robert C. Caldwell, R.B. McAlpine, W.T. Waller, W.G. Wolfe, J.D. McLean, R.C. Gilmore, J.L. Brownlee, W.C. Clark, W.H. Ziegler, W.J. Coleman, R.E. Fulton, and Erskine Jackson. The Reverend Isaac Hadden is buried at Bethel Church near Sumterville.

The choir of this church once had a noted quartet composed of Miss Ella Gaines Parker (Mrs. Going), Miss Aline Jones (Mrs. Sims), Albert Bedell and W.A.C. Jones. Miss Irene Park (Mrs. Charles H. Winston) was the organist.

[In 1955 the old church on the corner of Washington and North Streets was removed, and a new one built farther down the block.]

Methodist

The first mention of Livingston in connection with Methodism is in Conference Minutes of the year 1835 in these words: "Livingston. William A. Smith, one to be supplied." There is some earlier mention of a "Flatwood" Church that may have been in this region as there was a great stretch of forest near here known as the "Flat Woods."

A church building was completed early in the year 1838. Before then the congregation met in the log courthouse. The church stood near the present cemetery, on a site that has been much excavated by persons who wanted sand for building purposes. Back of the church was once a school building.

The church was built by Phillip Jones and John W. Adams, master carpenters of that day. No one knows what became of Jones, but Adams married Miss Elvira Ustick and died in Livingston in 1843. The trustees of this Church who entered into the contract with Jones and Adams were Seaborn Mims, Samuel B. Boyd, Peter Doty, John S. Jemison and John C. Cusack. The old church was made of hewed timbers and of whip-sawed planks, and there was a gallery for the slaves—unless the preaching was for the slaves especially and then the white people occupied the gallery.

Bishops Marvin and Pierce have preached in this old church and Bishop Robert Paine held District Conference here in 1877. Among the more noted of the early pastors were T.O. Summers, James O. Williams and J.H. Harmon. Mr. Harmon went to the Civil War as Chaplain of Dent's Company from Livingston.

The Civil War caused much damage to this Church in that many people moved away, many of the men were killed, and all were impoverished by the result.

About 1891 the old church was torn down and moved to Curl's Station by the late B.C. Hunter, and after some years, it was again torn down by Calvin Allen and used to build cabins at York.

A new church was built on the southeast corner of the intersection of Washington and Madison Streets while the Reverend Jeff Hamilton was pastor and was dedicated in 1892 by Bishop Galloway.

20

List of Photographs

List of Photographs, continued

PLATE I. Willie Martin, a Choctaw Indian who assisted Dr. Spratt with Indian names

PLATE II. Sumter County Courthouse, built 1902 (photo courtesy of John Craiger)

PLATE III. Bored Well Pavilion, before 1924 (photo courtesy Linda & Gregg Campbell)

PLATE IV. "New" Bored Well Pavilion

Plate V. Old covered bridge across the Sucarnochee River

PLATE VI. Sucarnochee River swimming hole near Captain Herr's farm

PLATE VII. Confederate monument on the courthouse square

PLATE VIII. Livingston Female Academy, the old building, which burned in 1894

PLATE IX. Livingston State Normal School, ca. 1928
[now The University of West Alabama]

PLATE X. Livingston Presbyterian Church, before 1955

PLATE XI. Livingston [United] Methodist Church

PLATE XII. Livingston Baptist Church, before 1948

PLATE XIII. St. James Episcopal Church

PLATE XIV. Sims' Place
[Now known as the Spence-Moon House, headquarters for Sumter County Historical Society

PLATE XV. Judge DeLoach House
[formerly on site occupied by the President's Home at The University of West Alabama]

PLATE XVI. Widow Lockard House [formerly on what is now Astrid Street]

PLATE XVII. Potts Place on Horn's Bridge Road [now in state of decay]

PLATE XVIII. Colonel Wetmore/Dr. Phillips House,
formerly on corner of Bibb Graves Hall lot

PLATE XIX. Captain Jones House with the Captain, seated
[formerly on lot now occupied by Presbyterian Church]

PLATE XX. M. C. Houston/Charles Bailey House on Washington Street

PLATE XXI. Thornton House on Monroe Street

PLATE XXII. Ustick/Scarborough House on Monroe Street [site of new public library]

PLATE XXIII. Lawrence House, formerly on corner of Washington and Monroe Streets

PLATE XXIV. Spratt House, formerly on corner of Spring and Monroe Streets

PLATE XXV. McMahon House [Mrs. Robert Ennis]

Prominent Methodists were Seaborn Mims, Samuel B. Boyd, Peter Doty, John S. Jemison, John C. Cusack, John W. Adams, W.K. Ustick, Lewis Parrent, H.W. Norville, J.L. Scruggs, Preston G. Nash, Judge James Cobbs, Judge A.A. Coleman, Judge James J. Garrett, A.W. Cockrell, L.A. Cockrell, G.W. Dainwood, D.L. Kirkland, Dr. S.S. Mellen, W.K. Pickens, John H. Norville, John Wesley Dubose, George B. Fellows, R.B. Callaway, W.S. Nichols, Henry L. Mellen, and George Wilson.

This about the Methodist Church is largely taken from a history of this Church written by the late Professor L.A. Cockrell.

The Methodist Choir once had a noted quartet of singers consisting of Mrs. D.J. Gregory, Mrs. W.S. Nichols, Thomas G. Makin and H.L. Mellen. Mr. Makin also served as organist.

Baptist

The late G.C. Gowdey once wrote a brief history of the Baptist Church of Livingston and the following is largely taken from it.

In 1834 the Baptists had a small log meeting house that soon burned and then they met in the log courthouse. The Reverend Mr. Ross, a missionary who traveled about this section, preached to them. Then for some time they met at Cooper's Spring some three and a half miles south of town.

In 1854 they built a frame church in Livingston and were doing well when the Civil War came and almost ruined the church beyond repair. It is said that after this there was but one member of the church left here. This was Mrs. R.M. Brasfield, who formerly lived in the Cooper's Spring neighborhood. In the Reconstruction era the church was given to the Negroes by the military authorities who controlled things. The church was recovered largely through the efforts made by the Reverend H.R. Autry.

In 1871 there was a re-organization with eighteen members. A pastorium was built in 1890, and a new church was built on the same site and was dedicated in 1892 by the Reverend A.H. McGaha.

Pastors of this Church have been Mr. Ross, Mr. Edwards, Mr. Latimer, J.K. Ryan, D.P. Bestor, H.R. Autry, J.B. Hamberlain, J.C. Wright, L.M. Stone, C.H. Sturgis, J.A. Howard, N.B. Williams, W.H. Smith (died 1933), B.F. Riley, W.G. Curry, A.R. Hardy, B.L. Mitchell, W.M. Blackwelder, H.B. Folk, Dr. A.C. Davidson, and David Bryan. A sister of the Reverend J.K. Ryan married Colonel Devereux Hopkins of Livingston. The Reverend D.P. Bestor was an uncle of Mrs. A.M. Tartt, who was one of the main supporters of the Livingston Baptist Church during her many years of residence here. Mr. Bestor was also the father of Mrs. Colonel I.C. Brown and of the late Daniel P. Bestor of Mobile. The Reverend B.F. Riley became noted as a teacher and as a writer. Mr. Folk was a brother of Governor Folk of Missouri.

Mr. Curry was here twice. He is buried in our cemetery. His son, W.A. Curry, married Miss Mary McKnight of Livingston. Another son, Capers J.

Curry, married a daughter of Lewis McLean who once lived near here. A daughter of Mr. Curry married Peter McLean of this place.

Dr. Davidson's daughter married T.F. Seale of this place, and his son Harry married a daughter of Austin Boyd, a prominent man who lives north of Livingston. A granddaughter of Dr. Davidson married Tartt Mellen.

[The old Baptist church was replaced by a brick structure on the same site in 1948, but many materials from the old church were used in the new one. This building burned in February 1965 and was replaced by the current church, which was dedicated in September 1967—*B.B. Williamson.*]

Episcopal

The St. James Protestant Episcopal Church seems to have had an organization prior to 1836, but owing to the loss or destruction of old records, it is difficult to find out much about the early history of this church. Many of the families that attended St. James in early times have moved away and their older members are dead. It is said that there was a sort of written history of the Church, but it was lost many years ago.

There is a tradition of a meeting place on the northeast corner of the hotel lot, opposite the residence of Mrs. A.M. Tartt. [This is at the intersection of Monroe and Jefferson Streets.]

In one of the 1836 issues of the *Voice of Sumter* is a notice that Reverend Mr. Wright of the Protestant Episcopal Church will (with Divine permission) perform the Services of the Church. A meeting of the Vestry was announced for the same day. These meetings were to be held at the schoolroom of Mr. Duncan, wherever that was.

In 1845 Willis Crenshaw, a Presbyterian, deeded the lot on which the St. James Church now stands. From the wording of the deed, Crenshaw gave them this lot. It also appears that there was a building of some kind already on the lot. It was said that the first bell the Episcopalians had was a large steamboat bell; whether the present bell is the same one is not known. The Bible now used at St. James was presented many years ago by Samuel M. Gowdey, uncle of the late G.C. Gowdey. Mr. Gowdey's name is on the flyleaf, the date being January 14, 1843.

It is said that Bishop Leonidas Polk consecrated this church. It is certain that there is a memorial window in the church for him. He was a graduate of West Point but became a clergyman and was Bishop of the Southwest and then was Bishop of Louisiana. When the Civil War came, he offered his services. He became a lieutenant general and was killed in battle in the latter part of the War.

Some of the families that attended and supported this church were the North Carolina Smiths, the Rhodes, Garbers, Gibbs, Thorntons, Cobbs, Murleys, Chapmans, Tankersleys, DeLoaches, Brownriggs, Whiteheads,

Wetmores and Abrahams. Judge Abrahams himself was a Presbyterian, and Colonel Wetmore was a Roman Catholic.

When the mineral region of North Alabama began to develop, this Church lost heavily, so heavily that it has never recovered, but it is in better condition now than for many years past.

Some of the clergymen who have served this church were Lucien B. Wright, J.J. Scott, I.H. Tichnor (died in Atlanta in 1881), Mr. Stickney, Mr. McCoy, Stephen U. Smith, Dr. L.L. Lurton, Mr. Lemon, Mr. A.K. Hall (drowned in 1881), Mr. Allen, Mr. Dye, J.J. Harris, Dr. J.T. Beard, Mr. Charles Penniman, and Mr. Waddill.

There are the following memorial windows:

On the north side, from west to east: Henry R. Thornton, Mrs. Mary Maury, Miss Constance L. Rhodes, Bessie Garber, Margaret A. Thom, and several Cobbs children (Maggie, Bettie, George, Julia, Wilmer); on the south side from west to east: Mrs. Rebecca Chapman (first wife of the Honorable Reuben Chapman), Judge Samuel Chapman and his wife (inscription reads *Mr.* and should be *Mrs.*), Bishop Cobbs, Bishop Leonidas Polk, William King Abrahams, and Kate Lucretia Abrahams.

Chapter 4

The Various Families and Their Homes

The Streets

[For much of the material in this chapter, it may be helpful to have some knowledge of the layout of the original streets, as explained by Dr. Spratt in the following two paragraphs.]

Washington Street runs northeast and southwest, and Spring Street parallels it on the west, while Lafayette, Jefferson and Church parallel it on the east. West Main leads off from the west side of the Square, and East Main leads off from the east side. The short street north of the Square is Franklin, and south of the Square is Marshall.

The main cross streets (running east and west), in order from north to south, are North, Monroe, Madison and South. North Street crosses Washington at [the former site of] the Presbyterian Church. South crosses it near the Scruggs house. Church Street was so named because it led to the old Methodist Church near the cemetery. Spring Street was so named because it ran past an important freshwater spring.

The Homes

Some seven miles north of town, near Jones Creek Church, was a large old house that was once the home of William Godfrey. He is said to have been of French Huguenot descent. He had a son who was the father of Dr. John Godfrey and of the late Solicitor L.D. Godfrey. One of William Godfrey's daughters married John E. Brown and another married George A. Brown. By a second marriage William Godfrey had a son, Dr. James M. Godfrey, who was the ancestor of the Godfreys of Sumterville. Dr. John Godfrey was a Confederate soldier in Stone's Cavalry Company, and after the war he became a surgeon in the old Marine Hospital Service, now the U.S. Public Health Service. Dr. John's two brothers, William and Lawrence D., also served as Confederate soldiers. This place was afterward owned by Hugh S. Lide, who married a daughter of Jerry H. Brown. This place is still owned by Mr. Lide's descendants, but the old house was demolished many years ago. Mr. Lide is said to have been a Confederate soldier in the Williams Company from Gainesville.

Nearer town, on a high hill, lived a Hutchinson family. One daughter of this family married F. H. McKnight, and they were the parents of W.T. McKnight. Another daughter married Robert Mason and this place became the home of the Masons. The children of Mr. and Mrs. Robert Mason were

Robert S. Mason, George Mason, Edward Mason, Mrs. Lewis Lancaster and Mrs. H.R. Foss.

Robert S., George, and Ed Mason were Confederate soldiers. Robert S. Mason married the widow of Judge C.S. McConnico, and among their children were Mrs. Wharton, Robert S., Jr., Miss Maggie, Miss Sadie and Will. George Mason had a son, Robert, who once lived in Livingston and worked for H.E. Little. Ed Mason married a sister of Mrs. A.B. Patton, a Miss Jessie Bolton, and they had a son Ed Mason, who once lived in Livingston and worked for W.S. Gulley.

H.R. Foss was a native of Ohio who served as a Confederate soldier. He was married before coming here, but this wife died leaving no children. After coming into this region he married a daughter of Joseph W. Jenkins, but she died childless. Then he married a daughter of Robert Mason, and she was the mother of Robert, Harry, Richard, George and Cliff Foss, who went to school here in their young days.

An Eskridge family lived nearer town. One of the daughters of this family was the mother of W.W. Smith of Epes. Two of the sons of the Eskridge family, Sam and Tom, served as Confederate soldiers. Samuel Eskridge, Sr., was born in Spartanburg Disrict, South Carolina, in 1798 and died near Livingston December 18, 1866. He and a number of his relatives and neighbors are buried on a high hill across the road from the old Eskridge house site. This burying ground is badly neglected—cattle have knocked down the stones, etc.

Nearer town was the home of Albert Lancaster, who married a sister of Joseph W. Jenkins. Among the children of this couple were Lewis, Ben and Miss Mattie. A sister of Albert Lancaster married Meredith Webb Lynn, who died near Millville in 1867. Among the children of this couple were Morgan Lynn and Mrs. Mitchell, the wife of the Reverend B.L. Mitchell, a former pastor of the Baptist Church here.

Most of the land from there to town along the Gainesville road belonged to former Governor Reuben Chapman, although he never lived here himself. This place was sold off by his heirs. Laco Lewis of West Virginia bought most of it and now lives on the place.

Judge Samuel Chapman, brother of Governor Reuben Chapman, once lived at what is now the "Pete" Jackson place. Among the children of Judge Chapman were the Honorable Reuben Chapman of Livingston, Mrs. Edmund W. Pettus and Mrs. Reuben Thom.

William Lockard bought this place and rented it to various families—the Wesley C. Dodsons, the Seelys, the family of Oscar Hord, the family of Judge P.G. Nash and possibly others.

Wesley C. Dodson and Amariah Seely were related. According to T.E. Lockard, Seely married Dodson's sister. Seely and Dodson were Confederate soldiers, Dodson being in the 40th Alabama, while Seely served in various commands as a substitute for Steve Potts, although Potts himself also served.

Mrs. Dodson taught at the old Female Academy and died at Bryan, Texas in 1867.

Then this place was the home of Robert P. Noble, whose sons, Nathan, Albert and Curtis, went to school in Livingston.

Some years after these moved, this place was acquired by the late Paul Gee, who lived there for some time. Mr. Gee was twice married. One daughter of his first wife married Marvin W. Parrent. Mr. Gee's last wife was related to the late Mrs. Lewis Parrent (Marvin's mother) and after Mr. Gee's death she married a Mr. Holder. She had one Gee child, a son who died recently.

John P. Jackson then acquired this place and built a new house. His name is John Percy Jackson, but for some reason he acquired the name "Pete" as a boy and it has stuck. The father of "Pete" was John Jackson, who lived east of town and was a brother of Andrew and of James B. Jackson. There were once three John Jacksons who lived around here and all of them were Confederate soldiers. These were John R. Jackson of Sumterville, the John Jackson who lived south of town, usually known as "Brock" or as "Mexican John" because he served in the Mexican War, and the John Jackson who lived east of town and whose son acquired this place. This John Jackson married a Miss Blakeney, and they had a number of children including William, Mrs. Dr. Phillips, James, John P., Jesse B., and Frank. James R. and John P. Jackson were twins, and both served as sheriffs of the county. James R. died December 20, 1929, and John P. died May 10, 1931. John P. Jackson married a daughter of the late Joe Patton of Brewersville, whose wife was a McMillan. The Jacksons have a number of children: Josephine, Janella, Nan Elizabeth, John P. and Andrew L.

[The Jackson house is now (1996) the Delta Chi fraternity house.]

To the south is a house built by Joseph W. Killian, whose grandfather, Joseph Maggard, once lived a few miles south of Livingston. Killian married a Miss Johnston, and their children were Mrs. William Douglass and Douglas Killian.

[The Killian house has been gone from the scene for many years.]

To the south stands a house that was once the home of Samuel W. Inge, a Congressman from this District. His uncle, William Marshall Inge, had been a Congressman from Tennessee and came here to practice law as a partner of Robert Harding Smith. Information is wanted as to where W.M. Inge was born, where he died, where he was buried, etc., in order to complete some sort of record of all who served in Congress. It is said by some that he died in 1842 and by others that he died in 1846, but nothing is known of his place of burial. He is thought to have been born in North Carolina, and in politics he belonged to the Whig Party. Samuel W. Inge removed to California and died in 1868.

About 1850 this place became the home of Socrates Parker, son of Captain James Parker of McCainville. His first wife, Mary Brown, was a sister of John E. and Colonel I.C. Brown, and she was the mother of Miss Fannie Parker.

After the death of this wife, Mr. Parker married a daughter of Joseph Lake, and she was the mother of Mrs. Going, James L. Parker, John L. Parker and Mrs. McMillan of Stockton.

Then Judge A.W. Dillard lived here. He was related to the Winstons and was Probate Judge. It seems the Probate Judgeship was established some time after the town was founded. The first Probate Judge was Ben Gaines, then came A.W. Dillard, Thomas R. Crews, C.S. McConnico, George B. Saunders, James Abrahams, W.R. DeLoach and P.B. Jarman. Judge Dillard's daughter married Reavis Woodson, and a daughter of Woodson married D.H. Hunter.

Then Mrs. Martha Horn Brockway bought this place. She was the widow of Dr. Augustus E. Brockway, who was a native of Connecticut and educated at the old Transylvania College in Kentucky. Dr. Brockway was a physician at Gaston for many years. Among the children of Dr. and Mrs. Brockway were Mrs. S.H. Sprott, Charles J. Brockway, and Dr. Dudley S. Brockway. Charles J. Brockway was a prominent lawyer and a good citizen. He married Miss Carrie Little, a daughter of Captain Ben B. Little, and among their children were Captain Ben L. Brockway of the U.S. Coast Guard, Mrs. Velma Chappelle, W.G. Brockway, James Brockway, and Charles Brockway.

Dr. D.S. Brockway practiced medicine at Coatopa and at Livingston for many years. He first married a Miss Patton, who died leaving no children. Then Dr. D.S. Brockway married a daughter of the late Colonel M.L. Stansell of Carrollton. This wife was the mother of Elizabeth and Helen Brockway. Helen died, and Elizabeth married a Mr. Charles Galbraith. The second Mrs. Brockway was a widow Pearson when she married the doctor, and she had one Pearson child, Ollie, who married Mr. Allan Sweet of Savannah.

Samuel H. Sprott, who married the daughter of Dr. and Mrs. A.E. Brockway, was in many respects a remarkable man. He was a son of Robert Sprott and his wife, who was Mary Bothwell. Among the children of Robert Sprott and his wife were Samuel H. Sprott, James Sprott, John Sprott, Mrs. W.T. McKnight and Mrs. Kincey (Miss Lou) of Texas. James Sprott was killed in the Civil War, leaving a son, William Sprott of Memphis. John Sprott married a daughter of Fred Evans and died leaving no children. He was a Confederate soldier. Mrs. Kincey left no children. There was some sort of a tradition of adherence to the Black Douglas and to Bonnie Prince Charlie in this Sprott family.

Samuel H. Sprott was a captain in the 40th Alabama, C.S.A. and, after the Civil War, was Circut Judge for many years. He married Miss Leonora Brockway, and among their children were Mrs. Thomas Long, Mrs. Thomas Robertson, Mrs. Jesse Long, Samuel H. Sprott, Jr., of Tuscaloosa, Mrs. Arthur Fite and Robert Sprott. Judge Sprott lived for some time at the place under discussion. S.H. Sprott succeeded James Cobbs as Captain of the 40th Alabama. W.T. McKnight, who married Miss Margaret Sprott, sister of Judge S.H. Sprott, was for many years a prominent businessman of Livingston and had served as a Confederate soldier. The children of Mr. and Mrs. McKnight were Mrs. W.A. Curry, Thomas H. McKnight of Memphis and Robert McKnight.

A Captain Azariah Abney of Choctaw County then bought this place and lived there a few years, but then sold it to the late Captain W.A.C. Jones. Captain Abney removed to Brevard County, Florida. He had a number of children, among them a son Robert and a son Billy.

Captain W.A.C. Jones came here as a civil engineer shortly before the Civil War and married the Widow McRea, who was a daughter of M.C. Houston. This lady's first husband was Dr. W.P. McRea, a brother of the former Governor McRea of Mississippi. She and Dr. McRea had two daughters, Mrs. Robert C. May and Miss Willie McRea. Dr. McRea died of yellow fever in Opelousas, Louisiana, and is buried here. Captain and Mrs. Jones had a number of children, among them Fred H. Jones, Mrs. W.A. Sims, Harden L. Jones and Miss Hettie Jones. W.A.C. Jones was a captain in the Confederate army and was a prominent citizen. Fred H. Jones married Miss Mary Hutchinson of Tuscaloosa, daughter of Captain Alfred Hutchinson, C.S.A., and a niece of J.J. Hutchinson of Dent's Company. Both Fred and Harden L. Jones were prominent but left no descendants. Captain Jones rented this place to various families. Among those living in the house was Dewitt A. Pruitt. He died, and his widow had a position at the Normal School for years afterward. Captain J.W.A. Wright also lived at this place for some time.

Miss Aline Jones, daughter of Captain W.A.C Jones, married Walter A. Sims, and in time this became their home. They lived here so long it became known as the "Walter Sims Place." Thomas Sims was a prominent man of Bluffport and Mobile in the days of Steamboating. He was married several times. His first wife was a Miss Shelton, and among her children were Mrs. S.B. Little (wife of H.E. Little), Walter A. Sims, Dr. Frank Sims, Shelton Sims and Mrs. Douglas McMillan. As stated, Walter A. Sims married a daughter of Captain Jones, and among their children were Mrs. Gregg, Fred, Frank and Shelton. After the death of Mr. Sims this place was bought by C.R. Moon, who was connected with the Normal School.

[This place, now known as the "Spence-Moon House," was acquired by the Sumter County Historical Society in 1987 and now serves as the headquarters for the organization.]

South of this house was a house built by W.R. DeLoach, and when it burned about 1901, he built another one very much like the first. This other house burned about 1934. W.R. DeLoach was one of the children of Dr. A.A. DeLoach and his wife. He served in the Confederate Army and was Probate Judge of this county for a number of terms. Judge Deloach married Miss Sue, daughter of Colonel Charles R. Gibbs, and they had several children, among them Dr. A.B. DeLoach of Memphis, Mrs. Nellie McClellan and Mrs. Florence D. Ennis. Judge DeLoach died in 1910. In his old age Judge DeLoach had removed to Memphis. Older men have told me that the Judge was quite athletic in his youth, and his son, Dr. A.B. DeLoach, was a skillful wrestler in his time. Judge DeLoach's widow died in 1933, and Dr. A.B. DeLoach died in 1933 also.

The DeLoach place was bought by the late J.A. McConnell, who had much to do with the early development of the town of York. Mr. McConnell married the daughter of Marcus Parker. This lady was a widow, her first husband having been Churchill Gibbs, who is said to have been related to Colonel Charles R. Gibbs. She and Mr. Gibbs had no children, but there were a number of children of her marriage to Mr. McConnell. Among the children of Mr. and Mrs. J.A. McConnell were John, Marcus E., the first Mrs. Dr. A.E. Young, Mrs. Dr. Morrow and Joseph A., Jr. Marcus E. McConnell has lived in Livingston for many years and has been Mayor of the town for a number of terms. He married Miss Julia Lawrence, and they have two sons, Marcus and John Reid, and a daughter, Mary Emily. [Marcus McConnell, Jr., who supervised the 1974 publication of this *History*, died in 1995 while this new edition was being prepared for publication, and his brother, John Reid, died this year (1996).] Mrs. Young was the mother of Joseph and Nan Young. Joseph A. McConnell, Jr., served overseas in the World War and was a captain when this war closed. On his return he married Kathleen Cobb, a grand-daughter of the honorable Reuben Chapman, and they had one son named Joseph. Captain McConnell died soon after the birth of this son, and his premature death was a cause of sorrow to many, as he was very popular. The DeLoach place now belongs to Mrs. Dr. Morrow.

[The site of the DeLoach place is now occupied by the University of West Alabama President's Home.]

Just to the south is a sort of street or road running to the west. Going along this, we pass some cottages used by the Normal School and then come to a queer-looking white house. This was the home of the widow of Thomas Lockard, Jr. It seems that in the very early times one Thomas Lockard of South Carolina came into this region. He married Mary Halsell, and among their children were Thomas, Jr., William, Edward, John and Mrs. Childers. William married Margaret Brewer, and Thomas, Jr., married Amanda Brewer. Thomas Lockard, Jr., moved to Aberdeen, Mississippi, where he died, and his widow returned to Livingston about 1855 with all of her children except the oldest daughter, who married a man named Betts in Mississippi. Her other children were Miss Addie, Miss Gertrude, Thaddeus E., Miss Adrianna, Orlando and Miss Amanda. The house mentioned was built for them, and they lived there a number of years. Thaddeus E. Lockard was a Confederate soldier, serving in Phelan's Battery. He is the last Confederate veteran living in Livingston. (That is, Mr. Lockard is the last veteran living here who went to war from Livingston.)

Edward Lockard married Amanda Chandler, lived awhile near the Tankersley Place, then near Horn's Bridge, then near Millville, and finally moved to Meridian, where he died and is buried. Edward served in the Mexican War and also served in the Williams Company from Gainesville as a Confederate soldier. Mrs. S.W. Scales of Starkville, Mississippi, is descended from Edward. Mrs. Ed Lockard was a daughter of G.W. Chandler, who once lived in this region and moved to Mississippi. John Lockard settled in South Sumter near old Gaston and was the maternal grandfather of Robert L. and Thomas F. Seale. It is said the Jones people of Panola are descended from Mrs. Childers.

Then this place was the home of D.L. Kirkland. He had served in the Confederate Army and was a widower when he came here. It seems that he had lived in the West in the very early days of that region and had been through many adventures. He married a daughter of William Lockard and they had a son, D.L., Jr., who was talented and popular but died when he was a young man. Mr. Kirkland's last wife was a Miss Jimmy Petty, who was a very religious woman. He became very religious also and frequently preached at places where there was no regular preacher. He did a good business at Livingston for many years and left a nice estate when he died.

Then B.F. Riley, a former Baptist pastor, lived at this place, and after him a Baptist missionary named S.O.Y. Ray. (Dr. Riley was an uncle of Mrs. Abner Hawkins.) The family of H.R. Foss also lived here at some time, and afterward it was the home of Mrs. Mary McDaniel. She was a daughter of Dr. J.C. Knox of Talladega and a sister of the late Mrs. John Lewis Brown. John, Asbury and George McDaniel were sons of Henry McDaniel, a wealthy planter of Sumterville. Among the children of Mr. and Mrs. John McDaniel were the late Mrs. Judge J.B. Newman, Henry McDaniel of Demopolis, John McDaniel, and Lewis McDaniel of Greenville, S.C. This place was then the home of the Clippard family, who came from Missouri. Joe, son of Mr. and Mrs. Clippard, married Miss Julia Stinson. The Clippards moved away in 1928, and this place was acquired by the Normal School.

[All the cottages and houses on this street, now known as Astrid Street, have been torn down in the course of developing the campus of the University of West Alabama.]

To the south, behind the Normal School site, was the home of the widow of William H. Green, a lawyer of the early days. William H. Green, Jr., known as "Bill," was their son and was a noted character. He was a Confederate soldier, and after the Civil War he taught a school that was established for the Negro children. Old Mrs. Green is said to have been a sister of the noted and wealthy Sim Giles, who had a wonderful mansion out on the Mississippi Line. Across the branch in a grove of pines was the site of Pine Ridge Academy, which has been mentioned. Mr. Robert Tankersley bought this place and built a small dwelling which he occupied until his death in 1894. He married Miss Eva Cunningham, and among their children were Mrs. W.K. Smith, George, Mrs. Bonney, Mrs. Henry Arrington and Mrs. Walter Wields, who later became Mrs. Dupuy of Arkansas. Various families have rented this place since that time.[This house is no longer standing.]

To the west is what is called the Hopkins Place. It was once the home of the noted Methodist preacher James O. Williams, who married a daughter of

Seaborn Mims and had two sons, named Johnson and Mims Williams. It is related that James O. Williams was once preaching in the old Methodist Church on the future state of the wicked. Outside in full view was a kiln where J.W. Harris was burning bricks. The kiln was doing its duty and was red hot. Mr. Williams told his hearers that this kiln was undoubtedly very hot but Hell was so much hotter that a sinner taken out of Hell and dropped into this kiln "would freeze to death in five minutes."

Then Captain B. B. Little lived here. He was a cousin of Major W.G. Little, and they were members of the noted and wealthy Little family of Warsaw. Captain Little was a prominent lawyer of Livingston and went to the Civil War as a member of Dent's Company (Company G, 5th Alabama). After a while he came home and organized a company of which he was elected Captain of the 22nd Alabama infantry. He was killed in battle near Atlanta. Captain Little married Miss Sue Tankersley, and their children were Mrs. Charles J. Brockway, Mrs. James B. Cobbs and Mrs. Baker.

Sometime after the Civil War, Colonel Devereux Hopkins acquired this place. He was a native of North Carolina and had lived in Choctaw County and in California before coming here. He married a sister of the Reverend J.K. Ryan. Colonel Hopkins served many years as Register in Chancery. Among the children of Colonel and Mrs. Hopkins were Mrs. Gaines, who afterward married Mr. Harden Lake; Miss Kate Hopkins, who succeeded Mrs. Hill as postmistress at Livingston; W.W. Hopkins, who had served as a lieutenant in cavalry in the Civil War and succeeded his father as Register in Chancery; Mrs. Addison G. Smith; Mrs Bryant; and Miss Julia. Mrs. Smith died in 1928 and Mr. Smith in 1933. [This home is now owned by Mr. and Mrs. Richard Thurn.]

A bit to the north was the home of John Connolly, an Irish boot-maker. He was an industrious old fellow who made fine boots for the dandies of that day. His son Tom was the father of Mrs. Carl Turk, i.e. the first Mrs. Turk. After the Connollys left, a family of Winns lived here. Old Mr. Winn died here suddenly. His son, R.A. Winn, was our first white barber. R.A. Winn married a daughter of Frank S. Lee. He died recently in Thomasville, Alabama. Since that time Negroes have lived at this place. [This house is no longer standing.]

Just beyond is a branch called "Passey's Branch," and it may be that the Passey family of long ago lived in this neighborhood.

Not far away was the home of Thomas Hill. One Thomas G. Makin, an Englishman who was connected with the Normal School for years, bought the Hill place and lived there. He and his sons, Harold and Clarence, left after Mrs. Makin's death. This place now belongs to the Hyatt interests.

Farther out was the home of Josiah Moore, who married a Miss Rebecca Ward. She is said to have been related by marriage to General Joseph Arrington's people. Josiah and Aaron Moore were brothers, and they bought this place from one Graham. Mr. and Mrs. Josiah Moore had one son, John W.

31

Moore, who lived in Livingston for many years and married Miss Bettie Harper of Gainesville. The children of Mr. and Mrs. John W. Moore were Mrs. Sharron, John Robert Moore of Meridian, Mrs. Paul Thomas, Mrs. Malone. All of them, excepting John Robert, live in Quincy, Florida. The widow of Josiah Moore married James Branch, and they had a son, Josiah Moore Branch, who has been a prominent business man of Livingston for years. He married Miss Fannie Harwood of Gainesville. The name Harwood comes down from the days of Hereward the Saxon, who put up such a determined fight against William the Conqueror. Mrs. Fannie Branch died in September 1931, and sometime later Mr. Branch married Miss Olive Mitchell.

About three miles from town, on this road, was where William Brewer settled about 1830. He lived here near Holihta Creek and was known in his time as "Holihta Bill" to distinguish him from another William Brewer living on Cedar Creek, who was called "Cedar Creek Bill." Mrs. Miriam Brewer Richardson of Montgomery, a daughter of the late Willis Brewer, informs me that "Holihta Bill" and "Cedar Creek Bill" were distantly related, and that Brewersville was named for "Holihta Bill's" brother, Matthew Brewer, who lived there in 1832. The wife of Holihta Bill Brewer was a Miss Bates, related, so it said, to Thomas Jefferson. The Brewers had a number of children, among them Robert Brewer, Mrs. William Lockard and Mrs. Thomas Lockard, Jr. Robert Brewer married a Miss Hadden, who was related to the noted Presbyterian preacher of that day, Isaac Hadden. Among the children of Robert Brewer and his wife were Lewis and Willis Brewer. Lewis served as a Confederate soldier, and Willis, in after years, served in Congress and wrote a history of Alabama.

Then the wealthy Tankersley family lived here. The name Tankersley comes from Tankerslea, a parish of Yorkshire, England. One Dolphyn de Tankerslea is mentioned in A.D. 1200, and two descendants of this family, Richard and George, came to America (Virginia) in or about 1700. Richard had a son Richard, who had a son George Edward, who had a son John, who was a soldier of the Revolution from Spotsylvania County, Virginia. John was born in 1764 and died in 1822. He married Susan Brooks in 1788. George G. who settled here, was a son of this marriage. George G. Tankersley married Sarah Frances Haley Jones, a daughter of Judge William Jones of Columbia County, Georgia. Their sons were William, Robert, George, James, Felix, Harrison, John and DeWitt. Robert died in 1894. George died during the Civil War while managing a plantation in Texas, and James, who had been serving as a soldier, succeeded George at the plantation. Harrison was a Confederate soldier with "Terry's Texas Rangers" and died in Texas, unmarried. Felix was killed in battle. He left an infant son at Chapel Hill, North Carolina. John ran away from the University and joined the Confederate forces. No doubt he belonged to Captain Little's command (22nd Alabama) when killed in Georgia in 1864. His Negro servant, Paige Hicks, brought his horse home. DeWitt died of some illness shortly before the war. Among the daughters of George

G. and his wife were Susan, who married B.B. Little; Carolina, who married Dr. Coleman; and Ellen, who was dragged to death by a runaway horse she was riding. William Tankersley (1825-1856) lived in Choctaw County and he and his wife, Rosina, were parents of Mrs. Oliver Ulmer of Butler. After William's death, his widow married J.B. Roach of Choctaw County.

At a later time, John H. Norville owned a part of the Tankersley place, and Mrs. Ulmer owned the other part. D.W. Hyatt of North Carolina bought Mrs. Ulmer's interest. H.L. Mellen and M.E. McConnell bought the Norville part.

Between the Tankersley and Parker plantations was a farm belonging to Daniel Greene, a prominent man of early times. He had relatives named Gunn and Andrews. Greene is buried at the Parker place.

Then came the McCainville neighborhood, where the following families lived: Brownrigg, Cockrell, Freeman, Hadley, Hopper, Kennedy, Lavender, Marten, McCain, Parker, Sledge, Spratt, Tartt, Thomas and Travis.

Dr. Brownrigg, a wealthy man, was twice married. His last wife was a Miss Prince of Mt. Sterling, Alabama. They had one daughter, Mrs. Maria B. Quarles, wife of the late Garrett Minor Quarles.

Jacob Cockrell of Nash County, North Carolina, had a son Nathan, and Nathan had two sons who settled in Sumter County, Alabama. These were William, who lived at Sumterville, and Demsey, who lived at McCainville. Demsey Cockrell married Millicent Carpenter, and among their children were Nathan, Augustus William, Leonidas A., Luther, Quintus, James and Mrs. Wrenn of Oklahoma. (Her husband, William Wrenn, was a brother of Messrs. James and Joe Wrenn of Sumterville.) All of the Cockrell sons served in the Civil War as Confederate soldiers, except Nathan, who died before the war. (This was the Nathan E. Cockrell who attended the University of Alabama and edited a newspaper.) Luther was so wounded that he died soon after and was buried at Old Side Church. Quintus was terribly wounded by sword and bayonet cuts but survived and left a family in Texas. James married a Miss Hendon and left descendants. Mrs. Wrenn had children.

Augustus William Cockrell was a lawyer of Livingston and later removed to Jacksonville, Florida. His first wife was Susan Spratt, who left two sons, including A.W. Cockrell, Jr., of Jacksonville, Florida. His second wife was a daughter of Judge P.G. Nash, and she left one son, Preston D. Cockrell of Miami, Florida. Mr. Cockrell's third wife survived him. She also had children, Alston and Evelyn.

Leonidas A. Cockrell kept the old place near McCainville and spent most of his life there. He served as First Sergeant of Company G, 44th [40th?] Alabama Infantry, C.S.A. He taught school at Livingston and in other places in Sumter County. His first wife was a Miss Taylor, and she was the mother of W. Leon Cockrell, Demsey Cockrell, Clarence Cockrell, Miss Mattie, Mrs. Dobbs, and Mrs. Northcutt. Mr. Cockrell's second wife was a Miss Hale, and she was the mother of Mrs. Frank Clark of Birmingham. Mr. Cockrell's third wife was Miss Bettie, daughter of E.S. Gulley, Colonel of the 40th Alabama, C.S.A. W. Leon Cockrell married a daughter of Charles H. Bullock and resides at McCainville. He and his wife have one son living, Frank Cockrell. W.L. died in 1939.

John Kennedy lived at the present Conde Boyd place, and Tom Kennedy lived where R.L. Giles afterward lived. (In early days, the name was seen as "Canady.")

A Mr. Freeman was the neighborhood blacksmith. His place is still called the Freeman place.

Dr. Hadley lived at the place afterward owned by John Lewis Brown. He was a physician and was a farming partner of Robert Desha. Columbus Hainsworth later lived here. He married a sister of J.E. Cusack.

The Hopper family moved long ago. The late John W. McAlpine, who was a lawyer of Livingston, married a lady of this family.

The late William Marten, who lived on the Brewersville road, was born at McCainville. He once told the writer an interesting tale of being captured by the Yankees during the Civil War and of escaping by swimming the Alabama River.

The Lavender name has almost disappeared, but there is a large family connection. Robert Lavender was the first settler. Herbert Lavender is a grandson.

Adam McCain of South Carolina settled at McCainville in 1831, and a house he built then is still standing. His wife was originally a Miss Elizabeth Marshall, and for years after Mr. McCain died she remained an influential member of the community. Among the children of Mr. and Mrs. Adam McCain were Weldon, George, William and Adam, Jr. Weldon McCain was the first teacher at the Mt. Moriah School and died prematurely. William, George and Adam, Jr., were Confederate soldiers and William was killed in battle. Adam McCain, Jr., married Miss Frances Lou Hodges, and among their children were A.C. McCain of McCainville, the late Clarence M. McCain, Dr. William J. McCain and Mrs. W.M. Kern.

A.C. McCain married a Miss Nixon and they had a number of sons and daughters. One of their sons, W. Claude McCain, served in the Spanish-American War and was a commissioned officer overseas in the World War. Clarence M. McCain was a former Sheriff and died at Livingston. He married a Miss Hinton, and they had three daughters, Mrs. John Neilson, Mrs. Travis Turner, and Mrs. David White. Dr. W.J. McCain has been a prominent physician of Livingston for many years. He has actively assisted in promoting the prosperity of this section in a number of ways. He had much to do with bringing in the improved beef breeds of cattle and with introducing the culture of alfalfa and of the pecan nut. Dr. McCain married Miss Julia White, and among their children are Mrs. James, Miss Louise, Mrs. Evans, Mrs. Reynolds, Miss Julia (Mrs. Lampkin), David, Mattie (Mrs. Martin) and Adfield. Mrs. Kern resides at the old place at McCainville and has a number of children. The wife of

Adam McCain, Jr., who was a Miss Hodges, had several brothers who served as Confederate soldiers, including Marion, Newt and Jasper Hodges. Marion Hodges was killed in battle.

Captain James Parker was the wealthiest man in the McCainville neighborhood. His wife was a Miss Mitchell, a great aunt of our County Solicitor, James A. Mitchell. Among the children of Captain and Mrs. Parker were Socrates Parker, Marcus Parker, Dave Parker, Conizine Parker, Volney Parker, and several daughters, including Mrs. Lewis B. Brown, Mrs. Robert L. Brown and possibly others. The families of Socrates and of Marcus Parker have been mentioned. A part of the old place is still called the "Soc Flat." Marcus Parker lived for a while at what is now called the Cusack place, a part of his father's old place. He married a Miss Hines and removed to South Sumter. His only child married a Gibbs and later married J.A. McConnell. Conizine Parker married Miss Mat Sherard and built the Carver house near the present McConnell Station. They had a daughter, Beulah, who married Sam E. Smith, an uncle of the present S.E. Smith of Epes. They had a daughter, Sammie, who went to the Normal School in Livingston. Captain Parker and his wife, Lewis S. Brown and his wife, Daniel Greene and various others are buried at the old Parker place burying ground. After the Civil War, Judge James Abrahams acquired the Parker Plantation and it is still owned by his heirs.

The widow of Joshua Sledge settled near McCainville at an early day. One of her sons, Albert, lived at the place near Horn's Bridge that had been the home of John Horn, who helped lay off lots in the town of Livingston. Albert was the father of Joe and Mark Sledge. Albert's wife was Eliza H., daughter of John Horn of Horn's Bridge. Among the other children of this Mrs. Joshua Sledge were Dr. William H. Sledge, Mrs. Bailey and Mrs. Bobbett.

Dr. William H. Sledge did a large practice in this region and was the father of a number of children, among them Mr. E.S. Sledge, Dr. William H. Sledge, Jr., of Livingston and Mobile, Mrs. Gardner, Miss Annie and Forrest. Mr. E.S. Sledge has lived in this same region all his life. For fifty-three years he and his crippled friend, the late P.O. Key, lived together, and it was always a pleasure to visit them. Dr. William H. Sledge, Jr., was the father of the present Dr. Edward S. Sledge of Mobile. Forrest Sledge went to school in Livingston, and after selling his property, went west. Mr. Parks O. Key died in October 1927. He was related to the Dial people and was afflicted by a disease resembling *Spondylitis deformans* which made him practically helpless for over forty years. He was cheerful and took a keen interest in what went on in the world, and he had a great many friends. He made his home with Mr. E.S. Sledge. Mrs. Bobbett lived where Cliff Seale now lives, and Mrs. Bailey lived at the adjoining place now owned by Conde Boyd.

Robert D. Spratt of South Carolina settled at McCainville about 1839. His wife was Lillis Barnett, and among their children who lived to be grown were Susan, who married A.W. Cockrell, James P. Spratt, Robert Barnett Spratt, Anna and Lillis Isabel. Mrs. Cockrell has been mentioned.

James P. Spratt served as a Confederate soldier, being one of the few from the county who saw the bombardment of Ft. Sumter, the first battle of the Civil War. He was at what is now the University of South Carolina and went down to the city of Charleston with a cadet company organized among the students. James P. Spratt married Miss Mattie Beggs, and their children were Robert D., Helen, Lewis B. and William P. Robert D., son of James P., is the author of this history. Helen died in early life. Lewis B. Spratt married Maggie Smith, and they have two daughters, Louise and Lillis. Louise Spratt married Charles H. Lanphier, Jr., of Springfield, Illinois. Lillis married R.A. (Andy) Allison. William P. Spratt was a partner of Wade H. Coleman of Livingston and volunteered when the World War came. He was made 1st Lieutenant of Company D, 1st Battalion, 325th Infantry, and was killed in action near St. Juvin in northern France, on October 14, 1918. He is buried at the National Cemetery at Arlington, Virginia.

Robert Barnett Spratt was on the Staff of the Confederate General Leonidas Polk, but became ill and died before he saw any active service. Anna and Lillis Isabel Spratt never married and spent much time in Europe. Anna died in Rome, Italy, in 1916.

Wade R. Thomas lived at what is still called the Thomas place. Mr. and Mrs. Thomas had a son, Wade, Jr., who was a Confederate soldier, and their daughter married the late Dr. Epes of Epes. Mrs. Thomas, Mrs. Bullock, Mrs. Albert Sledge and the first Mrs. Harris W. Killian were daughters of John Horn of Horn's Bridge.

James Tartt of Edgecombe County, North Carolina, is said to have been an older half-brother of Dr. Brownrigg and a brother of Elnathan Tartt. He married Sarah Barnes, and among their children were Elnathan, Enos, Thomas M. and Edwin B. James died in 1857 and is buried at Old Side Church.

One Joseph Johnston of North Carolina was a soldier of the Revolution who was killed at the battle of Stone. His daughter married one Andrews, and among her children were Margaret, who married a Turner, and Martha, who married Elnathan Tartt, said to have been the brother of James Tartt, who also had a son named Elnathan. This Mrs. Turner was the mother of the late Dr. Matthew Turner of Bladon Springs. Mrs. Tartt came to this county at a very early time. They settled on Bodka Creek and Elnathan died. His widow came to Livingston in 1832 and lived there awhile. Then she married one Welsh and removed to Bladon Springs, where she died at an advanced age. She had Tartt children who went to Texas. She was an intelligent woman and talked interestingly of the early days. She said that a Choctaw named Opelatchee lived on what we know as Baldwin Hill and that some of the Commissioners wanted to name the new town for him, but one of the members was a personal friend of Mr. Livingston, and he persuaded them to name the town Livingston. This name "Opelatchee" is undoubtedly the Choctaw *Apelachi,* which means "Help, to help, a helper, an ally, etc." She said that in early times rattlesnakes were very plentiful in the Bodka region.

Elnathan Tartt, James' son, merchandised in Livingston for many years. His own son Elnathan was for many years in charge of a soldiers' home at Biloxi, Mississippi. Thomas M. Tartt became a partner of his brother and later went into business for himself in Livingston. He married Miss Annie Jones, a niece of the Reverend D.P. Bestor. Among the children of Thomas M. Tartt and his wife were Mrs. H.L. Mellen, Mrs. James A. Mitchell, Thomas M. Tartt, Mrs. Charles Perry, Mrs. Darby H. Brown, W. Pratt Tartt. and Mrs. Charles Bell. Mrs. Perry and Mrs. Brown live in Birmingham. Mrs. Bell lives in Anniston. They have children.

Mrs. Mellen is the wife of H.L. Mellen, son of Dr. S.S. Mellen. The children of Mr. and Mrs. H.L. Mellen are W. Tartt Mellen, Henry L.Mellen, Jr., and Maude Mellen. Maude married Adam Summerfield (Adfield) McCain. W. Tartt Mellen married Frances Seale, a granddaughter of Dr. A.C. Davidson.

James A. Mitchell, who married Miss Alice Tartt, is County Solicitor and is a grandson of Augustus Winston. Among the children of Mr. and Mrs. Mitchell are Mrs. Charles B. Bailey, James A., Jr., Annie Bestor Mitchell and Martha Winston Mitchell.

The younger Thomas M. Tartt married Miss Jessie Cowin. He was born March 3, 1871, and died April 1, 1932. Since the death of A.C. McMillan he has been the active head of McMillan and Co., Bankers. The children of Thomas M. Tartt and his wife are Thomas M., Jr., Cornelia, Allen, Mrs. Knowles, Ted and Joe. Thomas Jr. married Gladys Stallworth, Allen married Louise Newton, and Joe married Dorothy Allison.

W. Pratt Tartt served a number of terms as postmaster at Livingston. He married Miss Ruby Pickens, and they had one child, Fannie Pickens Tartt.

Edwin B. Tartt, son of the original settler, James, served as a Confederate soldier and spent most of his life at the old home near McCainville. He and Morgan Lynn and Charles H. Bullock married the Burton sisters. When these three men got together at one of the old-time barbecues, they ate great quantities and had the best time of anybody. The children of Mr. and Mrs. Edwin B. Tartt were Edna, who died, and Anna, who married J.A. Shelby, a former Sheriff of the County. Mr. and Mrs. Shelby had two daughters, Edna and Mrs. Dew, and a son, E.B. Shelby. J.A. Shelby died suddenly October 16, 1931. After the death of E.B. Tartt, his widow married Charles H. Bullock, who was then a widower. There were no children of this marriage.

There was still another Burton sister who married John Kennard, brother of Nat Kennard. John Kennard and his wife had a daughter who married Andrew Shaw of Cuba. Shaw's daughter was the first wife of Malcolm Larkin.

Enoch Travis lived at an early day at what was later called the Bell place, and his brother Amos lived farther out on an adjoining place. The daughter of Enoch Travis married Ed Bell, who was killed in the Civil War, and then she married Dr. Turner of Bladon Springs, Alabama. She and Dr. Turner had a number of children, among whom were Mrs. J.C. Travis, Mrs. Esther Colston, Ben Turner, Miss Hattie, Travis Turner and Miss Matt.

Meantime, Amos Travis had moved to Gainesville and lived at what is now the John A. Rogers place. After the Civil War, Mr. Amos Travis and his family removed to California in the neighborhood of Los Angeles (Santa Monica). Some twenty years later he returned to Alabama and purchased the places near McCainville once owned by himself and his brother, and he lived there until his death at the old house built by his brother. The wife of this Amos Travis was a Coleman, akin to those of Eutaw. Among the children of Mr. and Mrs. Amos Travis were the mother of the late A.S.Vandegraff of Tuscaloosa; the mother of the Grimshaw boys who once went to school here; Mrs. Hutton of California; Thad Travis, who was a Confederate soldier; Messrs. Wiley and Jesse C. Travis, who returned to Alabama with their parents and spent many years here. Mr. Wiley Travis died unmarried. Mr. Jesse C. Travis came to Livingston and married Miss Maggie Turner. He succeeded the late W.W. Hopkins as Register in Chancery. Among the children of Mr. and Mrs. Jesse C. Travis are Eliza, Mrs. Holzborn and Matthew.

There was a noted school for boys at old McCainville called Mount Moriah Academy. The material of the building was hauled from a "peck mill" that once operated out near the Mississippi line. The school was located a short distance from McCainville on the Epes road, at a spot now marked by an old cistern.

Weldon McCain was the first teacher, and after he died, one James Harran had charge and became a noted teacher of that day. Then William A. Eakens taught here, and then a Mr. Rhodes. Schools were developed at Livingston and other larger places, and this Mount Moriah school was discontinued. After so long a time the old building was torn down and removed to McCainville and put together again, and it is still standing. The late C.M. McCain used this old building as a store building. R.B. Callaway taught in this building about 1878.

Among the boys of that day who attended this old school were "Sandy" Baldwin (son of Joseph G. Baldwin), Alf DeLoach, Mark DeLoach, Oscar Badley, Dave Hines, Nathan Cockrell, L.A. Cockrell, A.W. Cockrell, Quintus Cockrell, Dr. Jacob Huggins, Jim Hutchins, Jesse Hutchins, John Hutchins, Tom Hunter, William H. Hawkins, Bob Bass, Sam Carpenter, Adam McCain, Sam Neville, Dave Parker, J.D. Coleman, John Lake, J.P. Spratt, Harrison Tankersley, Felix Tankersley, Tom Prince and Nath Kennedy.

Alf and Mark DeLoach were brothers of W.R. DeLoach. Dr. Jacob Huggins became noted. Tom Prince was a very handsome man and was a brother of Mrs. Dr. Brownrigg and of Major Sidney Prince of Mobile. It is told of him that he once registered at a hotel in Scotland as "Thomas Prince of Mobile" and was accorded royal honors, as they read it "Prince of Mobile." (It may have been an older Prince about whom this story was told--see Brewer's *Alabama*.)

[At this point, Dr. Spratt's account shifts to the area south of town, across the Sucarnochee River.]

As previously stated, John Horn once lived near the Horn's Bridge and then Albert Sledge lived there. Albert's son Joe was in Stone's Company, and his son Mark had a narrow escape from being seized by Federal authorities who were after the Ku Klux of the Reconstruction era.

Across Horn's Bridge lived a Davis family and a Fitzpatrick family, and Tom Fitzpatrick and Hugh Davis were in Dent's Company. Hugh Davis was the father of Headly Davis.

Going toward town on what is called the Horn's Bridge Road, we come to what was once the Mallard place, where a Mr. Mallard had a school. He had a son named Gus Mallard who was in Dent's Company. This place was acquired by a Widow Moore. She had a number of Moore children, among them A.M. Moore, who was a Captain, C.S.A. This lady married a widower Allison who had a number of children, among them Robert Allison of the Stone Company. By this last marriage there was one child, a daughter named Henrietta Allison. She married Sam B. Turk of Kentucky, who had been a Confederate soldier. Among the children of Mr. and Mrs. S.B. Turk were Mrs. R.L. McCormick, Mrs. George Graham, Mrs. J.S. McGee, Mrs. R.B. Daniel, Houston Turk, Mrs. T.B. Weatherby, Bob Turk, Mrs. Sam Kubiack and Carl Turk. [This house has been torn down and the land is now used as a hunting preserve.]

It is said the Mims family lived at a place nearer town that was later owned by Ben Ivy, who died in 1858. Seaborn Mims had died in 1842. This place then became the home of Thomas A. Johnston, a native of New York State, who married a daughter of John H. Sherard. Among the children of Thomas A. Johnston and his wife were John S. Johnston, Charles T. Johnston, Mrs. George Fluker and Mrs. J.H. Hunter. Charles T. Johnston died in 1883 at the age of seventeen. Mrs. Fluker was the mother of our townsman L.S. Fluker. Mr. and Mrs. George Fluker lived at this place, and it, or at least the old home site, is now owned by their son, Leverett S. Fluker. Dr. William Fluker of Gaston was the grandfather of Leverett S. Fluker. Leverett S. Fluker married Miss Bettie Cooper, and they have one child, a son named George. The other surviving children of the elder George Fluker and his first wife are Miss Aurora and Emmet. [This plantation has been divided into several parcels. One is the Hunter place, with a house built about 1920, which is now the home of B.B. Williamson. The Story/Dorman camphouse is on a second portion, and the remainder is still in the Fluker family.]

About a mile and a half from town on this road was once a half-mile circular track where the young men of the 1880's and 90's tried out their horses, both running and harness. Among the more noted of the running ponies were those of J.H. Little and W.A. Sims, K. Allen and M.B. Rosenbush. Perhaps the fastest of the lot was Little Ella, owned by M.B. Rosenbush, but Big Henry and Texas Bill gave her serious opposition. Among the fast harness animals were A.C. McMillan's mare Bay Kit, R.W. Ennis' mare Red Bug, and several of J.W. Tisdale's stable, such as Prince William, John Boyd and Sam Jones. [Sunshine Arena, owned by the Williamson family, is built beside the site of this old track.]

Nearby on a high hill was the home of the handsome and dashing Steve Potts, related to the Mims people and a Lieutenant in Dent's Company. This is still called the Potts Creek place. A.P. Evans owned this place later, and then the late Stephen Smith acquired it. T.F. Seale bought part and Jenkins Jackson the rest. [The Potts house is still standing but in a very bad state of disrepair.]

A.P. Evans was a son of Fred Evans, and his mother was a daughter of General Joseph Arrington. A.P. Evans married a daughter of Joseph W. Jenkins, and they had a number of children, among them Joe Fred, Bessie, John Lee, Janie, Paul E., Add and Everitt. Mrs. John Sprott and Mrs. W.H.A. Voss were sisters of A.P. Evans.

About a mile from town on the Horn's Bridge Road was a place where Captain B.F. Herr was living at the time of his death. He built the present dwelling. Captain Herr was a native of Ohio of "Pennsylvania Dutch" stock. He sided with the South and was a captain in the Confederate Army. He settled in Livingston and for many years held county offices and was editor of *The Livingston Journal*, said to have been the best small-town newspaper of its day in the state. Mrs. Herr was a very capable woman. She and the Captain had several children, all of whom died, except one son, Frank Herr, of Mississippi, who died in 1937 at Greenwood. [The house built by Captain Herr is still standing but is unoccupied and in a state of disrepair.]

Returning to town, on Washington Street just south of the old Female Academy, there was a good-sized lot that belonged to William Lockard, and he lived here in a large two-story house. This house later burned, and J.J. Altman, who then lived at the place, built a smaller house that was finally taken over by the school. It either burned in one of the fires or was torn down. These houses stood about on the site of the present Webb Hall. William Lockard, as already mentioned, married Margaret Brewer, and among their children were Mrs. Sims, Mrs. Howard, Mrs. Kirkland, and Mrs. John J. Altman. There was also a son, Pembroke S. Lockard, who was a Confederate soldier and who left descendants in Texas. John J. Altman was of the Altman family of York. He was a prominent lawyer of Livingston and of Birmingham. He married Miss Cora Lockard, and they had several children, among them John W. Altman, who is a prominent lawyer of Birmingham at the present time. Captain J.W.A. Wright lived here a while after the Altmans left, and then the Normal School acquired the property.

South of this was a queer-looking house in a large lot. This was the home of Hiram Bardwell, a New England master carpenter, who lived here for many years and is buried in the cemetery. The late Stephen Smith acquired this property, and it now belongs to the Normal School. On the southeast corner of this Bardwell lot, Mrs. S.B. Little and her son-in-law, D.J. Gregory, built two cottages. These were acquired by the school and were moved bodily across the street.

To the south was a house built by Colonel T.B. Wetmore. He was one of Sumter's noted characters, being a fine lawyer and a fine man. He married Miss Octavia Hill, a granddaughter of Colonel Charles R. Gibbs, and among their children were Robert, James, Richmond P. and Mrs. Stone. In his later years Colonel Wetmore removed to Birmingham and died there. [This house, which is no longer standing, was on property now owned by the University of West Alabama.]

The story of Colonel Wetmore's cold shower bath has been handed down from early days. It seems that in those times of no water works, etc., the colonel was in the habit of taking a shower bath in the afternoons during the summer weather. He had a sort of bath house near his well, where he would have a keg of water hoisted up in the morning, and this water would be well warmed by the sun in a few hours. Then the colonel would enter and disrobe and pull on a plug and get a nice luke-warm shower. Some of the boys of that day knew the colonel's habit and sent to Mobile for some ice, which they put into the keg, and when the colonel took his shower that day, he got the shock of his life and ran out, forgetting his clothes.

Another interesting story about Colonel Wetmore I have heard from some of the older men in town. They say that on the night of his marriage he ate his own length in link sausage. Colonel Wetmore also owned the celebrated glass-eating dog Carlo. He was a common liver-spotted pointer, and people noticed his eating glass every now and then for a long time. A man had to see it to be convinced that it was so. In course of time he would be called upon to eat something nice and thin like a lamp chimney in order to convince some doubter, and he usually ate it. As there are not so many left who actually saw this dog eat glass, the writer got a signed statement to the effect that this was so and had it recorded in Miscellaneous Record Book 1, page 77, in the Probate Office. This statement was signed by a number of reliable citizens, and some of them are still living, so that anyone doubting the truth of this can consult them.

Mention of this dog brings to mind an amusing tale, especially amusing to one who knows the men involved. It seems that Dr. Sam B. Harris and Mr. W.K. Pickens once went to some distant city on business and Mr. Pickens went out, leaving the doctor at their hotel talking to some men in the lobby. In the course of the talk the doctor told of our glass-eating pointer in Livingston, and the men would not believe the tale, so he promised to prove it by Mr. Pickens. Then Mr. Pickens returned and listened to the tale very solemnly and said he "never heard of such a thing."

It might be said of Carlo that he lived to a reasonable age for a dog. He was left with W.K. Smith when Colonel Wetmore moved to Birmingham and he died in 1888 while Mr. Smith lived at the Wetmore place.

W.K. Smith lived at the Wetmore place for several years. He was a son of Captain E.W. Smith and married Miss Susie Tankersley, daughter of Robert Tankersley. Among the children of Mr. and Mrs. Smith were the late W.K. (Keirn) Smith, Jr., Mrs. Duncan, Mrs. Hobdy, Robert Smith and Captain Edward Smith, U.S.A. Then a family of Mathers rented the place.

Then Dr. J.T. Phillips lived here a number of years. He was born near Kewanee, Mississippi. His father was killed in the Civil War. He became a dentist and married a Miss Swain, who died leaving a daughter, Mrs. Tom Vaughan of Cuba. Then Dr. Phillips married Miss Lizzie Jackson, and she is the mother of Russell, Tommy, Mary Eliza, Mrs. Weston Sullivan, Virginia and Eleanor. Russell married a Miss Lucile Smith, a granddaughter of J.R. Phillips of Yantley. Tommy married a daughter of E.C. Vaughan of Curls.

To the south, a sort of street runs out to the colored Baptist churches, and on the south of this was a lot once owned by Matthew C. Houston. Mr. Houston was wealthy and influential and was twice married. Among the children of his first wife were Robert G. Houston and Miss Lizzie Houston. Robert was the father of Mrs. J.O. Scruggs. Among the children of Mr. Houston's second wife were Mrs. John T. Smith, Mrs. E.W. Smith, Mrs. Harden Lake, Mrs. Dr. W.P. McRae, Mrs. Dr. Robert Park and Mrs. Billy May. Dr. McRae died, and his widow married W.A.C. Jones, as has already been mentioned. Mrs. Park was the mother of the first wife of the late Charles Winston of Bodka. Mrs. Lake and Mrs. May left no children. These people were of the same family as the noted Sam Houston, Governor of Texas.

The north end of this lot was acquired by Clarence Cusack, who built a house which was purchased by Thomas F. Seale. Mr. Seale and his brother, the Honorable R.L. Seale, came here from South Sumter some thirty years ago. Thomas F. Seale is a prominent lawyer and married Mrs. Jones, a widow, who was a daughter of the Reverend A.C. Davidson. She had a daughter by her first marriage who married W. Tartt Mellen, and she and Mr. Seale have a son, Thomas. [The Julia Tutwiler Library of the University of West Alabama now stands on the site of this house.]

To the south of the Seale residence is the home of Dr. A.C. Davidson, a most popular and worthy pastor of the Baptist Church. Among the children of Dr. and Mrs. Davidson are Mrs. T.F. Seale, Dr. Marion Davidson of Birmingham, and Harry Davidson. [This house now belongs to the Livingston Presbyterian Church.]

To the south is the site of a Manse provided the Presbyterian pastor by M.C. Houston. Among others, the Reverend G.W. Boggs lived here. This house has been added to and for many years was the residence of Captain W.A.C. Jones. Miss Hettie Jones and her half-sister, Willie McRae, now live at this place. I have heard that the first Mrs. Boggs died here, and Mr. Boggs afterward married a daughter of Greene V. Mobley, a prominent character of Gainesville. [The "new" Presbyterian Church, built in 1955, now stands on the site of this house.]

As already stated, M.C. Houston donated the lot on which the Presbyterian Church now [i.e. 1928] stands.

After M.C. Houston died, various families lived at his old home, among them the family of Mr. Adolph Brown. Some time after the Civil War, one Samuel Brown, a German Jew from Bavaria, came here and went into business and was joined by his nephew, Mr. Adolph Brown. Samuel Brown moved to Mobile and Messrs. Adolph and Hugo Brown continued in business here as Brown Brothers. Brown Brothers established the first bank in Livingston about 1887, and this bank was succeeded by McMillan & Company when Brown Brothers moved to Mobile. Mr. Hugo Brown was a talented musician in his younger days. He never married. Mr. Adolph Brown married a Miss Hanan and among their children were Leo Brown, Mrs. Henly, Florence and Claudine. Adolph Brown died about 1930.

The late Stephen Smith acquired this place and lived there until his death in 1905. He was a son of Captain E.W. Smith and was for many years a prominent businessman of Livingston. He married a Miss Mary Phifer of North Carolina, and their children were Stephen, Jr., Phifer and Harold. Harold Smith graduated at the U.S. Naval Academy but resigned to enter business. When the World War involved the United States, he again became a naval officer and served as such through the war. Soon after the close of the war he again resigned and then died suddenly. Stephen Smith, Jr., had a family. He resides in California. Phifer Smith is an electrical engineer and has traveled extensively.

Then Mrs. S.B. Little lived at this place. She was a daughter of Thomas W. Sims and married H. Emmet Little. These were not related to the Warsaw Littles so far is known. H.E. Little came here from Forkland about 1885. Mr. and Mrs. Little had two daughters, Miss Lethe, who married D.J. Gregory (related to the Amasons), and Miss Mamie, who was very popular but died prematurely. Mr. and Mrs. Gregory reared an orphan boy, Jack, who served overseas in the World War. After the death of Mrs. Little, this place was acquired by the County Health Officer, Dr. J.S. Hough. He had seen service in the Army and in the Public Health Service, and soon after coming here he married a Miss Maxwell from Mississippi.

[The M.C. Houston house was occupied for many years by Mr. and Mrs. Charles B. Bailey (Alice Augusta Mitchell), but it was then converted to commercial purposes.]

West of the Presbyterian Church was the home of James Abrahams. The old house was much like that of M.C. Houston. Abrahams came here as a merchant in the very early days. He was a Union man, did not believe in secession, etc., but his sons all served as Confederate soldiers. This name is pronounced as if spelled Abrams. After the Civil War, James Abrahams was appointed Probate Judge, and his course was such as to make his old friends fall away. After he died, his people all moved away. Judge Abrahams married a Miss Ward of Georgia, and among their children were Ed Abrahams, Dr.

Lat Abrahams, Dr. W.T. Abrahams, Mrs. William Wayne, and Miss Lily. Ed Abrahams and Dr. Lat left descendants who reside at various places in the West. Dr. W.T. Abrahams lived for a while in Livingston. His wife was a Miss Crocheron, and they had several children who died.

Various families then lived at the Abrahams place, including the family of Reverend Mr. W.T. Allen, a former Rector of St. James Episcopal Church. Mr. Allen married a Widow Petty, said to have been a sister of the Weisinger who once managed the Artesian Hotel. Then Mr. George A. Brown lived here. He was the brother of John E. Brown, Colonel I. Chap Brown, etc., and his wife was Sarah Godfrey. Among the children of George A. Brown and his wife were Mrs. Dr. Watkins, the second Mrs. Captain James M. Henagan, Mrs. Cross and Miss Lula. There were also two sons, George and Clarence.

T.L. Smith bought this place and improved the house. His grandfather, William Smith, lived in Virginia and had a number of sons and daughters who came to Sumter County, Alabama. Among these were Ben (father of the late W.W. Smith of Epes), Thomas, Powhatan, Otaway (father of Jim Smith of Gainesville), Mrs. Thomas Hawkins, Mrs. William Winslett and Mrs. A.D. Fortner. Thomas, Powhatan and Otaway were Confederate soldiers. Thomas married Anne Berlin, and among their children was Thomas Long Smith, who bought this Abrahams house. T.L. Smith married Sarah, daughter of J. Reid Ramsay, and their children were Mrs. James D. Browder, Mrs. L.B. Spratt, Mrs. John E. Brock, Mrs. Feagin Rainer, Mrs. H.C. Kilpatrick, Thomas L., Jr., and Mrs. Dick Browne. This house burned in 1909 and a brick school-house [now Livingston High School] was built on the old site.

To the west was once the home of Dr. R.L. Hunter. His son Tom was in Stone's Company. One of Dr. Hunter's daughters was the last wife of Colonel J.M. Lee. Tom Hunter married and had a son Tom and died. His widow married a Cates.

Later on, this was the home of Major (afterward Chancellor) Thomas Cobbs. Thomas Cobbs was a Major of Militia in the Confederate Service. He was a younger half-brother of Colonel Hopkins, and his wife was a sister of Mrs. H.R. Thornton and of Reuben Thom. Among the children of Major Cobbs and his wife were Thomas D. Cobbs, James B. Cobbs and Miss Ellen, who was the first wife of the late Dr. J.H. Phillips of Birmingham. Thomas D. Cobbs went to Texas. James B. Cobbs married a daughter of Captain B.B. Little and became a banker of Birmingham. Dr. Phillips was a noted Superintendent of Schools in Birmingham. Judge James Cobbs was a brother to Major Cobbs, and his wife was a daughter of Joseph Lake. Among their children were a son named Boone and a daughter who married John Wesley DuBose. Judge Cobbs was a Captain, C.S.A., in the 40th Alabama. A Captain Brown succeeded E.S. Gulley, who was promoted. Brown was killed and Cobbs became Captain.

Then Colonel Isaiah Chapman Brown lived here. He was a brother of John E., George A., *et al.,* and his wife was a daughter of the noted Daniel P.

Bestor, the Baptist preacher. Colonel Brown was usually known as Colonel "Chap" Brown. Among the children of Colonel Brown and his wife were P. Bestor Brown and Windham Brown. P. Bestor Brown married a daughter of Major W.G. Little, and among their children were William Little Brown, Mrs. Reynolds, Mrs. Steele and Bestor.

This place became the home of Joel C. Dubose, the teacher, and after him the Reverend W.G. Curry lived here awhile. Then it was used as a school by Miss Bettie Richardson. Then Charles H. Allen lived here. He was editor of the *Sumter Sun* and had a nice family. Mr. Allen came from Gainesville and in his youth was a noted ball player and tournament rider.

The family of J.E. Cusack lived here for a time. It was while this family lived here that Clarence Cusack was almost killed by two Negroes who struck him over the head with a heavy picket taken from a nearby fence and then robbed him. The robbers were young and were sent up for life and one of them soon died. Their names were Ben Kennard and "Bully" Mooring.

Then the family of Charles H. Bullock lived here. He was a Confederate soldier who married a Miss Burton and lived at McCainville. Among his children were Mrs. W. Leon Cockrell, Mrs. W.R. Stinson, Frank Bullock, Ben Bullock and Mrs. Will Mason. His McCainville notes in Captain Herr's paper were enjoyed by all—he signed them "Rex." In his later years Mr. Bullock married the widow of E.B. Tartt and moved to Livingston, where he soon died. [This house has been gone for many years.]

What the early settlers called the "Big Gulley" runs in front of this last mentioned place. The gully begins on the square west of and in front of the Baptist Church and runs in a westerly direction, becoming gradually deeper until it gets to the river. It is quite deep with steep sides in front of this place, and when Major Cobbs lived here, the gulley was crossed by a bridge in front of his house so that his wife and her sister, Mrs. Thornton, could cross more easily—Mrs. Thornton living on the other side. This gully was from earliest times a place where small boys played. They dammed up the small brook running along its bottom, fished in the holes near the river, played Indian, built forts, searched for fossils in the steep limestone banks and went swimming in the river at the far end of the gully.

South of where Major Cobbs lived, across this "Big Gulley," was once the home of the Widow Brown. It seems that John Brown lived at Sumter, South Carolina, and died there. He married Julia (or Juliana) Windham, and they had a number of children, among them John E., William, Lewis S., George A., Robert, and Isaiah Chapman. There were also at least three daughters, Mrs. Jesse Womack, Mrs. James Mitchell and Mrs. Socrates Parker (her name was Mary). After the death of this John Brown, his widow and her children came to Sumter County, Alabama, and in the course of time she lived at this place under discussion. She died in 1836, and her son William died in 1838. It was said that she and her son William were buried on this place, in the orchard just to the west of the house, and that they once had headstones at their graves.

John E. Brown married Mary Godfrey, and among his children were Mrs. Julia Stewart, Mrs. Dr. R.M. Harris, Mrs. Major J.G. Harris, Mrs. Nettles, Mrs. Reynolds and Mrs. Lurton (afterward Mrs. Dr. Randall). Mrs. Reynolds was the mother of Alfred Reynolds and of Mrs. L.A. Ward. He also had two sons, John E., Jr., who was a Confederate soldier and died unmarried, and Arthur, who died quite young. Charles Stewart, husband of Mrs. Julia Stewart, was a Confederate officer and was accidentally killed by the blowing up of one of his own cannons. His widow lived to be over ninety years old. Dr. R.M. Harris and Major J.G. Harris were not related, and were not related to H.H. and J.W. Harris. Dr. R.M. Harris was a son of William Harris, who lived near the town of Cuba. The wife of this William Harris was related to General U.S. Grant. Among the children of Dr. and Mrs. R.M. Harris were Mrs. Perrow, John E. and Herbert L. Major J.G. Harris—known to his friends as "Gid" Harris—was a major in the Confederate Army and afterward served as State Superintendent of Education. His daughter, Mrs. Dawson, resides in Montgomery. A son of Mrs. Reynolds, daughter of John E. Brown, married a daughter of Dr. W.J. McCain. The Lurton and Randall children of Clara Brown, who married first Lurton and then Randall, were well known in Livingston in their younger days. These were E. Brown Lurton, Maud Lurton, Mabel Randall and Arthur Randall. Brown Lurton married a Miss Harrington and left two daughters. Maud Lurton married Mr. Blassingame and left children. Mabel Randall married James M. Wrenn, and after his death she married a Professor Thomas of Texas.

Lewis S. Brown married a daughter of Captain Parker, and among their children were William H. Brown, Mrs. Emma Massey and John Lewis Brown. William H. Brown was a Confederate soldier who married a Miss Henagan, and among their children were John L., Charles A., Darby H., Mrs. Isla Bancroft and Mrs. Julia Bancroft. Mrs. Massey was the mother of the wealthy Masseys of Birmingham. John Lewis Brown was a Confederate soldier and married Rosa Knox, sister of Mrs. Mary K. McDaniel. They had no children. Lewis S. Brown died in 1846 at the age of 33. His widow married H.W. Killian.

Robert L. Brown married a daughter of Captain Parker, and after his death his people all left except a daughter who married the late N.R. Battle. Her son, Jerry Battle, lives here now. A son, "Young Bob," left descendants in Louisiana.

The descendants of the other children of this Widow Brown have been mentioned.

In this connection it might be mentioned that John Brown of Sumter, South Carolina, had a younger half-brother named Jerry H. Brown who came to Sumter County, Alabama, married a Miss Hines and lived near Sumterville. Among the children of Jerry H. Brown and his wife were Mrs. Lide (afterward wife of Dr. J.G. Forster of Mt. Sterling, Choctaw County), Mrs. White and Ed Brown. Among the children of Mrs. Lide were Robert W., Leslie, Mrs. R.P. Wetmore, Mrs. Guy Blewitt and Walter. Among the children of Mrs. White were T.V., Mrs. Dr. W.J. McCain, Mrs. Dr. Reed, Professor James J. White, Mrs. James R. Jackson, W. Hubbard White, Mrs. Dickinson and David White. The husband of Mrs. White was Mr. David Campbell White of Kentucky, who served as a Confederate soldier in the noted "Orphan Brigade." Ed Brown served as a Confederate soldier and left descendants in other states.

Some time after the death of the widow of John Brown, her home in Livingston became the home of Reuben Thom, brother of Mrs. Major Cobbs and of Mrs. H.R. Thornton. It is said that his wife was a sister of the late Mr. Reuben Chapman. It is said that he served as postmaster and was a Confederate soldier. Reuben Thom has descendants named Berry living in Birmingham. Some people named Edwards were buried on this property a bit later and may have lived there.

Then this place was the home of H.R. Thornton. His brother was an officer in the U.S. Army and was killed during the Mexican War. This brother's body was brought to Livingston and buried. Among the children of H.R. Thornton and his wife were H.R. Thornton, Jr., Reuben T. Thornton, Miss Hortense, Mrs. John A. Johnston and Miss Lucy. Henry R. Thornton , Jr., and Mrs. Johnston had descendants. These people moved away in the middle 1880's, and this place was acquired by the late Judge S. H. Sprott, who lived there some twenty-five years.

After his time, it became the home of Mrs. Alice B. Patton. She was a Miss Bolton, and her mother was a sister of Colonel E.S. Gulley. The husband of Mrs. Patton was David Patton, one of the sons of Wayne C. Patton, who lived in the Brewersville region and was not related to General Patton of Sumterville so far as known. Mr. David Patton was a popular and successful lawyer of Livingston who died when he was about thirty-five years old. He and his wife had a number of children, among whom were W.W. Patton, Mrs. Hendricks of Athens, D.D. Patton of Carrollton, Roy B. Patton of Athens and Joe Patton. W.W. Patton became a prominent lawyer of Livingston and married Miss Anna Chapman, daughter of the Honorable Reuben Chapman. W.W. Patton and his wife have two daughters, Alta and Alice Dare. Roy B. Patton was a former Tax Collector, and he married a Miss Irene Foscue and they have children. Joe Patton has served as Tax Collector, and he married Miss Sara Law, a niece of Mrs. James L. Parker. Joe Patton and his wife have two children, Wayne and Lealis. Mr. David Patton had a brother, Joe Patton, of Brewersville, who married a sister of the late A.C. McMillan. Mrs. Beatrice White Jackson now [i.e. 1928] lives at this place. [The house is now divided into apartments.]

On land formerly a part of this lot, in front, so as to block up the west end of Monroe Street, is a house built, it is said, by Captain Ben F. Herr, and it later on was the home of John S. Johnston. Then it was the home of D.L.

Kirkland. After Mr. Kirkland's death, it was acquired by the widow of Mr. Daniel Mitchell, and she lives there with her daughters, Miss Sallie and Miss Olive. [This house now serves as the rectory for St. James Episcopal Church.]

This Mrs. Daniel Mitchell was originally a Winston. The Winstons were a prominent North Sumter family. William O., Augustus and James M. Winston were brothers and had at least one sister, Mrs. Dr. Dillard, who was the mother of the Judge Dillard mentioned. These people were cousins of former Governor J.A. Winston, who lived in the same neighborhood. William O. Winston was the father of the late Mr. Charles Winston of Bodka. Captain James M. Winston was the father of Mrs. C.W. McMahon and of Mrs. T.V. White, who both live in Livingston. Augustus Winston was the father of Mrs. Mitchell. Her husband, Daniel Mitchell, was a nephew of Mrs. Captain James Parker.

Among the children of Mr. and Mrs. Daniel Mitchell were County Solicitor James A. Mitchell, Mr. W.T. Mitchell, the second Mrs. Charles Winston, Dan Mitchell, Miss Sallie and Miss Olive. The younger Dan Mitchell spent a number of years in Livingston in his younger days. He worked for the former drug house of McMillan and Parker. Messrs. James A. and W.T. Mitchell went to school to Dr. S.S. Mellen when he taught in Livingston.

To the east of the Sprott or Thornton place is where Ned Ustick once lived. He was a brother of W.K. Ustick and of Mrs. John W. Adams. He had a son, Jim Ustick, who was a silversmith and is said to have gone to Eutaw. Then Robert Brewer lived here. He and his people have been mentioned. After the Civil War this became the home of Mr. W.T. McKnight, who has been mentioned. Then Woodson S. Gulley bought the place and lived there for some twenty years. He was a son of Colonel E.S. Gulley and married a daughter of Colonel J.M. Lee. The children of Mr. and Mrs. Woodson Gulley were Mrs. H.V. Hudson and Mrs. Seward.

Colonel E.S. Gulley was Colonel of the 40th Alabama Regiment of Infantry, C.S.A. Among his ancestors were the distinguished Slocums of North Carolina. He was married four times. His first wife was a Miss Thetford, sister of Dr. W.F. Thetford of Boligee. His second wife was a Miss Hinds. His third wife was a Miss Campbell. His fourth wife was a Miss Gulley of North Carolina, who had no children. The first wife was the mother of Woodson S. Gulley, Mrs. Dr. S.P. Hand and Mrs. Bettie Cockrell. The second wife was the mother of Mrs. W. H. Scarborough. The third wife was the mother of Zeke Gulley and of Mrs. Robert Campbell (afterward Mrs. Tidmore). Originally E.S. Gulley was a captain in the 40th Alabama under Colonel A.A. Coleman, then he was major, then colonel. After Mr. W.S. Gulley's death, this place became a part of the Allison property.

Dr. J.F. Allison lived at what was later called the Jack Williams place below Bellamy. His wife was a sister of Oliver Wylie, formerly a prominent man of South Sumter. Among the children of Dr. and Mrs. Allison were Charles, Evan F. and Miss Jennie. Charles Allison married a Miss Curl and was the father of Henry, Robert and Mrs. J.C. Greenwood. Evan F. Allison became wealthy and owned much property in the county. He married Miss Mary, daughter of Captain A.J. Derby, and they had a son named Richard who married a daughter of Dr. J.L. Williamson of Tuscaloosa. Richard Allison died prematurely, leaving three children, Andy, Dorothy and Jimmy.

Captain A.J. Derby was born in Canada but came to this region and served as a Confederate soldier. He married a Miss Campbell, and among their children were Mrs. E.F. Allison, Robert C., James, Andrew and Frank. The children of Captain Derby went to school in Livingston, and Mr. Robert C. Derby, who has for a long time served as Tax Assessor, resides in this town.

Across Spring Street to the east was the home of Mr. William Ustick. Among the children of William K. Ustick and his wife were Mrs. David Rast, Mrs. G.W. Dainwood, Mrs. Virginia Carré and Lilbern Ustick. Mrs. Rast's husband was a teacher. Among the children of Mr. and Mrs. Dainwood were Miss Lydia, Bob Lee and Mrs. Hardaway. Bob Lee Dainwood married Miss Bettie Richardson. Mrs. Hardaway married a son of that Colonel Hardaway who was for many years Professor of Civil Engineering at the University of Alabama. She and Mr. Hardaway had three children, Robert, George and a daughter. The Hardaways moved to Texas.

Mrs. Carré was the widow of Robert B. Carré of Purvis, Mississippi, who was of French descent and died of yellow fever in Mississippi in 1878. She returned to Livingston and for a number of years conducted a private school. She finally moved away. All of her people, with the exception of her son, Lilbern, live in El Paso, and he lives in Anniston, Alabama. The children of Mrs. Carré were Miss Alice, Lilbern, Robert, May and William U. Robert Carré was deaf, but was a fine ball player in his youth. He was Livingston's pitcher in the early 1890's. Lilbern Ustick was a member of Dent's Company and was killed in battle during the Civil War.

Mr. and Mrs. G.W. Dainwood lived at this place for many years, and then various families rented the place. It is now the home of Mr. and Mrs. W.H. Scarborough. Mr. Scarborough, a son of the Reverend Abner Scarborough, was twice married. His first wife was a Leitch. She was the mother of Mrs. Herbert Lavender. After the death of this wife, Mr. Scarborough married Miss Beckie Gulley, daughter of Colonel E.S. Gulley. The Reverend Abner Scarborough was a prominent citizen of the Bluffport community. Among his children were John and Jim Scarborough, who served as Confederate soldiers, Mrs. John Hawkins, Mrs. Zane Hoit, Mrs. William H. Hawkins, William H. Scarborough, A. Porter Scarborough and Andrew Scarborough, who married Miss Emma Winslett.

[The Ustick place has recently been purchased by the city of Livingston as the site for a new public library building.]

To the east is what was one of the early log houses, which was boarded up and improved into its present form. At an early time it was the home of a noted character named Bob Johnson, who kept a stable. Then it was the home of Bill Kirkland, another noted character who kept a stable also. Bill was not related to D.L. Kirkland so far as known. Among the children of Bill Kirkland were Bill, John and Bob, who served as Confederate soldiers, and also some daughters, one or two of whom married members of the "Bayley Troupe." This was a theatrical organization which came every year in the old days and stayed two or three weeks, giving such plays as *Major Jones' Courtship, Ben Colt*, etc. This troupe pitched a tent on a vacant lot between the store of Shearer and Lake and that of the Houston Brothers. The vacant lot was about where Branch's store and the post office now stand. [The site was on Franklin Street.] The Bayleys also played at the old courthouse.

Dolman, a plasterer, then lived at this house. He went to the Civil War in Dent's Company and was killed. Then J. Zimmern lived at the place for some time. He sold it to Captain James M. Henagan. Captain Henagan lived in South Carolina and came here after the Civil War. He had three brothers who lived in this county. These were Major Charles Henagan, Dr. Darby Henagan and Eph Henagan. He also had a nephew who was named Eph Henagan. Captain Henagan married Miss Kate Brown, daughter of George A. Brown, and they had no children. Captain Henagan moved away and this place became the home of H. Emmet Little, who has been mentioned. Sam Perry Henagan, son of Captain J.M. Henagan, married Lizzie Hill, daughter of Foster Hill of Tuscaloosa. He served in the World War and later on completely disappeared.

Various families rented the place until it was acquired by William Haywood Lawrence, who came here from Tuscaloosa in the middle 1890's and took charge of the old *Livingston Journal* of Captain Herr and changed the name of the same to *Our Southern Home*. Mr. Lawrence was a son of Captain William H. Lawrence of Tuscaloosa, and married Miss Emily Reid, daughter of Samuel and Clara Reid of Montgomery. These people are descended from Haywoods and Reids of Continental fame who lived in Raleigh, North Carolina. Mr. and Mrs. Lawrence have two daughters, Mrs. Auld and Mrs. Marcus E. McConnell. [This house was removed some years ago, and the site is now occupied by a commercial establishment and a parking lot.]

To the north of this lot was once a stable kept by Johnson and then by Owen. Captain Henagan built a dwelling here which was rented by various families. W.K. Smith, M. Tannenbaum and W.W. Bell, a Postal Telegraph employee, all lived here at different times. Then it was acquired by Dr. W.J. McCain and has been his home for many years. [This house was removed some years ago, and the site is now occupied by a commercial establishment.]

Across Monroe Street, south of the William K. Ustick or W.H. Scarborough place, is where Willis Crenshaw once lived. Old residents such as Mrs. Eason and Tully Cornick, the lawyer, said this was the first frame dwelling built in the town. Crenshaw sold the place to Wayman Staples, the sadler. Robert D. Spratt bought this place for his daughter, Mrs. A.W. Cockrell, and after her death it was bought by the late Major J.G. Whitfield, who lived in the house awhile and then rented it to the Wetmores, to the Cusacks and to Colonel Clanton, who had married a daughter of former Governor Reuben Chapman.

James P. Spratt bought the place and lived there until his death, and then it became the home of his son, Lewis B. Spratt. [This house was removed some years ago, and the site is now a city parking lot.]

To the south was once the home of Mrs. John W. Adams, who was a sister to the Ustick brothers. At a later time one Rawls lived here. He married one of the older daughters of George Wilson. Then Dr. H.B. Leverett lived here and did a big medical practice in the 1850's. Dr. Leverett served as a Confederate soldier in the latter part of the War. After the Civil War a Mrs. Underwood lived here. It seems that her father, Edward Herndon, was Register in Chancery here. Mrs. Underwood had a daughter named Malvina who died in 1876 and was buried in the Livingston Cemetery. Then this place became the home of Mr. Addison G. Smith (1851-1933). He was a son of Captain E.W. Smith and married Miss Florence Hopkins. The children of Mr. and Mrs. Smith were Edward D., Mrs. Stokeley, Addison and Sidney. Edward D. Smith is now a prominent lawyer of Birmingham. Sidney served overseas as a commissioned officer during the World War.

Mr. A.G. Smith moved to Birmingham and this place was bought by Colonel E.S. Gulley for his two daughters, Miss Bettie and Miss Beckie, and when these married it passed to Miss Bettie, who married Mr. L.A. Cockrell. The Cockrells lived here some years but were renting it to a family of the name Smith when it burned in 1921. Frank Bullock bought the lot and built a residence for himself. He married Miss Olivia Trippe of Marengo, and they have one child, Frank, Jr. [The former Bullock house now serves as offices for the State Department of Human Resources.]

To the east of this was once an office used by Dr. Griggs, a dentist, and by Dr. Reub Arrington. It was used by W.P. Billings, the carpetbagger, who was killed near Grindstone Prairie in August, 1874. Dr. James R. Garber also used this office. Mr. W.R. (Dick) Arrington converted this into a small dwelling and lived there a number of years. He married Miss Lucy Bell and they had no children. She was a sister of the last Mrs. Andrew J. Arrington. Along about 1901 the late A.C. McMillan, P.N. Horn and W.W. Patton lived here. Horn died, Patton married, and Mr. McMillan lived here himself until he died.

Allen Clifton McMillan, born in 1854, was a son of Drury McMillan and his wife, who was a McDonald. He came to Livingston as a young man and became prominent in business. He was interested in a number of enterprises and for years was the active head of McMillan & Co., Bankers. Mr. McMillan died in 1911, aged 57. He had a number of brothers and sisters, among whom were Mrs. I.W. Horn, Mrs. Dr. B.B. Seale, Mr. Felix G. McMillan and Mrs. Joe Patton of Brewersville. Mrs. Horn was the mother of the late Curtis Horn, John L. Horn, the late Preston N. Horn, the late Felix Horn, the first Mrs. John P. Scales, Mrs. Frank Derby, etc

Mrs. Seale had several children. Buford Seale is said to have been the original settler of this family. He lived near old Gaston and among his sons were Robert, Dr. B.B. (Ben), Thomas, and Arnold. Dr. B.B. Seale was the one who married Miss McMillan, and their children were Robert McMillan, Mrs. Fannie Beville (Mrs. Stone), Clifton C., T. Ben and Linwood. After the death of this wife, Dr. Seale married the widow of a Mr. Thetford who once lived at Payneville, a brother to Dr. W.F. Thetford of Boligee. This lady was a sister to the Captain Curry who married Miss Melissa Dent. She and Dr. Seale had a son, Howard, who lives at Coatopa. Dr. Seale was a dentist. Thomas Seale married a daughter of John Lockard, and among the children of these were Robert Lockard, Mrs. Eddins, Miss Cora and Thomas Franklin. Arnold was the father of Emmet Seale.

Felix G. McMillan was Tax Collector at one time. He was twice married. Among the children of his first wife were Mrs. Clarence Larkin and Dick. The only surviving child of Mr. McMillan's second marriage was Mrs. Arthur Hall.

Mrs. Joe Patton of Brewersville was the mother of Ike Patton, Mrs. John P. Jackson, Miss Janie Patton, Mrs. David Davis, Mrs. Ella Nixon, etc.

After the death of A.C. McMillan, one Gus Koppius, a German blacksmith, lived here. Gus and his brother Otto came here about 1905 or 1906. Otto attended school and finally went north, where he became a Professor of Chemistry. Gus remained here some thirteen or fourteen years. He married and had a son named Otto. About 1915 Gus Koppius brought the first electric lighting system to Livingston. His wiring was done by Harold Makin and Bill Johnston. The town bought Koppius' light plant when he left and some years later sold out to the Alabama Power Company.

The town once had old-time lamps on posts on various street corners. These lamps used gasoline and were picturesque, but gave out very little light. Just before dark the lamplighter would pass from one street lamp to another carrying a short ladder and filling and lighting each lamp. Then about 1900 what was called the "Kitson Light" was used. This was a system of gasoline under pressure and gave a good light, but required much care. Then for a time acetylene lights were tried, mainly in homes.

Gus Koppius brought Frank Kruse here. Kruse was a sailor on the then German Steamship *George Washington.* During the World War, Kruse was interned here. Later on, he took out citizenship papers, married Sallie Allen, and became a good American. They have two children. After Gus Koppius left, the place under discussion became the home of Mrs. David Davis, who was a niece of A.C. McMillan.

Across Spring Street, to the west of the Frank Bullock Corner, is a house built by the late Dr. W.H. Sledge, Jr., who practiced here awhile and then went to Mobile, where his son, Dr. Edward S. Sledge, is now a prominent physician. This place became the home of Dr. D.S. Brockway, who has been mentioned. Dr. Brockway sold it to the Bradshaws and they lived here some time. Mr. John Bradshaw was of an old Gainesville family and was a Lieutenant in the Confederate Army. He was captured and was in prison with Judge W.R. DeLoach and with Captain Hutchinson, father of Mrs. Fred H. Jones, at the Johnson Island prison. Mr. John Bradshaw married a Miss Dunlap, who was also of an old Gainesville family, and among their children were Mrs. John A. Rogers, Mrs. William G. Little, Mrs. S. Phillips Verner, Miss Mamie, Mrs. Dr. H.B. Smith, Mrs. B.C. Jones of Bessemer and John Bradshaw of Fairfield. A sister of Mr. Bradshaw lived with the family. This was the late Miss Lizzie Bradshaw, who conducted a business in Livingston for a number of years.

T. Ben Seale bought this place and lived here for a time and then sold it to his sister, Mrs. Fannie Beville. She sold it to D.M. Hyatt of North Carolina, who now lives there. T. Ben Seale was a nephew of the late A.C. McMillan and married a Miss Gordon, and they have two children, Newsome and Martha. Mrs. Beville was the widow of the late Woodie Beville and had one child, Melna Beville. Mrs. Beville afterward married a Mr. Stone of Nashville. [The house built by Dr. Sledge has not survived. The site is now occupied by a home built by the late Judge and Mrs. Wilbur Dearman.]

To the north was once a stable, and then the lot was acquired by W.K. Smith, who built himself a residence and after some years sold it to the late Mrs. Laura Little, widow of Major W.G. Little. Major Little was a cousin of Captain Ben Little and was prominent in his day. He served as a Confederate soldier in a Mississippi organization. Among the children of Major Little and his wife were James K. Little, Mrs. Bestor Brown and W.G. Little of Livingston. The younger W.G. Little married Miss Bessie Bradshaw and they have two children, William G., Jr. and Janie Mooring. William G., Jr., married a daughter of Henry Leland of Tuscaloosa, and they have a son who also bears the name of William G. He, too, has a son named William G. Major Little and his wife are buried at Shady Grove near Warsaw.

While Mrs. Little lived at the place under discussion, a number of her young relatives lived with her and attended the Livingston schools. Among them were the Watrous brothers, Will and Theodore, from British Honduras. Will Watrous was drowned on June 21, 1894, while on a fishing trip near Mt. Hebron in Greene County. He was about sixteen years old at the time. Theodore Watrous became a prosperous exporter of Central American mahogany.

Mrs. Little removed to the country, and this place was then owned by Mrs. Anna Battle of Texas, who lived here for some time with her sister, Mrs. Lemuel F. Whitehead. After Mrs. Battle's death, this place was inherited by Mrs. W.W. Patton, who had been Miss Anna Chapman, and the Pattons lived here many years. W.W. Patton died in 1937. [This house is now occupied by Dr. and Mrs. James Patrenos.]

The house now owned and occupied by Mrs. C.W. McMahon once had a large lot that included the W.W. Patton lot and the Hyatt corner lot. It is said that Price Williams built this house. He was a prominent man of early days and is said to have married a sister of Judge Nash. Then this place was the home of Dr. A.B. DeLoach. He and his wife died, and their children were looked after by Mr. and Mrs. Daniel Ayres. One of the sons of Dr. and Mrs.

DeLoach remained in Livingston and became prominent—the late Judge W.R. DeLoach who has been mentioned. Then Dr. Hal (H.F.) Arrington owned this place and rented it to various families. Colonel William M. Stone lived here for some years. He was a brother of Thomas B. Stone and married a daughter of R.F. Houston. Colonel Stone had been Captain of Company D, Jeff Davis Legion of Cavalry, C.S.A., which will be mentioned later on. The late John E. Brown purchased this place, and it was inherited by his daughter, Mrs. Lurton, who afterwards married Dr. N.F. Randall. These people have been mentioned.

Various families rented the place for some years. The Dunlaps of Eutaw had it as a sort of hotel for a time. Then it was acquired by the late Captain J.M. Winston, who left it to his daughter, Mrs. C.W. McMahon. The late C.W. McMahon was of an old Gainesville family and married Miss Gage Winston. Among the children of Mr. and Mrs. McMahon were Mrs. Morton, Miss Lilah, Winston McMahon, Captain Carl W. McMahon, Mrs. Fallow, William O. McMahon and Donald McMahon. Carl served as a Captain of Infantry and died soon after the war was over. [This house is now the home of Mrs. Robert Ennis.]

To the west is a house said to have once been the home of Robert Desha, a prominent man of wealth, said to have occasionally stayed here as he owned much property in the county, and some of his people are buried in our cemetery. There is some sort of a tradition that he was related to the Duke of Marlborough. He owned this place, the Hadley place at McCainville, and a place east of town. To all of these he sent flowers to be set out, and among them were seeds of the nut grass which has spread over the country from these three places.

Then a Sanders, an uncle of W.S. Nichols, owned this place and sold it to Captain E.W. Smith. Captain Smith was a son of Stephen and Sallie Ann Smith of North Carolina. He was captain of a military company here before the Civil War, but the company went to war under John H. Dent. Later on, Captain Smith organized another company of which he was captain, but it was in the latter part of the war and it was impossible to equip the company, so it never saw active service as an organization. Captain Smith married a daughter of M.C. Houston and their children were Messrs. Addison G., Stephen and Walter K. Smith, who were all prominent and whose people have been mentioned. Captain E.W. Smith saw active service as a Confederate soldier with Captain Jones' Company, 40th Alabama.

Then this place became the home of Major J.G. Harris. Major Harris married a daughter of John E. Brown. He is said to have introduced Johnson Grass into this section. For some time before leaving here, Major Harris lived at what is now the McMahon place, while this other place under discussion became the home of Mrs. Lydia Amason, widow of Asa Amason, a wealthy man of the Sumterville neighborhood. The children of this Mrs. Amason were Mrs. Robert Neilson, S.C.M. Amason and Miss Kate. Mrs. Neilson left a daughter, Nellie, who married J. Hamilton Hoit. S.C.M. Amason was a lawyer and was once a representative in the State Legislature. These people went to Birmingham and the place was rented to various families until it was acquired by Mrs. Fannie Beville (now Mrs. Stone), who sold it to her brother, T.B. Seale, who now lives here. [This house is now the home of Mrs. Jerry Dorman.]

To the west is said to be the site of an old jail. Later on, H.H. Harris, known to his friends as "Chub" Harris, built a dwelling and lived here. Mr. Harris married a Miss Park, a sister of Dr. Robert Park, John Park and Mrs. Dr. Hebard (wife of an early dentist). The mother of this Mrs. Harris was originally a Miss Mason and married Robert Park (who died in 1835) and then William M. Cunningham, and she had two widowed sisters, Mrs. Bedell and Mrs. Goodman. Mrs. Bedell married Ben S. Barker, and Mrs. Goodman married R.C. Howie. Among the children of Mr. and Mrs. H.H. Harris were Park M. Harris, Henry Harris, Robert Harris, Dr. Sam B. Harris, Dr. Norflet T. Harris and Miss Eva. Park M. Harris served as a Confederate soldier and married a Miss Loula Gordon. They had two sons, Gordon and Frank Harris, who went to school in Livingston in their young days. The widow of Park M. Harris married John H. Norville. Henry Harris left descendants in other states. Robert Harris died unmarried and so did Dr. Norflet, who was a dentist. Dr. Sam Harris, also, was a dentist who was twice married, and both wives had children. Miss Eva adopted a relative, Bessie Underwood. Bessie, a pretty girl, married a Dr. Johnson and was drowned with her three children in a ferry boat accident in Jacksonville, Florida, in 1914. Dr. S.B. Harris died in 1928, aged 71. Miss Eva Harris died in 1933, the last of this family.

After the death of Mrs. Harris, W.K. Smith and various others rented this place until it became the home of Julian B. Ennis, who lived there some time. Julian was a son of Robert W. Ennis and married Miss Juanita Pickens, who was related to the late W.K. Pickens. T.V. White bought this place from Ennis and has made it his home since that time. Mr. White is a grandson of Jerry H. Brown and his people have been mentioned. Mrs. T.V. White is a daughter of the late Captain James M. Winston. The children of Mr. and Mrs. T.V. White are Mrs. Robert Barnes of Eutaw, Winston White, Olive, Addie, Cameron and Hubbard White. Winston White served overseas during the World War. He married Marie Williams. [Addie now lives in this house.]

West of this, a sort of lane leads to what is called the Hooks place, where Thad E. Lockard, our last Confederate veteran, who died November 26, 1929, has lived for such a long time. W.D. Battle, Sr., lived at this place about 1847, but it had been built and occupied by others before that date. Then it became the home of John C. Gillespie, said to have married the daughter of Francis Foard. The Gillespies had two daughters and one of these is said to have married Johnson Williams, Jr., son of Johnson Williams, the lawyer. Francis Foard owned most of the land around Livingston in very early times and is said to have been the original owner of the Planters Hotel. He was buried in the cemetery in an overground vault made of marble. This vault was cracked long ago so as to expose the bones, and the writer's father has told of going there as a boy to peep in at the bones.

At a later time this was the home of Dr. M. C. Kinnard. There were two related families here; one spelled the name "Kennard" and the other "Kinnard." In this region both names were accented on the first syllable. This Dr. Kinnard married a Miss Kennard, and among other children they had a son named Jim who was a noted character in his youth.

At one time this home was rented by J. Hafter, who became the father of triplets while living here. Then this was the home of David Hooks. Mrs. Hooks was related to her husband, and her maiden name was Hooks. These people were related to the Slocums of North Carolina. The children of Mr. and Mrs. Hooks were E.W. Hooks, Coster Hooks and two daughters who both married the same man, Rogers. The last Mrs. Rogers had two daughters who both married the same man, a Mr. Canterberry of Linden. George W. Rogers was a Confederate soldier.

E.W. Hooks—his name was Erasmus and he was known to his friends as "Ras"— was a quiet, gentlemanly person who never married. He served as a Confederate soldier with Ed Lockard in the Williams Company from Gainesville. Coster Hooks left a daughter, Mrs. Holaday, and a son named Warren. E.W. Hooks and T.E. Lockard lived at this place for a number of years. Mr. Hooks died about 1919.

South of this last place was the home of Squire Bob Arrington. He was a brother of Dr. Hal Arrington and is said to have been a very forceful person. Among his children were a son, Joseph, who died; another son who was a physician and was named Robert H. Arrington; and a daughter named Rebecca, who was the first wife of the Honorable Reuben Chapman.

Then this was for years the home of Dr. Reub Arrington. He married a daughter of John H. Sherard, and their children were Henry, Solon and Miss Julia. Henry married Miss Eva Tankersley and left two daughters, Mrs. Stevenson and Mrs. Roberts. Solon Arrington lived in Mississippi. He married and had a daughter. Solon died in 1933. Miss Julia married Robert A. Barnes and they had two sons, John and Robert. John died and Robert lives in Meridian. The widow of Dr. Reub Arrington married Mr. J. Clint Houston and moved to Meridian. Mrs. Henry Arrington lived at this place a number of years and taught in our schools. As stated, she was a daughter of Robert Tankersley.

She sold this place to W.R. Stinson, and he has lived there since. Mr. Stinson was born at or near Aberdeen, Mississippi. His first wife was a daughter of John R. Jackson of Sumterville, and among her children were Mrs. Will Gardner, Mrs. Joe Clippard, Mrs. Hendley of Mississippi, and W.R. Stinson, Jr. After her death, Mr. Stinson married a daughter of Charles H. Bullock, and she is the mother of Murray Stinson and Elizabeth.

South of this place is a house built by the late Robert A. Barnes. Various families have rented it since his death. It is now owned by the Hyatts. Frank L. and Burlin R. Starnes, who went to school in Livingston, were nephews of Robert A. Barnes.

The Arringtons have been mentioned several times, and it might be well to say something about this family now. The name has about disappeared, but the family connection is extensive. It seems that General Joseph Arrington of North Carolina had twenty-one sons and daughters, eighteen of whom grew up and married. General Arrington came to Sumter County, Alabama, and settled at what was once known as Arrington's Station on the "Little Southern" Railroad. The place is now known as Woodford.

Dr. Hal Arrington and Squire Bob Arrington, who were brothers, were related to General Joseph Arrington, being, it is said, cousins in some degree. Mrs. Jim Mason and her sister, Mrs. W.D. Battle, Sr., and their brothers, Crawford, Bennett and Jesse Arrington, were nieces and nephews of General Joseph Arrington. It is said that Mrs. Josiah Moore, who was afterward Mrs. Branch, was a niece of Squire Bob and Dr. Hal. Her mother was their sister, Mrs. John Ward.

General Joseph Arrington and Crawford Arrington, Sr., were sons of Arthur Arrington. Betsy Arrington, a sister of Squire Bob and Dr. Hal Arrington, married John Ward, and Rebecca Ward, their daughter, married first Josiah Moore and then James Branch. After the death of this John Ward, his widow married her cousin, Crawford Arrington, Sr., General Joseph Arrington's brother, and thus became the stepmother of Mrs. W.D. Battle, Sr., Mrs. Jim Mason, Crawford Arrington, Jr., Bennett Arrington and Jesse Arrington. The wife of Squire Bob Arrington was named Patience Ann Wright. Bennett Arrington died in Texas. Jesse Arrington died in Demopolis.

Among the children of General Joseph Arrington who affected the history of Livingston in a greater or lesser degree were William Arrington, Edward Arrington, Dr. Sam Arrington, Andrew J. Arrington, Mrs. Fred Evans, Mrs. J.L. Scruggs, Mrs. John H. Sherard, Joseph Arrington, Mrs. M.E. Whitehead, Mrs. Anna Battle and Mrs. J. Clint Houston (Mr. Houston's first wife).

William Arrington was the father of Messrs. J.C. and W.R. (Jim and Dick) Arrington, who were Confederate soldiers. Edward and Andrew J. Arrington were prominent in the county. This Mrs. Scruggs was the mother of Mrs. Billiou, Mrs. Kate Chapman, Mrs. W.D. Battle, Jr., J.O. Scruggs, Dr. Sam Scruggs and Mrs. Lyle. Mrs. Evans was the mother of A.P. (Apollos) Evans, Paul E. Evans, Mrs. John Sprott and Mrs. W.H.A. Voss. Mrs. Battle spent most of her time in Texas, where she had much property. Mrs. Whitehead, widow of Lemuel Whitehead, was for many years prominent in church and social affairs. Joseph Arrington seems to have been married several times. He went to Mississippi many years ago and was the father of the Miss Ethel Arrington, later Mrs. Allen of Memphis, who attended the Normal School here in her younger days. Edward Arrington was the father of the last Mrs. Dr. R.H. Hale of York. Mr. and Mrs. Houston had no children.

The name Battle has been mentioned. This family came from North Carolina. W.D. Battle, Sr., married a Miss Arrington, daughter of Crawford Arrington, Sr., and niece of General Joseph Arrington. Among their children were W.D. Battle, Jr., Ned R., Dave T., Crawford A., Mrs. Jessie Lawhon, Mrs. Mattie Battle and Soc Battle. W.D. Battle, Jr., was of distinguished appearance and was known as "Major" Battle. He served in the Sengstak (afterward Barrett's) Battery, C.S.A., along with John Trott, Wellington Murley, Bob Kirkland, Jim Hoit, Henry G. Harris and Bob McDonald from York. Major Battle married Miss Ludie Scruggs, and among their children were Mrs. McKay, Mrs. Oscar Gray, Mrs. W.S. Nichols and Jodie. Ned Battle married a daughter of Robert Brown, and they had a number of children, among them Ned, Jr., who married a daughter of Jim David, and Jerry, who is the only one of this family now living here. D.T. Battle married Miss Mollie Kornegay, and they had a number of children, among them Gray, Dave, Frank, Bessie, Crawford, Dan, Jeff and two younger girls who married away from here. Dan and Jeff served as soldiers overseas during the World War. Crawford was doing some special work during this war and died, probably as a result of exposure, as he was of delicate physique. Bessie married P.M. Nelson, a Confederate veteran, and lives near Livingston. Ben [?] and Crawford A. Battle did not marry, and Soc has not lived in the state since his youth, but resides at West Palm Beach, Florida.

Mrs. Lawhon had one daughter, Ruby, who married Huriosco Austill of Mobile, descended from old Jeremiah Austill, one of the heroes of the "Canoe Fight" in the Creek War days.

Mrs. Mattie Battle's husband was one of the Tuscaloosa Battles. They had two children.

South of and across West Main Street from the T.V. White place was the home of William H. Cunningham. He was a cabinet maker and, among other things, he made and sold coffins. It is related that some planter in the neighborhood had told him that he was going to send a Negro for a coffin early the next morning, so Mr. Cunningham rose up early and went to his shop to prepare for the Negro's coming. It seems that during the night an Irish working man of the town got very drunk and fell asleep and the boys got some blacking and blacked his face most thoroughly. This Irishman was named Jim something or other. Jim woke up, still dizzy, and roamed about until he saw a light in Mr. Cunningham's shop and went in. Mr. Cunningham thought it was the man coming in for the coffin and so addressed him, but when the man spoke in an Irish accent, he knew what had happened and sent Jim to a mirror to look at himself. Jim was so frightened that he ran out and got under a nearby house and was dislodged with difficulty—he thought he had turned black.

Mr. Cunningham married the Widow Park. She was originally Evelyn Mason, daughter of John and Sophia Slaughter Mason. Her father is said to have brought the first steam sawmill to this county, and her brother, Jim, who also operated a mill, was killed in some kind of a sawmill accident near the old covered bridge site. Among the children of Mr. and Mrs. Cunningham were Mrs. Robert Tankersley, Tully, Frank and Miss Ida. Tully was named, it is said, for the old lawyer, Tully Cornick, and was a Confederate soldier.

Jim Mason, the brother of Mrs. Cunningham, married a sister of Mrs. W.D. Battle, Sr., and they had two daughters, Bettie, who married H. Otto Voss, and Mollie, who married Daniel Underwood of the Sumterville region and was the mother of the Bessie Underwood before mentioned. The Underwoods lived between Sumterville and Emelle, where Arch Boyd now lives.

The widowed sisters of Mrs. Cunningham also came here. They were Mrs. Goodman and Mrs. Bedell. Mrs. Goodman married R.C. Howie, and Mrs. Bedell, who had a son named Albert Bedell, married Mr. B.S. Barker. Barker had a large carriage factory here once. He was a Confederate soldier and served as Mayor. Among the children of Mr. and Mrs. Barker were Mrs. Davidson, Benjy and Billy. Mrs. Barker lived at this Cunningham place for awhile but then moved away, and various families rented it. Among them was the family of "Marse" Tony Cleveland, who made a good living shipping our Bored Well water. Mr. Cleveland was twice married. His first wife was the mother of Charles Henry Cleveland. This place is now owned and occupied by the widow of B.C. Hunter. She was Miss Lizzie Cusack and lived at this place with her widowed sister, Mrs. Helen Smith. [This house is now the home of Mrs. Margaret Walburn.]

The Cusacks were early settlers. Thomas Cusack of South Carolina settled at what is now the Manley Farm near Epes. Thomas Cusack and Thomas Lockard, Sr., came from the same place in South Carolina. After Priscilla, Cusack's first wife died, he married the widow of Obadiah Hand. His son, John C. Cusack, said to have been handsome and talented, married the daughter of Judge Sion L. Perry. Two of their children survived to leave descendants. These were the late J. Eugene Cusack and the late Mrs. Columbus Hainsworth. This daughter of Judge Perry was a remarkable person. After the death of John C. Cusack, she married a man named Foster and lived near Moscow. Mr. Foster died and she bought the Mark Parker place near McCainville and moved there, but she soon married Mr. Jack Eason of that neighborhood and was known to all in her old age as Mrs. Eason. (She lived to be 84.)

J. Eugene Cusack (1834-1924) married Miss Corinna, daughter of J.W. Harris, who was a brother of H.H. Harris. Among the children of J. Eugene Cusack and his wife were Mrs. Helen Smith, Mrs. Lizzie Hunter and Clarence Cusack. Mrs. Hunter was the second wife of B.C. Hunter, who was a native of Kentucky and fought in the Confederate Army. Mr. Hunter located in Sumter County, Alabama, and married Miss Anna Trott. She was the mother of D.H., B.C, and Charlie Hunter, and there was also a daughter, Anna T., who married George K. Little of Tuscaloosa. After the death of this wife, Mr. Hunter married Miss Lizzie Cusack and she is the mother of Eugene Hunter of Mobile.

Mrs. Columbus Hainsworth was survived by a daughter, Mrs. Suydam, who left descendants.

There was a day when the Hainsworths and McGrews of the Moscow region were a law unto themselves. The writer's father said they would come to town when he was a boy, and he would follow them about in silent admiration, as they were picturesque and very fascinating to the youthful mind. They would come in well-mounted, wearing pistols, spurs and big hats, and their hair was worn long in the fashion of the old-time scouts.

James L. Hainsworth married a Miss Theodosia Trigg. He and Mr. Thomas Scales, father of Dr. J.P. Scales, had some trouble and it led to an encounter between them in which Hainswoth was killed and Scales was desperately wounded but lived many years after this. This took place on October 19, 1857, near the W.H. Coleman and Company corner, i.e. the northwest corner of the intersection at West Main and Washington Streets.The widow of Mr. Hainsworth married Captain James Mooring, and after his death she spent many years in the family of Major W.G. Little, whose children and grandchildren called her "Aunt Doe."

A story is told of Miss Sallie Hainsworth, a sister of this James L. Hainsworth, showing that she was a woman of spirit. It seems that she had to cross the Tombigbee River for some reason or other, and two of the younger and wilder McGrew boys were rowing a boat. The boys rowed out into the stream and then let the boat drift while they took out their pistols and threatened to shoot the boat full of holes unless Miss Sallie got upon one of the seats and danced jigs for their amusement. She danced and danced until the boat drifted some distance, and then they laid their pistols down and began to row. She managed to get their pistols and then compelled them to swim to shore for her amusement—and the water was very cold. This Miss Sallie Hainsworth married Dr. Estill of Coatopa and was the mother of Sam Estill.

To the east is a house where the widow of Napoleon Sherard, who had been a Dinkins, once lived. She had a son Jack who married a Miss Beebe, and she also had a daughter who married Alonzo Kornegay. Mr. and Mrs. Kornegay had three children, Jesse, Fannie and Napoleon, generally known as Nep. Nep died in 1923. The family of Major Cox, a Union veteran, lived at this place awhile. Mrs. Cox was a Miss Debardeleben, related to those of Birmingham, and she had several daughters, including Louise and Annie. Louise Cox married Frank Bancroft. Later on, W.G. Coop lived at this place. Coop was an Englishman and could do many things well. He was a good carpenter, a good painter, and a fair musician, being able to play the violin, the piano, and the ordinary church organ. Coop moved to Birmingham and died.

Along about 1904, O.G. Breitling acquired this house and has lived there since. He married a Miss Cordelia Cooper, and among their children were Robert O. Breitling, Mrs. William Beebe, Mrs. Thigpen, Frank, Mrs. Hodgson, and Mrs. James L. Scruggs. Mrs. Breitling died in 1930. [This house is now the home of Mrs. Kelly Land and her sister, Mrs. Orlean Tartt.]

Next to the east is a house built and occupied by Dr. Hal Arrington, one of the early physicians of the town. His wife was a Jemison, and since they had no children, this place passed to Dr. Arrington's niece, who married the Honorable Reuben Chapman, son of Judge Samuel Chapman. This Mrs. Chapman was the mother of Miss Alta and of Robert A. Chapman. After her death Mr. Chapman married Miss Catherine Scruggs, and she was the mother of Mrs. Cobb, Reuben Jr., Mrs. W.W. Patton and Miss Lulu. The Honorable Reuben Chapman was a captain in the Confederate Army. Miss Lulu married John H. Sherard of Coahoma County, Mississippi. Various families rented the place after Mr. Chapman died—the family of C.M. McCain, the family of John P. Ramsay, Mrs. Cobb, and possibly others. It is now used as a sort of apartment house.

To the east is a house built by M. Shulman, who lived here a number of years. Various families rented it after the Shulmans left, and finally it was bought by P.B. Jarman and was later the home of his son, Mitchell C. Jarman. Mitchell was Clerk of the Circut Court and married a daughter of the Reverend F.A. Rogers. She died in 1929, and this house was bought by G.W. Brock. [It is now the home of Mr. and Mrs. Bob Holycross.]

To the east is where Rains once had an inn. It is an old log house boarded up. It is said that Colonel Cooper also lived here once. Then it was the home of Tom Ward from Georgia, a brother of Mrs. Judge Abrahams. Then it was the home of B.M. Emanuel, said to have been related to the Rosenbush family and a rabbi. His daughter married Herman Tannenbaum. Then Mr. Adolph Brown lived here, and after him, the Tannenbaums. Mr. Moses Tannenbaum was married, and Mr. Ben, his brother, was single. Mr. Moses married a Miss Levi, and their children were Mrs. Levy, Herman and Mrs. Goodman. Solly Levi was a nephew of Mrs. Tannenbaum. J.K. Shelton bought the place and lived there. He was a son of Robert Shelton, and his mother was a McDonald. His brother Andrew married a daughter of J.O. Scruggs, and J.K. married a niece of T.F. Seale. William G. Little, son of W.G. Little, bought this place about 1920, and since then has lived there. His people have been mentioned. [This home is now owned by Mr. and Mrs. Greg McNider.]

To the south was once a large lot, on the north [South?]end of which is the old spring that originally tempted the weary traveler to settle here. This spring is still used as a water supply, being largely used for cooking and washing purposes.

Waldo W. Shearer once had a fine house on this house lot, and it was afterward occupied by Mr. Lemuel F. Whitehead, an early lawyer, who had married a daughter of General Joseph Arrington. This house burned. [The home of Mr. and Mrs. Robert P. Upchurch and the parsonage for the Livingston United Methodist Church now occupy this lot. In the 1930's this area became the site of Livingston's first municipal swimming pool, with the old spring providing a constant source of fresh water.]

The spring was located in a sort of gully where there was never any dwelling, but at a later time, just south of the spring, was a house occupied by W.H.A. Voss, who married a daughter of Fred Evans. Mr. Voss and his brother, H.Otto Voss, came from Germany and served as Confederate soldiers, and W.H.A. Voss lost an arm in this service. He once told the writer of an interesting encounter between two armed steamers on the Mississippi River. He was on one of the river steamers. Mr. and Mrs. Voss had no children, but this place was acquired by William S. Nichols, the banker, who married Mollie, a daughter of W.D. Battle, Jr. [The Nichols house had, at one time, been divided into apartments, but it was bought by Dr. and Mrs. James Pate—Dr. Pate was a Professor and Dean at Livingston University, now the University of West Alabama—and they restored it.]

To the south was a house once the home of Mrs. Virginia Ustick Carré, whose people have been mentioned. She was the widow of Robert Carré, who died in Purvis, Mississippi of yellow fever. P.J. Jarman bought this place. He came from near Cuba and has served as Sheriff, Tax Collector and Probate Judge. He married a Miss Gordon, and their children are Peterson, Mrs. Hubert Dent and Mitchell C. Peterson served as a commissioned officer in France during the World War and was wounded in battle. [He also served for some years as Congressman from this district.]Mrs. Jarman was related to the late Probate Judge Thomas R. Crews. She died in 1931. Judge Jarman sold this place to the late Mr. Fred H. Jones, whose people have been mentioned, and the widow of Mr. Jones, Mrs. Mary H. Jones, sold the place to Mr. Wade Coleman. The Colemans now live in this place. [The Coleman house is now the home of Mr. and Mrs. Gary Busby.]

To the south, down under the hill, is a house built by the late Jesse Butler Coleman, a kindly and useful citizen who was accidentally drowned during the high water of 1892. Mr. Coleman served as a Confederate soldier and married a Miss Kynerd. Among the children of Mr. and Mrs. Coleman were Webb, Wade Hampton, Mrs. Herbert, and Mrs. Heard. This place became the home of Wade H. Coleman. He married Miss Lillian Jackson of a prominent Montgomery family, and their children are W.H., Jr., Jeff, Sarah Hart, Nell and Clayton. Another daughter of J.B. Coleman married Dr. Scott of Birmingham, and they have children.

A number of families of the name Coleman have lived in this town. One of the first settlers was Dr. William Harris Coleman, said to have been from Washington County. His first wife, who is buried in the cemetery, is said to have left two sons. Dr. Coleman later married a daughter of George G. Tankersley, and she was the mother of a number of children who attended the Livingston schools in their young days. Then there was Circuit Judge A.A.

Coleman, who once lived near Livingston and married a Phares. Another Dr. W.H. Coleman, who left descendants in the Coatopa section, is said to have lived in Livingston at one time. His wife was a Shackleford, and their son married a McCarthy. So far as known, these people were not related to each other, nor were they related to Jesse B. Coleman's people.

East across Spring Street from the W.S. Nichols home was once a large lot on which grew a number of cedar trees. There was a brick house on this lot that was at various times occupied by a family of Campbells, by the family of Colonel Charles R. Gibbs and by Captain E.W. Smith. Mr. A.G. Smith says that he and his brother Stephen were born here.

About 1882 a school building was put up and was added to a year or so later. Dr. S.S. Mellen taught here, and it was known as Cedar Grove Academy and later as the Livingston Military Academy. M.E. McConnell and J.H. Norville bought the lot about 1912, demolished the old school building and built a house which was rented to various families including Strand, Haralson, O.F. Adams and perhaps others. This house is now owned and occupied by G.H. Grant. [The Grant house is now the home of Mr. and Mrs. Robert M. Seale.]

Across Madison Street to the north from Grant's place is one of the old log houses boarded up. This was at an early time the home of D.H. Trott, a newspaperman. Mr. Trott's wife was a Jemison and the children of Mr. and Mrs. Trott were John J. Trott, Mrs. B.C. Hunter, D.H. Trott, Jr., Mrs. Harrison Johnston, Mrs. W.W. Smith, Mrs. Lewis Murray and Mrs. Sid Williams. John J. Trott was a member of the Sengstak Battery, C.S.A., and was a noted character. Some of his sayings and doings were quite out of the ordinary, and I would that I had the words. Mr. Trott moved to the Major Battle corner and was succeeded at the place under discussion by John H. Dent, a son of General Dennis Dent of Tuscaloosa.

A militia company at Livingston was commanded prior to the War Between the States by Captain E.W. Smith. John H. Dent succeeded to the command of this company, and it was the first organization to leave the county for this war. It seems that when they were ready to go, Captain Dent was taken ill, and General Dent, his father, took the command temporarily. The company went to Pensacola, Florida, where one of its members, James L. Parrent, died of measles. Then it went to Virginia and remained there until Lee surrendered. There was some sort of a public ceremony when this company left, and a flag was presented by an aunt of this writer. Susan Spratt was this aunt's name, and she married A.W. Cockrell. The flag was received by Charles DuBose, who had clerked for J.L. Scruggs, the druggist. This company was Company G, Fifth Alabama.

The wife of Captain Dent was a Travis, and among their children was a daughter, Melissa, who married a Captain Currie of Missouri, and their son, the late Dr. Donald H. Currie, was a valued officer of the U.S. Public Health

Service. Captain Dent had a younger brother named George who was a member of the Dent Company and was killed in battle.

The Dent family left here, and this place became the home of W.J. Nichols, who married a Miss Sanders, and their surviving children were Mrs. Ed L. Mitchell and William S. Nichols, the banker. After the death of Mrs. W.J. Nichols this place became the home Mr. and Mrs. Ed. L. Mitchell. [This house is now the home of Mr. and Mrs. Robert E. (Bob) Upchurch.]

J.W. Arnold and Ed L. Mitchell once had a business at the Bob Witt Hotel and later on in the Harris Brick store. H.C. Abbott, of Birmingham, was employed by them as a watch repairer. Mr. Arnold married Miss Hettie Hazelwood, a niece of the last Mrs. George Wilson, and their children, Henry and Gertrude Arnold, were well known here in their early days.

It was once a matter of common knowledge throughout this region that the grandfather of Ed. L. Mitchell, Mr. Ben Mitchell, was the hero of the *Eliza Battle* disaster, which happened in 1857 or, as some say, in 1858. The *Eliza Battle* was the finest steamboat on the Tombigbee, in the days when steamboats were steamboats. This vessel was on her way to Mobile with a crowd of passengers and a load of cotton bales. Cotton of that day was put into bales tied with ropes. The river was high, being out in the low places, and there was a cold wind blowing. Opposite James Bluff in Choctaw County the boat was found to be on fire. According to Captain Eugene C. Hunter the *Eliza Battle* was burned about halfway between Naheola and Tompkins Bluff, about 185 miles above Mobile. The tiller ropes burned so that it could not be steered, and the wind blew it over to the eastern bank, which was low and covered with water. The ropes around the cotton bales burned and the cotton bulged out and caught fire everywhere. Many people perished. Some swam into the flooded forest on the east bank and climbed trees, and a number of these died of exposure.

Mr. Ben Mitchell pushed cotton bales overboard and placed people on them so they could float away to possible safety. Then he plunged into the river and swam across to the west bank, where he went along the bluff until he found a place he could climb and then, after some time, he found people who brought small boats and made fires along the bank. He returned with a small boat and rescued a number of others. He said it was warmer in the water than in the wind.

This Mr. Ben Mitchell died about 1859 and is buried at Bethel near Sumterville. He had several sons who were Confederate soldiers, among them two who were well known in Livingston, J. Montgomery Mitchell and Dave W. Mitchell. A daughter married Dr. Silliman. J. Montgomery Mitchell, known as "Uncle Mun," is ninety-five years old at this writing and has retained his faculties well. Among his children was Ed L. Mitchell, who came to Livingston as a young man and married Miss Jessie Nichols. Dave W. Mitchell was a former Sheriff. His first wife was the mother of the late Ernest L. Mitchell of

Epes, and Mr. Mitchell's last wife was the mother of Minnie Mitchell, who married the late Vernon Tutt.

To the north of this last place, there were two saloons in the early days of the town. A part of the present lot there was Captain Dent's horse lot. After the saloons had moved elsewhere, Dainwood, Sanders and Nichols had a woodworking establishment here, and the upstairs part of the building was used as a school by Newton J. Hamill, Davis Rast and other teachers. Then Captain B.F. Herr lived here and had his printing office in the same building. Mrs. Dr. J.G. Forster, a daughter of Jerry H. Brown whose first husband was H.S. Lide, bought this lot, had the old building removed, and put up a good-sized residence here. After her death it was sold to Mr. John Bradshaw and after his death, his people sold it to Dr. D.S. Brockway. Dr. Brockway died April 15, 1929.

To the east were three small offices used in early times by various lawyers and doctors, among them Squire James Hair, Dr. H.B. Leverett and A.W. Cockrell. Later on they were used by Dr. Forster, Dr. Reub Arrington, Dr. J.T. Nash, the *Sumter Sun*, Sam O. Harkness, Gus Koppius, W.H.A. Voss, Major Levy and possibly others. Now and then a traveling photographer did business in one or the other of these. Finally R.B. Callaway bought them and combined the three into a small dwelling and lived in it. [Most of this block on West Main, east from the corner of Spring Street, is now occupied by the Regions Bank.]

Robert Baker Callaway was reared at Greensboro and has taught school in various places. He has been Superintendent of Education in Sumter County for some thirty-five years. He married Miss Margaret Edmunson, daughter of John King Edmunson of Nashville, Tennessee. Mrs. Callaway's brothers, J.K., Jr., and W.B. Edmunson, were once well known here. These Edmunsons are related to the family of Alabama'a statesman, William Rufus King. The surviving children of Professor and Mrs. Callaway are Helen, who married Graham Putman of Birmingham, and Marguerite, who married Bryan Whitfield of Florida. Both of these daughters have children. R.B. Callaway died suddenly at the courthouse on July 30, 1928. He was 76.

To the east, on the southwest corner of the intersection at West Main and Washington Streets, is a double store building erected soon after the Civil War by W.J. Nichols and later owned by his son, W.S. Nichols. Various persons have rented these premises and done business in them. At the present time one side is used by Ed L. Mitchell and the other by Tom A. Phillips. [This corner is now occupied by a parking lot.]

To the south is a much older building now used as a storage place for coffins, etc. This place was once the saddle shop of Wayman Staples, and later on Buck Anderson had a saddle shop here. It is said that soon after the Civil War, Park M. Harris had a grocery business here. Then it was used as a tin shop by H.D. Fellows, assisted by his son Harry. One Mager, a German tinner, also helped here. The name *Mager* became corrupted to "Majors." (In the original name the "ager" of *Mager* sounds like the "ager" of *lager*.) Harry Fellows conducted this shop for awhile after his father died. There was a hall upstairs used as a Masonic Lodge.

South of the old saddle shop was once a small office used as a drug store by Dr. William Harris Coleman and later on used as a drug store by W.J. Nichols. Dr. Reub Arrington and R.W. Ennis clerked for Dr. Coleman here. Dr. M.C. Kinnard is said to have succeeded to W.J. Nichols' drug business, and he moved to the old Gibbons Tin Shop to be mentioned later.

South of this was the store of James Abrahams. This is said to have been the first frame store in the town. In 1875 this old store was removed and was succeeded by a larger store with a hall upstairs. This hall was such a noted place that the whole building became known as Abrahams Hall. The hall was used as a place for rollerskating, dances, suppers, shows of all kinds, etc.

H.M.S. Pinafore was once given here by local talent. Captain W.A.C. Jones, Dr. R.D. Webb and Mrs. Mary C. Short were directors and managers, and among the performers were Miss Aline Jones (Mrs. Sims), Miss Ella Gaines Parker (Mrs. Going), Miss Florence Hopkins (Mrs. A.G. Smith), a Miss Cook from Gainesville, Colonel T.B. Wetmore, Major Thomas Cobbs, Albert Bedell, Boone Cobbs, Captain James M. Henagan and possibly others. Miss Aline Jones was Buttercup. (The students at the College also gave *Pinafore* in 1932.)

About 1884 "Blind Tom," the Negro musical prodigy, gave a performance here. Tom was blind from birth, but he could play anything on the piano that he ever heard. Some time later, James O'Connor gave a performance of *Richelieu* at the hall. It seems that he was a rather noted actor of his day who became mentally deranged so that he traveled about with a number of attendants. Whenever the notion to act struck him, he would give a performance, no matter how small the town. Also, one Raspe taught dancing at the hall in the early 1890's.

After Judge Abrahams died, various people rented the store part of the Abrahams Hall Building. Among these were T.E. Lockard; Seymour, Norville and Jenkins; D.L. Kirkland; Captain Abney; and possibly others. Then the building became a livery stable and passed into the possession of the late M.B. Rosenbush. Soon after his death the old building fell, and Edwin Rosenbush converted what was left of it into a storage place for automobiles.

South of this is another very old building. It was once used as a grocery store by the Harris brothers, J.W. and H.H. Then it became a saloon, and then was used as a restaurant. Joe Jowers lived in it for a time, and it is now a Negro hotel (the Deer Saloon), kept by Bob Witt, the drayman.

The Jowers family were rather strange people who lived in this region. In some respects they resembled Gypsies, and no one knew anything about their origin. Joe, who lived in this house just mentioned, had brothers by the names of "Doc," Hiram and "Hook," and there were also a number of sisters.

To the south were two small houses of brick. One was used by Mr. Cunningham and one by Mr. Connolly, the bootmaker. Connolly, for a time, was postmaster, and the post office was here. These brick buildings fell down and were replaced by frame cabins.

South of these is a small house built by Jerry Brown, son of Robert, for his sister, Mrs. Battle.

On the corner to the south is an old house that has been variously used. A Habercorn family once lived in it. Newton Hamill once had a school here. J.W. Harris used it as a post office. William Beggs bought it and was living in it when his wife died. [This building is currently in use as law offices for the attorney Robert M. Seale and his father, Judge Thomas F. Seale. All the other old buildings in this block on the south side of Washington Street have been replaced by modern facilities used as law offices, the County Health Department, and a dry cleaning establishment.]

Across the street to the south, on the southwest corner of the intersection at Madison and Washington Streets, is what for many years has been known as the "Major Battle Corner." There was an old dwelling here with an office that stood right in this corner. [This site is now occupied by an apartment building.] The office was used as a school room by Hamill and as a dental office. It was also used as a rooming place by various young men about town and by some of the older boys who came from distant places to attend the schools here. Among those who roomed here might be mentioned W.A. Sims, P.N. Horn and Fincher Bobo. Bobo married a sister of John E. Brock. At an early time D.H. Trott lived in the dwelling, and later it was the home of the Purdys. It is said one Purdy married a Widow Ratigan, who was a sister of Judge Nash and the mother of Dan and Emmet Ratigan, who were in Dent's Company.

Then Buck Anderson lived here, and then it was the home of Dr. Berryman Hawkins, a dentist who had served as a Confederate soldier and is buried in the Livingston cemetery. He was a very large man, not fleshy but with an almost gigantic frame. His wife spoke to and of him as "Mist' 'Awkins," and it sounded alarming to bashful gentleman patients of the good doctor, as they thought she was referring to her stockings, unless they knew her and her manner of speaking to her husband.

Later on, the place became the home of W.D. Battle, Jr., usually known in his later years as "Major" Battle. He and his people have been mentioned. After the death of Major Battle, this place was bought by Mr. E.C. Vaughan, a wealthy man of Curl's Station. Mr. Vaughan had three daughters who married men living in or near Livingston. One married W.H. Gould, one married Robert O. Breitling, and one married Tom A. Phillips.

West of this place is a house built by Tom Phillips, and south of the Battle corner house is another house built and occupied by Robert O. Breitling. [The Phillips home is now a duplex apartment building, and the Breitling house is now the home of Mrs. Johnnye Scott.]

South of Rob Breitling's is a house built by William Wayne, who was a son-in-law of Judge Abrahams. It was built soon after the Civil War. Before, this was merely a large vacant lot. Joseph W. Jenkins bought this place for his son-in-law, H.R. Foss, and after Mrs. Foss died, Mr. Jenkins made it his home until his death. Joseph W. and Leroy Jenkins were brothers, and their sister, Elizabeth, was the wife of Albert Lancaster. These people came from around Fredericksburg, Virginia, and so far as known, they were not related to Dick Jenkins. Leroy Jenkins had a son Jimmy, who was killed in the Confederate service. Joseph W. Jenkins married a Miss Logan, and among their children were the second Mrs. H.R. Foss, who left no children; Mrs. A.P. Evans; Mrs. James C. Arrington; Mrs. Mitchell Eason, who was later Mrs. James B. Jackson; and Mrs. W.G.J. Everitt.

Mrs. Everitt inherited this place. She was the mother of two sons, W. Blanks and Clem Everitt. She sold the house to the late J. Lewis Brown and moved to California with her sons. Mr. Brown was of the Sumterville family which has been mentioned. He died in 1917. During Mrs. Brown's lifetime, after her husband's death, this place was rented by the late A.M. McGehee, a veneer manufacturer, and then to the late Judge P.B. Jarman, and after the death of Mrs. Brown in 1928, the place was purchased by William G. Little, grandson of Major Little and son of the late Probate Judge W.G. Little. After a few years, he sold the place to L.B. Spratt and moved to Tuscaloosa. [This is now the home of Mr. and Mrs. James McGahey.]

South, across South Street, were two small lots and what was called "Jenkins' pasture." One of the lots belonged to Miss Norville Dinkins. Miss Connie Hall later built here, but the house burned. Mrs. Lawrence acquired the lot and then Dr. Brock, who sold it to Mr. Schoel, who built here. Next west was where Mrs. Elizabeth Lancaster lived. She was a sister of J.W. Jenkins. Her people have been mentioned. The Jenkins' pasture passed through the hands of Mr. Brown, Mr. Little and Dr. Brock. It was recently acquired by Mr. J.R. Anderson, who built a residence on the higher part next to the street. [The Anderson house is now the home of Mr. and Mrs. Tom Luke, Jr.]

Between the Jenkins and Jarman pasture land was once an old road leading to the covered bridge site. On either side on the higher ground are some Negro houses. It was in this quarter that Stewart Allison, the courthouse janitor, was killed by his wife, and a few years later Cleopas Gray, a noted Negro man, was killed by Jesse and Oliver Wright, and his body thrown into the river.

Near the river on the Jenkins side was the old tanyard of Squire Hair, where Coblentz worked, and near this was a large chinaberry tree on which Steve Renfroe was hanged.

On the other side of the river, the first steam sawmill of the county stood. It was operated by James Mason, who was a brother of Mrs. Cunningham. Mr. Mason, as has been mentioned, was the father of Mrs. Otto Voss and of Mrs. Daniel Underwood. Mr. Mason's mother, Mrs. Sophia Slaughter Mason, and her daughter, a Mrs. Sarah Mason Allison, are buried just north of the

Cunningham burial lot in the cemetery. Mrs. Mason was the mother of Mrs. Cunningham, Mrs. Barker, James Mason, etc.

What is locally called "the river" is a rather large creek which has been variously spelled "Souken Hatcha," "Sucarnatchie," "Sucarnoochee," etc. The first spelling (Bernard Romans in 1771) probably approximated the true original pronunciation more than do the others. The common present-day pronunciation is "Suky notchy." [The standard spelling today is "Sucarnochee."]

Because *hog* and *opossum* were "shukha" (shooka), there has always been an effort to derive the name from some connection with these beasts. If the *Sh* had been used in Romans' time, he would no doubt have used it instead of spelling it "Souken Hatcha." Furthermore, opossums and hogs are no more common here than elsewhere in the region, and hogs are a comparatively recent introduction. The name of a prominent Indian who went west in 1840 was similar in sound and was called "Sucarnatchie" by the white people. According to the Reverend H.B. Cushman, the real name of this Indian was *Shuka niachi*—"Hog fattener."

The name of the watercourse is much older. It was doubtless given the stream long before hogs were brought in and the opossum—also *shuka* in early days—was no more common here than elsewhere and could, so far as one can now see, not be characteristic things. Now the banks of this creek, which were not cleared, are lined with muscadine vines. The writer, after a good deal of study and investigation, ventures to differ with other authorities and has come to believe the original was *Suko i hvcha*, which was no doubt contracted by the Indians themselves to *Suk' in 'vcha* or *Sukinacha*, which very well agrees with the old spelling of Romans and with the present-day pronunciation. This name means "Muscadine their river" or "Muscadine river." Several intelligent Choctaws have agreed that such a name would be grammatical, would preserve the original sound and would describe an outstanding characteristic. (Compare with *Tichumbum* in Choctaw County from *Iti hika umpohomo—T' ik' ump' om*—"Sweet gum trees make a roof over it.")

On what is still known as "Baldwin Hill," lived the noted lawyer and writer, Joseph G. Baldwin, related by marriage to Dr. Garber. He removed to California, and then William Kirkland lived at this place. The old house burned long ago. This place is said to have a ghost. [A poem relating to the ghost, written by Mrs. W.H. Coleman, appears in Appendix B.] W.A. Williams built and lived there and sold to Mrs. Julian Ennis. She moved to Tennessee after her husband died and rents the place out. [This house is now the home of Judge Thomas F. Seale.]

W.A. (Alex) Williams was of South Sumter, a son of George W. Williams, a Confederate veteran. He was first married to a Miss Walker. Mrs. Couch, George, Carrie Lee and Mrs. Thorn were her children. The second wife of Mr. Williams was a daughter of J.K.P. Rushing. She is the mother of Marie, Martha, Mary Lula, Ruth and Della.

Chess Smith, a colored citizen, once lived on the next hill. He was a powerful swimmer and taught the art to many white boys.

Nearby, Bob Johnson built a house much like the old Lawhon house. After his time, this was the home of E. Troup Sturdivant. He was related to the Potts family, and his sister married James R. Smith. Later, this was the home of Robert H. Seymour, a forceful man of means who made friends and enemies. He was shot in a difficulty with the Scott brothers, Bob and Will, and died as a result. His wife was a Miss Leah Harris. Their children were W. Henry, Mrs. T.B.F. DeGraffenfried, Littleton, Mrs. Hurt and Horatio. W. Henry Seymour taught school in Livingston, went to the State Legislature and served as consul at Palermo. He married a Miss Almerdine of Montgomery. Mrs. Hurt lives in Marion, Alabama, and has descendants. Littleton died as a young man. Horatio is a prominent businessman of Meridian and has descendants.

M. Luke of Pickens County bought this place and lived there until his death. His wife was a sister of Dr. Reed of Epes. Their children were Jim, Mary Clanton, Tom, Mrs. Lewis McLean, Myrtle and Nancy. These still own the place but rent to others. The old house burned in Mr. Seymour's time, and a new one was built by him. [This is now the home of Mr. and Mrs. Preston "Man" Minus.] The late Oscar Cobb had a tourist camp here at the time of his death. Mr. Cobb married a daughter of the late Austin Boyd. His sons continued the business at this place. One of his sons, Smith Cobb, a very pleasant-mannered young man, was killed in an automobile accident while the family lived here.

Across the road was the home of Colonel James Rhodes. He owned several plantations and married two sisters of George Kornegay. Among his children were Mrs. Dr. Garber, Mrs. Joseph Borden, Miss Constance, Mrs. Ivy Lewis, Captain Eugene Rhodes and Mrs. Sidney T. Prince. It is told that Colonel James Rhodes, who was quite deaf in his old age, rode up to a cabin and asked for a drink of water. Then he asked some question and placed his ear trumpet to his ear and the woman poured the water into the trumpet. Major Prince was a brother of Mrs. Brownrigg. Eugene Rhodes served as a captain in the Confederate service. At a later time John T. Smith lived here, and it now belongs to his grandson, Dr. Hadden Smith. Alex Williams bought a part of the place and built two small dwellings. He died while living at one of these.

Along here the road forks. One branch goes on to York and the other runs to the south and goes on to Choctaw County. This branch is locally known as the Bellamy road. Bellamy is a town formed about 1900 by the Allison Lumber Company and named for Volney Bellamy, a Confederate veteran.

Farther along the York road lived a Murray family related to Richard (Dick) Jenkins. Later T. Harden Lake lived here. He was a partner of Waldo Shearer, and his first wife was a daughter of D. Hopkins. Mr. Lake moved to Mobile many years ago. Some younger cousins lived with Mr. Lake at this place. Later, Mr. Emmet owned this place, and then Laporte Hall from Indiana bought it and built the present house. Hall sold this house to Earl Godfrey and moved to Birmingham, where he recently died. His brother, Arthur, married Alice McMillan. [This house is now the home of Mr. and Mrs. Alfred L. Puzak, Jr.] Earl Godfrey is a son of the late William Godfrey of Sumterville and a grandson of Dr. James M. Godfrey. He married a daughter of the late Mr. Simms of Emelle and has served at least two terms as Sheriff.

Yellow Creek runs across the York road just beyond the last mentioned place and then cuts across the Bellamy road. Just across this creek on the right is the old John T. Smith place later owned by William Ellis. He was a brother of the late Gray Ellis of Gainesville. John T. Smith was a brother of Dr. Joseph and Captain E.W. Smith. His wife was a daughter of M.C. Houston, and among their children were Thomas, C. Brooks, Mrs. Ella Ferrell, Mrs. Dr. Sam Scruggs, Mrs. Leslie Lide and Mrs. Smith of Georgia. Mr. John T. Smith was a Confederate soldier. Thomas B. Smith, who recently died at an advanced age, served as Mayor, as postmaster, and as Register in Chancery. He married a daughter of Dr. Lewis Hadden of Belmont, and their children were Walter B., Dr. Hadden B., Cullen, the first Mrs. A.G. Horn, Mrs. Dr. Pinson and Mrs. Brown. Hadden B. Smith studied dentistry at Vanderbilt and married Miss Jean Bradshaw. Their children are Hadden, Louis, Lena, Jean, Tom ["Tip"] and John. C. Brooks Smith, former State Auditor, spent most of his life in Montgomery.

Hixon was formerly known as "Hooks Crossing." Near this place was the home of Joseph Maggard, maternal grandfather of the late J.W. Killian. It was near this crossing that the Negro Tom Ivy was killed in the Reconstruction days.

Also, along this road lived families named Armstrong, Praytor and Brown. Farther down were Scotts and Harpers. W.J. (Jabe), H.B. (Hugh) and Middleton Praytor were well known in Livingston. John G. Brown was known as "Hell Roaring" Brown—he came to Livingston to sell fresh beef early in the morning and advertised in a loud voice.

Dick Jenkins lived farther down the York road where Alonzo Kornegay's widow lived later. He was not related to Joe and Leroy so far as known. His sons were Dr. John, Oliver, Albert and Bill. All of these sons served in Dent's Company. Dr. John (J.T.) Jenkins had clerked for J.L. Scruggs, the druggist, and married a sister of Major W.G. Little. While Dent's Company was in Virginia, two of its members, W.R. DeLoach and Bill Jenkins, had a fist fight, and Dr. John Jenkins ran up to separate them. Lilbern Ustick thought he was going to attack his friend DeLoach, so he struck Dr. Jenkins with a ball bat and killed him.

Returning toward town and then going down what is now called Bellamy Road, we come to where Dr. A.M. Garber lived. He married a daughter of Colonel James Rhodes and lived at this place for many years. Dr. Garber came from Virginia about 1837. Among the children of Dr. and Mrs. Garber were Dr. James R. Garber, Joseph B. Garber, Buckner L. Garber, Mrs. James C. Browder, Judge Eugene Garber and Colonel Alex M. Garber.

Dr. James R. Garber was a lieutenant, C.S.A., and was the father of Dr. James R. Garber of Birmingham. Mr. Joseph Garber removed to Hale and Marengo Counties and never married. Mr. B.L. Garber removed to Hale and Marengo Counties and married a Miss Browder, and they had a number of children. Mrs. Browder, whose husband was a brother of B.L. Garber's wife, continued to live at the old home near Livingston. Her children were James D. Browder, Joe Browder, Mrs. Dr. W.T. Cocke and Mrs. John Watkins. James D. Browder lives at the old place now. He married a daughter of the late T.L. Smith and their children are Sara, James and Tom. Judge Eugene Garber lived in California and had met with much success there before he died prematurely. Colonel A.M. Garber taught school for awhile in Livingston and then went to Talladega, where he was a lawyer. He became Attorney General of Alabama and afterward removed to Birmingham. He married and has two sons, Alexander and Eugene.

In connection with the Browders is an interesting story. It seems that a French family of the name Chapron lived in Haiti, then a French colony. In 1804 a boy of this family named Frank (or John?) Chapron was sent to Philadelphia to attend a school. About this time there was a terrible insurrection of the slaves in Haiti and nearly all the white people were killed. The Chapron family is said to have been warned in time to get aboard a ship, but the ship was lost and the family disappeared, except the boy, who was at school in Philadelphia. This Frank Chapron went to work for some tea importers, and by the time he was grown, he was in that business for himself and made a success of it. His daughter married Dr. James D. Browder of Richmond, Virginia, and Dr. Browder and his wife moved to Alabama. James Chapron Browder, who married Miss Annie Garber, was a son of this Dr. James D. Browder and his wife, who had been a Miss Chapron.

Farther out this road, across Yellow Creek and Hannah's Branch, was the home of George Kornegay, related to the wives of Colonel Rhodes. Among the children of Mr. and Mrs. Kornegay were Alonzo, Mrs. Levy, Mrs. Wessenburg, Mrs. Dave Battle and Henry. Alonzo married a daughter of Napoleon Sherard. Mr. and Mrs. Wessenburg lived at this place for a time, and while they lived here the old house burned. It was much like the Parker house in Livingston. Wessenburg built a smaller house, which has been added to and is still in use. Wessenburg was a Scandinavian and was a noted engineer. It is said that he built the New Orleans and Northeastern Railroad trestle across Lake Pontchartrain. Mrs. Battle seems to have inherited this place upon Mrs. Wessenburg's death and the Battles have lived there since then. Mr. and Mrs. Battle had a daughter, Bessie, who married a Mr. Nelson, and the Nelsons now live at this place. Mr. Dave Battle spends much of his time with the Nelsons.

Nearby is the Cooper's Spring mentioned earlier, and not far off is what is known as the Wat Chiles place. It seems that an early mill man named Chiles had a number of children, among whom were William, Walter (Wat) and Mrs. R.N. Brasfield. William had a mill on Alamuchee Creek, and his son, W.S. Chiles, spent most of his life operating mills. Wat Chiles had a son named Fred who became prominent in Arkansas.

Out on the other side of Piney Grove Church was the home of the widow of Stephen Smith of North Carolina. She was a sister of Colonel James Rhodes, and among her children were Dr. Joseph A. Smith, the Reverend Stephen Uriah Smith, James R. Smith, John T. Smith, Captain E.W. Smith, Mrs. James Houston and Miss Anne Smith. Dr. Joseph A. Smith was one of the early physicians of Livingston. He is said to have been an intellectual man who accumulated considerable property and died unmarried. The Reverend Stephen U. Smith had no family. He was at one time rector of the St. James Episcopal Church here, and at the time of his death was rector of the Eutaw Church. James R. Smith is said to have been married twice, and both wives had children. His people left here. Captain E.W. Smith and John T. Smith have been mentioned. Captain E.W. Smith's son, Walter K., was born at this country place under discussion. Mrs. Houston's husband was a son of R.F. Houston, and this family went to Louisiana. Miss Anne Smith spent much of her time with her nephews in Livingston.

A.W. Cockrell acquired this place in some way, and after awhile formed a farming partnership with J.P. Spratt, who lived on the place, and in course of time Mr. Spratt bought the place. They called it their "Greeley Farm." About that time Horace Greeley of the New York *Tribune* was a prominent man. He gave advice to farmers in one part of his paper, about farming. Mr. Cockrell claimed to know no more about farming than Mr. Greeley did, and so the name originated. No family named Greeley ever lived there.

Jerry Brown, son of Robert, bought this place, and it has passed through many hands since his time. Kittrell, Northcutt, and Wilson lived there at various times. Kittrell was from Tennessee, and one of his daughters married Tom Wright, who clerked for L.S. Fluker and was one of the first persons in this region to lose his life in an automobile accident. Northcutt was from Georgia and returned to that state. Richard D. Wilson was a Confederate veteran who left this place to his daughter, and after so long a time it was purchased by a Mr. Armstrong of York.

To the east of this place was the Hooks country place, owned by David Hooks, who has been mentioned.

Nearby was the home of Daniel White. He was a Confederate soldier, and his wife had a brother, Lieutenant Colonel J.K. Norwood, C.S.A., buried in the Livingston Cemetery.

Rufus M. Brasfield, who lived near, was a Confederate soldier. He was related to the Brasfields of Hale and Marengo Counties. Rufus Brasfield's brother married the widow of Woodson Garrett, who was a brother of Mrs. R.W. Ennis.

Colonel Cooper is said to have lived about where Chestleigh Kennard, a colored citizen, lived.

Francis Foard once owned what is now called the "Lockard Place." Foard is said to have been buried in the front yard, and his body was later moved to Livingston. In Civil War days a man named Caldwell bought this place and died. Then Phillips and Joseph W. Jenkins bought it, and eventually Jenkins owned it. Judge James Abrahams acquired it and Mr. T.E. Lockard rented it and lived there for many years. Yellow Creek runs into Alamuchee not very far from the house site. The Allison interests now own this place.

To the southeast of and adjoining the Dr. Garber Place is what was known as the Pickens Place. Who this Pickens family was is not known. Francis Foard, E. Troup Sturdivant, Joseph W. Jenkins, H.R. Foss and others have owned it. J.H. Norville acquired it about the time gold was discovered in the Klondike region of Alaska, and he named it "The Klondike." Frank Harris lived here for awhile after Mr. Norville died. Later this place was owned by Little and Nixon.

Returning to the northern part of the town of Livingston, on the east side of Washington Street, we can begin at what is called the Rogers Place. This is twenty acres formerly belonging to Colonel Gibbs. His son-in-law, W.R. DeLoach, lived here awhile, and afterward it was the home of Henry Rogers of Warsaw. Mr. Rogers married a Miss Hallie Williams of Mobile and their children were Harry Ross, Will, Jim, Richmond, and a daughter who married. This place has for many years belonged to a brother of Mr. Rogers, Jim Rogers, of Warsaw. Harry Ross Rogers is a sawmill man of Mobile.

To the south was the home of Colonel Charles R. Gibbs, who came from Virginia. He was twice married and some of his first wife's children never came here. Among this first wife's children were Mrs. Hill, the mother of Mrs. Colonel Wetmore, Mrs. George B. Saunders, Dr. R.T. Gibbs, etc. Colonel Gibbs' second wife was a Thornton and her children were Miss Charlotte, Miss Eleanor C. (Miss Nellie), and Miss Sue, who married W.R. DeLoach.

A good many years later, Colonel Gibbs died and this place was acquired by the late Nat Kennard. His widow still owns it and lives there. This is one of the old log cabins boarded up. Nat Kennard was a son of James Kennard and was a Confederate soldier. James Kennard lived east of town and was married at least twice. Among his first wife's children were Mrs. Dr. M.C. Kinnard and Mrs. Judge C.S. McConnico. James Kennard's second wife was the widow of Ennis, and she was the mother of John and Nat Kennard. Nat Kennard's first wife was a sister of the late W.D. Johnston, Sr., of Boligee. His second wife was a distant relative from Georgia. Both wives had children.

James Pinckney Kennard is said to have been married four times. One wife is said to have been a Miss Nancy D. Oglesby, and she was the mother of that Smith Oglesby Kennard who attended the University of Alabama and is buried in our cemetery. Another wife was a Miss Miller, and she is said to have been the mother of Mrs. McConnico, who was later Mrs. Robert S. Mason. Mr. Kennard's last wife was Mrs. Ennis, who was originally Miss Phillips. As has been mentioned, another of James P. Kennard's daughters married Dr. Michael C. Kinnard, and after Dr. Kinnard's death this family removed to Texas. Dr. and Mrs. Kinnard had several children, among them the late Judge James P. Kinnard of Haskell, Texas, who now and then revisited his old home at Livingston, Alabama.

Here a road runs out to the east. This road formerly led to Epes and to Bluffport. Along this road near the railway is a small house that was once used by Judge Saunders. Later, R.L. Giles lived here. He married a sister of W.T. McKnight. This family went to Mississippi, where the girls married and his two sons, Will and Robert, died. Then a Willis family lived here. After many years J.K. Shelton bought this place, lived there awhile and sold it to W.R. Stinson, and sometime later he sold it to Ed Wrenn. Ed Wrenn is a brother to Jim and Joe Wrenn of Sumterville. There was a rather large Wrenn family at Sumterville. Jim, Joe, Gus and Ed were brothers. Also George and Elias were brothers. Just what relation these two branches of the family were to each other is not known to the writer. George Wrenn was the father of the James M. Wrenn who married Mabel Randall. Ed Wrenn married Miss Mattie Wilson, who was related to Mrs. Asa Amerson. Her brother, Ike Wilson, was a noted ballplayer in his youth. Mr. and Mrs. Ed Wrenn have one child, a son named Earl, who lives in Mississippi. Then a Mr. O.M. Martin, who had lived in Idaho and in Louisiana, bought this place and lived there. He had two sons, Winford and Granville.

Farther out, John E. Harris bought some land and built a house. He is a son of Dr. R.M. Harris and married Miss Kathleen Hooper of Birmingham. They had three children—John E., Jr., Mrs. George Fouche and William. John E. Harris, Jr., was in training during the World War and died.

Farther out was a place owned by Squire James Hair, who came from Tennessee in 1834. Marks on the old house, which burned in 1927, indicated that it was erected in 1846. Squire Hair's first wife was a Miss McCullock of Virginia, and among their children were Mrs. I.D. Hoit and Sam Hair. Several others of them never came to this part of the country. Sam Hair is said to have been gay, festive, and quite popular. A story is told in this family about Sam's going out with the McGrews and breaking up a church meeting at Prospect. The old Squire was a very religious man, and when he heard of what Sam had done, he gave him a good thrashing. It is said that the Squire wore out an entire blackjack thicket beating Sam. Squire Hair's second wife is said to have been an aunt of Marten Jenkins.

J.D. Hoit was a northern school teacher who came into this region and married. He and his sons Zane and James served as Confederate soldiers. James Hoit belonged to the Sengstak Battery and was killed. Zane Hoit married a daughter of the Reverend Abner Scarborough and died leaving a number of children, among them J. Hamilton Hoit, I.D. Hoit, Mrs. Ellis and the first Mrs. Will Turner, mother of John and Zane. This name was also spelled "Hoyt."

I.D. Hoit, Sr., lived at the Hair Place, and then it was the home of Thomas B. Stone, an unmarried brother of Colonel W. M. Stone. Mr. Stone was a staunch Presbyterian and raised Jersey cattle. He served as a Confederate soldier in his brother's company. After living here for many years, he went to Mississippi and died in Meridian in 1925. Judge James Cobb lived here awhile. He succeeded A.A. Coleman as Circuit Judge, and served for a time as Captain in the 40th Alabama, C.S.A.

On a part of the Hair land, which he bought, R.G. (Garrett) Ennis built a dwelling and lived there many years. He was a son of Robert W. Ennis and was twice married. His first wife was Miss Florence DeLoach, and she was the mother of Richard and Florence. The second wife of R.G. Ennis was a Miss Florence Irwin of Tennessee and she is the mother of Cornelia Ennis. The Garrett Ennis house burned in 1928.

A Beazely family lived farther out. They had a daughter who married James E. David. Mr. David in his younger days was a very powerful man physically and was quite active also. He could carry an ordinary cotton bale and do other such things. Mr. David was also quite musical and could make good dance music on a piano. He and his wife had two sons and two daughters—Jim, who lived in Meridian; Laurie, who lives in Greene County; Clara, who married Young Ned Battle and died some years later; and Polly, who married a Mr. Bellis of Greene County and resides in Tishabee, Greene County, Alabama. Polly's daughter married a son of John McQueen of Tuscaloosa.

The Cates family lived farther out as mentioned. A Mr. Cates married the widow of Tom Hunter, who had been a Miss Burchard.

This takes us into the New Prospect and Bluffport regions. Families named Scarborough, Porter, Autry, Gary, Hawkins, McLean, Lewis, Sullivan, May, Leitch and Gould lived here. Also, B.G. Cook, the silversmith, is said to have lived out here and introduced Bermuda Grass into Sumter County. B.G. Cook had a son, J.M. Cook, known as "Doc," who was in Stone's Company, C.S.A.

The Porters were related to the Scarboroughs and had two daughters named Sue and Annie. Sue Porter married Newton Hamill, the teacher, and after his death she married C.T. Roan, who had served as a Confederate soldier under General Forrest. Annie Porter was the first wife of John Lawhon and was the mother of Mrs. Walton, Miss Rosa Lawhon, and Miss Annie Porter Lawhon.

Newton J. Hamill was born at Eutaw, March 31, 1836, and died here in 1867. He was lame and unable to do military service in the war of 1861-65. He taught a school for boys and practiced dentistry. His wife was Miss Sue Porter, and after his death she married C.T. Roan. Hamill resided at what is now called the Roan Place some three miles east of town. There were both Hamill and Roan children, all of whom left here. The Roan children were John, Forrest, Susie, Jim, and C.T., Jr. John died in Tishomingo, Oklahoma, leaving descendants. Forrest is buried here. Susie married and lives in the North. Jim lives near Marion, Alabama. C.T., Jr. lives in Australia.

The Reverend H.R. Autry and his great services to the Livingston Baptist Church have been mentioned. H.B. Leitch afterward lived at the old Autry place. He was the father of Will, Jim, Horace and John Leitch, and he had a number of daughters, among them the first Mrs. William H. Scarborough and the second Mrs. Will Turner.

John H. Gary, son of M.E. Gary, a former Sheriff, lived out here. The younger Gary had a son, Samuel, who was in the Stone Company. This family was related to the first husband of the second Mrs. J.L. Scruggs, so it is said —she was a Widow Gary. The Reverend Mr. Scarborough afterward lived at the Gary Place, and it is now the home of his grandson, I.D. Hoit.

Two Gary brothers, Matthias and John H., came to this region in early times. John H. Gary settled at Bluffport and built the house recently owned and occupied by the widow of Mr. Zane Hoit. This house was burned in 1932. John H. Gary married Eliza Monette, and they had a number of children, among them Samuel H., who attended the University of Alabama and served as a Confederate soldier in Stone's Company and died as a result of exposure in 1864. This family left here about 1866 and settled in Meridian. Some of the descendants now live in the West. Eliza, who married John H. Gary, was a sister to Captain James Monette of Livingston.

Matthias Gary married (1) Sarah Melton, (2) Amanda White and (3) Rachel Seale, (originally a Miss Seale, she had been married twice before). This family left this region long ago and some of the descendants live in Mississippi, Texas and other states. Mrs. Judge C.R. Brice of Roswell, New Mexico, is descended from Pernetia, a daughter of Matthias Gary, who married David Maggard, a brother of Joseph W. Killian's grandfather, Joseph Maggard.

Thomas Hawkins was the father of John and William H. Hawkins, who married daughters of the Reverend Abner Scarborough. Mr. and Mrs. John Hawkins had a number of children—Abner, Jim, John, Will, Ernest, Mrs. Johnson, Miss Ruth, Miss Rhoda, and possibly others. Abner Hawkins, who died in 1927, was a successful farmer and was highly thought of all over his home county.

Mr. Lewis McLean's mother was a Lewis. He married a Miss Turner, and among their children were Mrs. W.M. Sullivan, W. Peter McLean, Mrs. E.C. Gulley, Lewis McLean, Jr., Mrs. Cliff Curry, Mrs. Capers J. Curry, Turner McLean, etc.

Mr. James M. Sullivan was a Confederate veteran. His first wife was an Ethridge and they had a son John. Mr. Sullivan then married a Miss Terell, and she was the mother of Wesley M. Sullivan, Jim, Billy, Mrs. Lavender, Miss Mary, Miss Clint and Mrs. Wall.

The Sullivan, Monette, and Phares families were related. The old Phares home near Belmont that burned recently was one of the few really fine antebellum homes in this county.

The two May families lived in this region. They were known as the "Black Mays" and the "Speckled Mays." Robert C. and Billy May, who have been mentioned, were of the "Black Mays." The mother of M.D.—Malachi D., known as "Mack"—Gould was of the "Speckled Mays." Her brother Phil was a Captain of cavalry in the Confederate Army. M.D. Gould married a Miss Beebe, and their children were William H., Mrs. Lanham, Mrs. Blalock, and M.B. Malachi D. (Mack) Gould joined the Confederate Army in the last days of the Civil War, but the war ended before he saw active service. Mr. and Mrs. Lanham were killed in an automobile accident on Christmas Eve night in 1924. This occurred on the Gainesville side of the Mason Hill, some five and a half miles north of town.

Returning to town, just south of the Colonel Gibbs or Nat Kennard Place, across the road mentioned, was the home of Jordan Short, a former Sheriff, who came from North Carolina at an early time. He married a Miss Mary Chiles, daughter of a widowed Mrs. Chiles who kept the old Planters Hotel in early days. Mrs. Short was well educated and taught at the old Female Academy and also conducted a private school for some years. Among the children of Mr. and Mrs. Short was a daughter, Miss Fannie, who married W.K. Pickens. Mr. Pickens came here as a young man and became prominent in business and in county politics. Mr. and Mrs. Pickens had two children, W.O. (Champ) Pickens and Miss Ruby. Miss Ruby married W. Pratt Tartt. Champ Pickens married Miss Blanche Hopkins of Louisiana, and they have a number of children. Mr. and Mrs. W.P. Tartt have one daughter, Fannie Pickens Tartt.

South of this place, on what was a part of the old Short property, one King of Birmingham built two small concrete block houses. James L. Scruggs lives in the one nearest the Pickens Place. He is a son of J.O. Scruggs and married Miss Lizzie Breitling, and they have a son named James. Raymond Hylton, a grandson of W.W. Smith, lived in this house for a short time before Scruggs. The next house, also built by King, has been occupied by Dru McDonald, principal of the high school. He is a son of Moses McDonald of South Sumter, who married a Miss Busche of Ohio.

All this portion of the old Short lot was once used as a ball ground and as a sort of playground for the Normal School. In 1892 there was a Columbus Day celebration held here with oratory and a dinner under the trees. By the way, the trees were then covered with long Spanish moss, which entirely disappeared a few years later.

To the south was another very large lot on which Joseph Lake built a large two-story residence. Among the children of Mr. and Mrs. Lake were T. Harden Lake, John Lake, Mrs. Elizabeth Parker, Mrs. Margaret Cobbs, and Mrs. Crawford of Mobile. A sister of Mrs. Crawford's husband married Commodore Vanderbilt. T. Harden Lake was a partner of Waldo Shearer, and his first wife was a daughter of M.C. Houston. His second wife was the Widow Gaines, a daughter of Colonel Devereux Hopkins, and this second wife had a number of children. John Lake was an officer in the Confederate Army and was being congratulated for some exploit by his superior officer when a ball came along and killed him. He is said to have been a fine man. Mrs. Parker was the second wife of Socrates Parker, and their children have been mentioned. Her son, James L. Parker, now owns and occupies this old house. Mrs. Cobbs was the wife of Judge James Cobbs, who has been mentioned as a brother of Major Cobbs.

After the Lake family dispersed, Robert F. Houston lived at this place. He was a brother of Matthew C. Houston and was a very popular man, being, it is said, about the only Democrat in the county able to beat the Whigs for the Legislature. Among the children of Mr. and Mrs. Robert F. Houston were James, J. Clint, Robert, Mrs. W.M. Stone, Mrs. Marten Jenkins, and the second Mrs. Dr. Robert Park. James Houston married a sister of John T. and Captain E.W. Smith. J. Clint Houston married a daughter of General Joseph Arrington, and in his old age he married the widow of Dr. Reub Arrington. He was an officer in the Confederate Army, and his first wife had a number of children. Robert Houston recently died in Meridian, Mississippi. Colonel William M. Stone was a prominent man in his day. He was Captain of Company D, Jeff Davis Legion, C.S.A., and moved to Meridian after the war. He and his wife had a number of children. Colonel Stone and his brother, T.B. Stone, came here from Tuscaloosa. Mr. and Mrs. Jenkins lived in Meridian and left a number of children. Dr. and Mrs. Park also had children.

Then this became the home of Mr. Socrates Parker, who has been mentioned. He once lived near McCainville, moved to Livingston and lived at the S.W. Inge place, then went to Mobile. He returned to Sumter County and resided for a time at farms he owned, one being east of town and another being in the Bear Creek neighborhood. Then he acquired the Lake home in town, and it is now the home of his son, Mr. James Lake Parker. James L. Parker married Miss Lily Ashe of Greensboro, and they had three children of their own. These are James L. Parker, Jr., of Panola, Mrs. Sid B. Jones, and another daughter, Lily, who died during childhood. [The Lake place is now the home of Mr. Parker's granddaughter, Mrs. Lily Ashe Jones Richardson, and other members of the Parker family.]

Just south of this home was once a good-sized open space where the boys played baseball. It is quite likely that this was the ball ground when the game began to be played substantially as it is today. What was perhaps the first real baseball team in town was composed of the following players:

> J.C. Travis, catcher
> W.C. Travis, pitcher
> James L. Parker, first base
> W.S. Nichols
> Solon Arrington
> Ed Abrahams (grandson of the Judge)
> Soc Battle
> John L. Parker
> Walter Harris

There were a few cabins on Washington Street along here. These were torn away long ago and the late J.A. McConnell acquired that part of this land on the street mentioned and built two dwellings. One of these is now the home of M.E. McConnell. Dr. G.W. Brock of the Normal School lives in the other. [These houses are no longer standing.] Dr. Brock's first wife was a Miss Luttrell, and she was the mother of Mildred Brock, who married Mr. A.L. Lippett of Atlanta. After the death of this wife, Dr. Brock married a Miss Mary Boyd.

To the south a road or street runs east to the colored Methodist church neighborhood. There is quite a settlement in this neighborhood, which is really a part of the old "Smith Flat" to be mentioned later on.

To the south and across this street from Dr. Brock's house was the home of Nehemiah D. Stockley—(pronounced "Stokeley"). He was a prosperous tailor of the old days, and his wife was related to the Usticks. Later on a Mrs. Adams lived here. Mrs. Mary F. Adams was killed by lightning on February 23, 1866. She was a daughter of William and Margaret Routt of Orange County, Virginia. She was born September 18, 1813, married James Cockrell in 1834, and later married Aaron Adams. Her daughter is said to have married Oscar Hord, father of Jim Hord, who died suddenly after an encounter with bandits on July 5, 1932. Jim Hord lived at Brewersville, and his daughter married Will Tom Hylton of Epes. Hylton is a grandson of W.W. Smith.

Tom Myers, a colored citizen, who was Mr. G.B. Fellows' wood worker, afterward lived about where this house stood.

Along Washington Street to the south are the two houses moved across the street from the Bardwell lot, owned and used by the Normal School.

To the south is a large lot where Dr. John H. Webb built a house away back from the street. Captain Samuel Webb came here from old Patton's Hill, now called Sumterville. Captain Webb had two sons who were physicians, Dr. John H. Webb and Dr. Robert Webb. After living in this house for awhile, Dr. John Webb left the state and then James Houston lived there for a time. Then it was the home of Robert Beck, whose wife was related to our Travis people. Then Thomas R. Crews lived here. He was a Probate Judge and had a son, James, who was one of the lieutenants of Dent's Company and who afterward served under General John H. Morgan. The writer's father said this James Crews was the bravest man he ever knew. Thomas R. Crews died in 1866. Then this became the home of C.S. McConnico, who was another Probate Judge. He seems to have been married twice. His last wife was a daughter of James Kennard and she was the mother of several McConnico children, among them Jim, Ben and Shelby McConnico. The widow of C.S. McConnico married R.S. Mason, and their children have been mentioned. The Masons lived at this place for many years. Then various families rented it, and the old house burned about 1924.

To the south a small house was built by Professor Moulder, who preceded Dru McDonald as principal of the high school. This place is now a part of the Normal School property. This house is built of material from the old Ennis Store. (Principals of the high school have included Professor E.B. Calhoun, Professor Moulder, Dru McDonald, and Mr. Tidwell.)

To the south is where the Widow O'Neil lived. She was a sister of Captain Abney, who has been mentioned. Then one Copley is said to have lived here. Finally, the Presbyterians acquired this place for use as a manse. It is probable that Dr. W.H. Zeigler, who recently resigned, lived in this house and served this church longer than any other pastor in the church's history, so far. Dr. Zeigler was reared near Carlisle, Pennsylvania, but came south and married a lady from Albany, Georgia. He was a broadminded, kindly and scholarly man, and was fond of hunting, fishing and of all other healthful sports.

To the south was where Robert Harding Smith once lived. He was a teacher and became a lawyer. After some years he moved to Mobile. There was once a sort of office in the yard of this place, and in this Mrs. Dr. Truehart, a sister of Mr. Smith, taught school. About the time of the Civil War, Captain Jim Monette lived at his place. He had a son named George and a daughter named Mollie. Mrs. Monette was related to the Cedar Creek Brewers. George Monette was accidentally killed by his friend, Robert Harris. They were boys and went off on the railroad to play with an old pistol. They were somewhere near the Pickens Crossing when Harris aimed the old gun on a rail, while George leaned over to see what happened. The pistol went off and George was dead in a little while. These people went to Mobile.

Some time after the Civil War this place became the home of Robert W. Ennis. He was born in the Warsaw neighborhood, and his widowed mother married James Kennard of Livingston. Mr. Ennis learned the drug business under Dr. Coleman and Mr. Scruggs. He was a Confederate soldier in Vandergraaff's Company and became, so I have been told, Brigade Apothecary under Dr. Gray Little. Mr. Ennis was a business partner of the elder T.M. Tartt and then went into business for himself. He married Miss Annie Garrett, sister of William and Woodson Garrett, of Greene County. The surviving children of Mr. and Mrs. Ennis were Mrs. W.J. Hendley, R. Garrett Ennis, Mrs. Joe Little of Washington, D.C., Woodson L. Ennis and Julian B. Ennis.

Woodson Ennis now lives at this place. He is a prominent businessman and married Miss Tempie Scruggs. They have two sons, Woodson, Jr., and Robert. [This was the home of Woodson Ennis, Jr., for many years, and his widow, Jean, still lives there.]

To the east of this last house, on North Street, is where Mrs. Hill, mother of Mrs. Colonel Wetmore, lived. Mrs. Rosina Hill afterward married J.B. Roach. Later on, the Widow Tankersley lived in this house, and then it became the home of Stephen W. Murley. His first wife and several children are buried in our cemetery. His son, Wellington A. Murley, was a member of the

Sengstak Battery and was killed. His body is said to have been brought home and buried. S.W. Murley was also postmaster at one time and once resided at the Harden Lake place south of town.

Dr. Robert D. Webb bought this place and lived here a number of years before he moved to Birmingham. He was a son of Captain Samuel Webb and married a Miss Julia Fulton. They had one daughter, Miss Bettie, who married the famous Senator from Mississippi, John Sharp Williams. Dr. R.D. Webb was a student and an investigator. In one of the *Transactions* of the Medical Association of the State of Alabama—I believe it is that of 1881—Dr. Webb has a very interesting paper on the subject of malaria fevers. He discussed every possible thing that might cause the disease except the mosquito. His investigations into this disease led him to study the various types of soils, the water supply, the vegetation growing in various districts, etc. His maps of this county are still used by the County Board of Health.

After Dr. Webb left, this was the home of Mr. David Patton, and after he died, Mr. Charles J. Brockway lived here for many years. Mr. Brockway's daughter, Mrs. Velma Chappelle, sold this place to Mr. E.C. Vaughan, who now lives there. [This house has been removed and replaced by a modern dwelling, which is now the home of Mr. and Mrs. Tim Giles.]

To the east is some low-lying ground where many Negroes live. It was once known as the "Smith Flat." [The houses which were once on North Street here have been removed, and much of the "Smith Flat" area is now commercial.] Captain W.A.C. Jones had a grist mill down here, and it blew up, throwing a colored fireman an amazing distance without hurting him seriously. This fireman was John Kimball, son of Jesse Kimball, who was once Captain Dent's waiting man. In his old age Jesse Kimball served as sexton at the white churches. John Kimball married Poky (Pocahontas), who cooked for Dr. McCain for many years. Poky was the daughter of a free woman, also named Pocahontas, who once lived in that section of Monroe Street known as "Dog Street."

A road or street runs along the railroad here toward the colored Methodist church, and one of the tragedies of Reconstruction times took place about the middle of this street. This was the Coblentz killing, which will be mentioned later.

East of this spot, across the railroad, was the home of H.W. Norville, an early settler. He married a Miss Hodges, and among their children were Lorenzo Dow Norville, John H. Norville, Mrs. Chatfield, Jordan S. Norville and Miss Hardenia. John H. Norville kept this place as his home for a number of years and left it to his heirs. He was Mayor of Livingston and was a prominent businessman here for years. He married the widow of Park M. Harris, but they had no children. She was the mother of Gordon and Frank Harris.

It is said that a Dr. Davidson, a dentist of long ago, tried out a flying machine in the pasture connected with this place. It is also said that William L. Yancey, the noted orator of antebellum days, once spoke here. According to Mr. John H. Sherard of Sherard, Mississippi, his uncle, Mr. Joseph Arrington, was associated with Dr. Davidson in building his flying machine. It is said this machine had wings which were worked by pedals like those of a bicycle. A tramp mechanic who came along about then volunteered to fly it. In the attempt, it fell on the mechanic, breaking his leg.

This Norville place was known as "Grampian," as the following lines from Home's tragedy, *Douglas,* seemed somehow to apply:

> My name is Norval; on the Grampian Hills
> My father feeds his flocks; a frugal swain,
> Whose constant cares were to increase his store,
> And keep his only son, myself, at home.

North of this Norville house, but nearby and on the same lot, was a house where a family named Eastland once lived. J.C. Travis was living in this house when it burned about 1900.

East of Grampian was the Bolling place. A Mr. W.R. Bolling was married twice, and a daughter of his first wife married Samuel A. Hale. The second Mrs. Bolling was a sister of the Lees of Lilita. Her Bolling daughter married I. James Lee, not related to the Sumter County Lees. I. James Lee and his brother Frank S. came from Tuscaloosa. Samuel A. Hale became a widower and married the Widow Bolling and lived at this place, so that it came to be called the Hale place. W.R. Bolling (or Boling) is buried at Brewersville. Samuel A. Hale died at the home of I. James Lee near town and no one now living remembers where he was buried. His first wife is buried here. His last wife left here with I. James Lee and died in Tuscaloosa.

Samuel A. Hale was a native of New Hampshire, and his brother, John P. Hale, was a U.S. Senator from that state, served as Minister to Spain, and was a prominent Abolitionist. Samuel A. Hale was immortalized by Joseph G. Baldwin as "Samuel Hele" in *The Flush Times of Alabama and Mississippi.* It has been said of him that he "was wonderful in his power of invective and disposition to animadvert upon the community about him." In Baldwin's book is the account of how he was induced to tell such alarming tales to a troublesome school teacher that she left town the next day. Hale had been a newspaperman in Tuscaloosa who came to Livingston in 1843.

Felix G. McMillan then owned this place, and after he died his people sold it to Frank Derby, and he sold it to Dr. Elisha A. Young. Dr. Young died in an automobile accident in 1930, and John P. (Pete) Jackson was badly injured in the same accident. [This house was removed some years ago, and the area was developed as Shady Heights subdivision.]

Dr. Young has been connected with the Normal School for many years. He is a grandson of the noted Professor Henry Tutwiler [and a nephew of Miss Julia Tutwiler]. Dr. Young's first wife was Martha, daughter of J.A. McConnell, and she was the mother of Joseph Young and of Nan, who married C.H. Schaeffer. Dr. Young's second wife was a daughter of the Reverend W.C. Clarke, a former Presbyterian pastor here. Their children are William Crawford Clarke Young, Adair (Mrs. Louis) Y. Wood, Monroe (Mrs. Lyle) Y. St. Amant, Martha (Mrs. Don) Y. Campbell, Agnes Young, and Gessner (Mrs. Ed) Y. Galloway.

To the east, John H. Sherard, an early settler, built. He was married at least twice, and among his older children were Mrs. Thomas A. Johnston, Chris Sherard, Napoleon Sherard, and Mrs. Con Parker. Mr. Sherard's last wife was Miss Malvina, daughter of General Joseph Arrington. She was the mother of Mrs. Dr. Reub Arrington, Solon Sherard and John H. Sherard of Mississippi. Solon Sherard was a member of Dent's Company and died unmarried. Mrs. Arrington was the mother of Henry, Solon and Mrs. R.A. Barnes. Mr. John H. Sherard, of Coahoma County, Mississippi, is a prominent and wealthy man. He has preserved a tender feeling for his native town and visits Livingston every year. He married a Miss Dubose, and after her death, he married Miss Lula Chapman. After the death of the elder John H. Sherard, his widow married a Mr. Wooten and they had a son, the late Joe Dick Wooten.

Mr. Joseph Arrington seems to have lived at this place for some time and to have looked after the interests of the Sherard heirs—in fact, a part of the old Sherard place has been known for years as the Arrington place, although Mr. Arrington did not own it. Mr. Joseph Arrington was married two or three times, one of his wives being the Widow Godfrey, the mother of Dr. John William and Lawrence D. Godfrey. All of her sons served as Confederate soldiers and were prominent in their day. Dr. John Godfrey spent his last years in Detroit, and L.D. Godfrey married a Miss Woodson and lived at Gainesville. Mr. Joseph Arrington and the younger John H. Sherard moved to Mississippi.

Then this place was the home of Lemuel F. Whitehead, who was a lawyer and gentleman farmer. He married a daughter of General Joseph Arrington and they had no children.

Then Mrs. Laura Little, widow of Major W.G. Little, bought the place and died there. Her son, W.G. Little, sold it to the late Hugh A. Haralson. Haralson came from about Selma and was of a prominent family. His first wife was a sister of the late W.R. Larkin of Coatopa, and after her death he married a Miss Woods of Florence, and she was the mother of a number of children. After Mr. Hugh Haralson's sudden death this place was acquired by Mrs. Richard Allison, and she rented the dwelling place to J.A. Shelby, a former Sheriff. About 1928 all that part of this place north of the Livingston and Brewersville Road, amounting to some sixty-five acres, more or less, was purchased by Mr. R.H. Southerland, connected with the Normal School. There are about 235 acres in the whole place. Southerland succeeded R.B. Callaway as Superintendent of Education. [This house was leveled in the very destructive tornado of February 1945.]

PLATE XXVI. Desha House [Mrs. Jerry Dorman]

PLATE XXVII. T. V. White House on West Main Street [Addie White]

PLATE XXVIII. Cunningham/Hunter House, formerly on West Main Street
[Margaret Walburn]

PLATE XXIX. Reuben Chapman House, formerly on West Main Street

PLATE XXX. Ward/Little House on West Main Street [Mr. and Mrs. Bob Holycross]

PLATE XXXI. Cedar Grove Academy, formerly on site occupied by Grant House
[Mr. and Mrs. Bob Seale]

PLATE XXXII. Dent/Mitchell House on Madison Street [Mr. and Mrs. Bob Upchurch]

PLATE XXXIII. Forster/Brockway House, formerly on corner occupied by Regions Bank

PLATE XXXIV. U. S. Highway 11, between Livingston and York, ca. 1928

PLATE XXXV. Nat Kennard House, formerly on Washington Street

PLATE XXXVI. "Lakewood," the Lake/Parker House on Washington Street
[Mrs. Thomas Richardson]

PLATE XXXVII. Ennis Corner at Washington and North Streets

PLATE XXXVIII. Webb/Vaughan House, formerly on North Street

PLATE XXXIX. Smith Flat Area, off North Street, ca. 1928

PLATE XL. "Grampian," the Norville House, formerly off Highway 28

PLATE XLI. Bolling/Hale/Young House, formerly in Shady Heights area

PLATE XLII. Sherard/Southerland House, on Highway 28, destroyed in 1945 tornado

PLATE XLIII. Allison House on Washington Street [Mrs. Horace Hunt]

PLATE XLIV. Tartt/Mellen House, formerly on Monroe Street

PLATE XLV. Gowdey/Patton House on Monroe Street

PLATE XLVI. Lawhorn House, formerly on East Main Street

PLATE XLVII. Taking cotton to the gin

PLATE XLVIII. Cotton warehouse, formerly near the depot on Church Street, 1866

PLATE XLIX. Cotton bales before the warehouse. Standing on top: Andy Moore (l.) and W. Champ Pickens (r.); other (l. to r.): "Kootchum" Brown, Frank Hudson, Aus Coleman, William "Slick" Dale, "Jiner" Tartt, Dick Gowdey, "Big John" Moore, Joe Jones, Will Moore, "Little John" Moore

PLATE L. Harrris/Beggs House, formerly on Church Street

PLATE LI. Scruggs/Giles House on South Street [Hiram Patrenos]

PLATE LII. Parrent/White House [Mr. and Mrs. Gray Holycross]

PLATE LIII. George Wilson House and "Tankersley Corner," once on E. Main and Jefferson

PLATE LIV. Steve Renfroe House on Jefferson Street [Mrs. Clarice Hillman]

PLATE LV. Alabama Inn, formerly on Lafayette Street

PLATE LVI. Franklin Street, looking east toward Alabama Inn

PLATE LVII Artist's drawing of Choctaw Tavern, formerly on Marshall Street, ca 1880

PLATE LVIII. One of the "office rooms" of the Choctaw Tavern

PLATE LIX. ca. 1906: (l. to r.) Ed Wrenn, James R. Jackson, Charles J. Brockway, M. E. McConnell, Thomas F. Seale, W. W. Patton, R. B. Patton, J. C. Travis, Capt. W. A. C. Jones

PLATE LX. Preparing barbecue, ca. 1928

PLATE LXI. Rose Thetford, washerwoman

PLATE LXII. Walter Cook

PLATE LXIII. Ben Brown

To the east is a place that was first owned by one Shelby Corzine, and after him it passed through a number of hands until it became the home of Judge A.A. Coleman, who married a Phares and has descendants in Birmingham. He was the first Colonel of the 40th Alabama, C.S.A. This place then became the home of Major W.G. Little, who was a very prominent man in his day. His people have been mentioned. The widow of Major Little sold this place to the late Walter K. Smith, and the old house burned while Mr. Smith lived there. Then it passed into the hands of Felix G. McMillan and was inherited by his daughter, Mrs. Clarence Larkin. She sold the part north of the road to R.W. Ennis, who gave it to his daughter, Mrs. W.J. Hendley, and Mrs. Hendley sold it to R.D. Spratt. This place contains about 180 acres. [Dr. Spratt, the author of this history, lived in a house on this place until his death in 1950. His house stood approximately where the home of Mr. and Mrs. C. David Larkin now stands.]

A.A. Coleman succeeded the late Senator E.W. Pettus as Circuit Judge, and he was succeeded by James Cobbs, who is said to have been removed by the authorities in Reconstruction times and a "Radical" named Luther A. Smith appointed. Then W.S. Mudd was elected, and he was succeeded by S.H. Sprott. Then came Bernard Harwood, A.S. Vandergraaf, R.T. Jones, John McKinley, and F.B. Elmore.

Farther east was a part of the Battle place, about sixty-seven acres. W. Peter McLean bought this place and built there. He was a son of the late Lewis McLean and married Miss Susie, daughter of the Reverend W.G. Curry. Among the children of Mr. and Mrs. McLean are Mrs. Myron Scales and Peter, Jr. W. Peter McLean died in 1935. Morgan Stickney bought this place and sold it to W.M. Sullivan. Mr. Sullivan died in 1936. [This is now the home of William Dew.]

Farther east is what is called the Desha place. It once belonged to Robert Desha. James B. Jackson acquired it and lived there. He married the widow of Mitchell Eason. Mr. Jackson traded this place to his brother John and, in course of time, it belonged to Woodson L. Ennis, who has lived there himself and rented it to various families. Andrew Shelton lived here awhile and Conde Boyd now rents the place. It contains about 167 acres. [The house on this site was replaced by a modern dwelling, which is now the home of Mr. and Mrs. Thomas McDaniel.] Mr. Boyd is named Conde Caldwell for the old Presbyterian paster of the 1880's, and is the son of Mr. Austin Boyd. He married a Miss Neeley, a sister of Mrs. Philip Willingham, and they had ten children, several of whom are grown and married. Their oldest son, Ralf, was accidentally killed in a football game at Auburn, and their youngest son, Caldwell, was accidentally killed by some other boys who were playing with a shotgun.

To the east of this place is what is known as the Sprott place. The mother and brother John of Judge S.H. Sprott lived here after the Civil War. This came to belong to William G. Little, and he took W.J. (Jim) Nixon as his partner, so the business is styled Little & Nixon. Mr. Nixon lived here for a number of years, and there is usually some white man living on the place acting as a sort of superintendent. [The home of Mr. and Mrs. Ray Hamrick now stands on this place.] The Nixons were related to the McDaniels of Sumterville. William Nixon married a sister of Jeff Boyd, and among their children were Dr. Bascomb, W.J., Moreland, Percy, Leland, Leslie and Cameron B. Nixon. There were several daughters also, among them the wife of J.A. Mitchell, the farmer, who has lived at the old McLean place for a number of years. W.J. Nixon married Miss Ella Patton, daughter of Joe Patton of Brewersville.

To the east a road runs out to the Bluffport neighborhood passing the Roan place, the Gould place, the McLean place, the old home of Pinckney Brewer, etc. Newton J. Hamill, the teacher, who married a Miss Porter, once lived out this way, and his widow married C.T. Roan, who also lived at the same place, so it is known as the Roan place.

The main road keeps on down to Brewersville and onward.

East of the Sprott place is a farm now owned by Mr. J. M. Branch, which was once the home of M. Boyd McDonald. His first wife was a Miss Hale, and she was the mother of Cliff McDonald, who went to school in Livingston in his youth, and there were at least two daughters. Mr. McDonald's second wife was Miss Sally, a sister of the elder Lewis McLean. Mr. McDonald was a Confederate soldier.

To the east is a place where Mr. Robert H. Lide once lived. For a long time it belonged to W. Tureman Wallace. [This place is now owned by Mr. and Mrs. Robert B. (Ben) Elliott.]

To the east is a Negro church known as Shady Grove, and east of this is what is called the Beebe Place. It was the home of William Beebe. He was twice married, and his first wife was the mother of W.C. Beebe, who married Miss Clarice Breitling. The second wife of Mr. Beebe was the mother of Woodie, John and Jim.

Across the road to the south is what is called the Lee place. At an early time John S. Jemison lived here, and afterward it seems to have belonged to Joseph and Leroy Jenkins. It passed into the possession of I. James Lee, who married into this other Lee family. Colonel Lee was originally from Tuscaloosa and was an officer in the Confederate service. He had a brother, Frank S. Lee, who lived near Livingston also. Frank S. Lee also was a Confederate soldier and left a son John, who lives in Eutaw. Mr. Robert W. Ennis acquired the Lee place and several of his children lived there at various times. This place is now a part of the Allison properties. [The Lee place is now a part of the Grubbs estate.]

To the west of the Lee place was a small farm where A.D. Fortner lived. His wife was an aunt of T.L. Smith. Mr. Fortner is said to have served for a short time in the Confederate Army.

To the west of this was the home of James Kennard, who has been mentioned. Among the children of his first wife were Mrs. Dr. Kinnard and Mrs.

C.S. McConnico. Among the children of his second wife were John and Nat Kennard, who served as Confederate soldiers. Susan Kennard, famous as a nurse of the sick in her day, had been a slave in this family and was Mrs. McConnico's maid. She was a good woman and was liked by all. She lived to be around one hundred years old, dying in 1924. Some time after the Civil War this place became the home of John Jackson, father of Mrs. Dr. Phillips and of "Pete." His people have been mentioned. Then Mr. W.S. Nichols acquired it and various families have rented it.

Across the road from the Sprott place was a farm that once belonged to the Sherard estate and later was owned by Major W.D. Battle. It is now owned by Little and Nixon. To the south is that portion of the Sherard land known as the Arrington place. John Jackson moved here from the Kennard place and sold it to his brother, James B. Jackson, and it is now a part of the Allison property.

To the west is a farm once owned by one of the older Tartts. Mr. Soc Parker bought it and lived there for some time. He sold it to W.D. Battle, Sr., who lived there until his death. This place now belongs to Marcus E. McConnell.

A part that reached across the Livingston and Brewersville Road was sold off to W. Peter McLean, as already mentioned. Another tract of about forty acres, in front of where McLean built, was sold off to J. Hamilton Hoit, who built and resides there. He is a son of Zane Hoit and married Miss Nellie Neilson, and they have three sons, Robert, William and John.

On another part east of Hoit's, Dr. Galt, a veterinarian, built a home. His wife was a Miss Ivy, and one of their sons was drowned in a pool on the old Hair place. R.O. Breitling bought this and sold it to W.L. Ennis.

West of Hoit's is a place of about thirty-five acres on which Mrs. Clarence Larkin built a residence. She lived there a while and sold it to W.J. Nixon, who now lives there. [This is now the home of Mr. and Mrs. Max Jones.]

To the west is a place of about ten acres belonging to Dr. H.B. Smith, who lives here. [The Smith subdivision was developed in this area.] To the west is that part of the old Sherard place lying south of the Livingston and Brewersville Road.

To the west is a place where Daniel Ayres, a former sheriff, lived. Daniel Ayres and his good wife, Ann, had no children of their own, but they cared for the children of Dr. and Mrs. A.B. DeLoach when their parents died, and they are said to have cared for the children of S.W. Murley when his wife died. Mr. H.S. Lide bought this place and lived there. His widow married Dr. Forster and built a new house in town on the southeast corner of West Main and Spring Streets. Mr. Robert H. Lide then lived here for a number of years. He married a lady from Virginia and finally moved to Virginia, where he died, leaving a son and a daughter. Mr. Lide sold this place to his cousin, Mr. T.V. White, and after some years Mr. White sold to Dr. J.T. Phillips. [This house was removed some years ago and several modern dwellings are in the area.]

West of this place was once a large building used in early times by the elder John H. Sherard as a place for making plows, etc. Later on Hamill used it as a schoolroom. It is said that Mr. Sherard manufactured old-fashioned cotton gins here.

J.H. Lee acquired a lot and built a house here. He is of the Lilita family and his wife, a Miss Parker, was related to the Blakeneys. Among the children of Mr. and Mrs. Lee are Miss E.S. Lee, Mrs. Stitt, Mrs. Atkinson, Mrs. W.G. Brockway, Goldsby, Miss Erin, Mrs. Morris, Mrs. Orr and John Robert.

To the west was formerly pasture land that was acquired by a company formed to manufacture cotton quilts and comforters about 1900. This company built and operated a factory. Later on, this factory was converted into a heading and veneer plant and was operated as such by a Mr. Strand and then by A.M. McGehee. [This site was approximately where the Livingston Stockyard is now located.]

Passing under the railroad trestle here and west along North Street, we come to the Baptist pastorium, built about 1890 and first occupied by the Reverend W.G. Curry and his family. A Negro workman by the name of Gus King fell from this roof while it was being built and was impaled on the picket fence below, so that he died shortly. [The old pastorium was located on the corner of the present Livingston First Baptist Church lot—i.e., on the southeast corner of the intersection of North and Lafayette Streets.]

West and across Lafayette Street from the pastorium was where Bill Batton, a former jailer lived. The Habercorn family is said to have lived here awhile, and possibly others. Then the old house was removed and a new one built by P. Bestor Brown, who married Mamie, daughter of Major W.G. Little. It was known as the Bardwell property when Mr. Brown bought it about 1881. Then a Mrs. Smith, a widow, lived here and her son Walter attended Dr. Mellen's school. Mrs. Smith had been a Mrs. Hibben and had one or two Hibben daughters. Then Dr. R.M. Harris lived here for a number of years. His wife was a daughter of John E. Brown and these people have been mentioned. Then L.O. Breitling lived here and owned it, and then it was acquired by the Reverend John Henson, a retired preacher. Mr. Henson died, and his widow sold it to his sister, Mrs. W.R. Larkin, of Coatopa, and she rents it out. [This is now the home of Mrs. Malcolm Larkin, Sr.]

To the west is where Dr. Truehart once lived, and then it became the home of Dr. William Harris Coleman. Dr. Coleman was twice married and both wives had children. Dr. William Harris Coleman's first wife was Emma Thompson, sister of the noted Harvey Thompson, a former sheriff. She was the mother of two sons, George K. and Harris. These lived near what is now Panola, Alabama. George K. attended the University of Alabama. His last wife was Miss Caroline, daughter of G.G. Tankersley. Several children of the last marriage lived with the family of Mr. Robert Tankersley after the deaths of Dr. and Mrs. Coleman, among them James, Dan, Miss Maggie, Mrs. Fox and Sterling. Then B.S. Barker lived here. It has been mentioned that he married the Widow Bedell. Then it was acquired by Mrs. Brownrigg, and she lived here for a time, rented it to various families and then came back and lived here again until she moved to Mobile.

Mr. R.B. Callaway bought this place and lived there and then sold it to Mrs. McCain, widow of C.M. McCain. In 1917 it was struck by lightning and was burned. Mrs. Richard Allison bought the lot and built a brick house, where she lived for awhile, and then she moved to Birmingham. She returned to Livingston in 1930. [This house is now the home of Mrs. Horace C. Hunt.]

To the south, on the corner of Monroe and Washington Streets, was once a sort of office. B.S. Barker lived there in his last days, and then it became the home of J.C. (Jim) Arrington. He had served as a Confederate soldier and married a daughter of Joseph W. Jenkins. Among the children of Mr. and Mrs. Arrington were William H. Arrington and Miss Alpha Lloyd Arrington. William H. Arrington married a daughter of Gus Nash, and they had two daughters, who now reside in Washington, D.C. William H. Arrington died in 1932. Then the late M.B. Rosenbush acquired this place and lived there until his death. He was born in Hasse-Cassel in Germany, and came here as a young man, being related to the late B.M. Emanuel. Mr. Rosenbush married Miss Lena Eli, and their children were Bernard, Edwin and Ike. Edwin now resides at this place. [This site is now occupied by Rosenbush Plaza, a commercial development.]

To the east, about the middle of that section of Monroe Street known as "Dog Street" was the home of Pocahontas, a freed woman who was a seamstress. At a later day T.S. Childs, who had worked for Barker, had a carriage shop here and Marcellus Speight was his blacksmith. Mr. Childs was a Quaker, and he accumulated considerable property.

On the corner to the east was where Mr. Lewis Parrent had the first blacksmith shop in town. At a much later time, two Negroes had shops here, Alan Arrington and Minter Dodson. Another colored man named John Campbell now does business here. [This corner is presently the site of the Drug Store.]

To the north is where the town once had an acetylene light plant, and to the north is a store built and used by the Breitling brothers, L.O. and O.G. Mrs. L.O. Breitling was a Gallagher, and two of her nieces, Louise and Rose Gallagher, became rather noted, Louise as a writer and Rose as a dancer.

Across the street east from the Alan Arrington or John Campbell corner was where the Houstons had a shop. Mr. H.D. Fellows had charge of this shop and Marcellus Speight, who has been mentioned, learned his trade here.

D.W. Mitchell acquired this corner and put up a stable. After his death the late Mrs. A.M. Tartt bought the lot and built a house, which has been rented by various families. Among these was the family of John R. Smith, who was a very popular businessman here. He had two sons, Eugene and Felix. Mr. Smith's sister-in-law, Miss Bettie Richardson, married Bob Lee Dainwood.

To the east is where Dr. Robert D. Webb once lived. In his time an octagonal room, used by him as an office, stood in the yard. This was moved into the Baptist church yard for use as a pastor's study, and was afterward bought by W.S. Gulley and moved to his lot, where it became a tenant house. Mr. Webb decided to go to some other town and sold this place to the elder Thomas M. Tartt, but Mrs. Webb objected to the move, so the Doctor bought the Murley place and lived there some years. Mr. Tartt died at the place under discussion, and for many years it was the home of his widow, the late Mrs. A.M. Tartt. Mr. and Mrs. Henry L. Mellen now live at this place. [This house, which was, for many years, the home of Mr. and Mrs. Tartt Mellen, has now been removed and the lot belongs to the Baptist Church.]

To the east was the home of Captain Samuel Webb. Then it became the home of William Tureman, and it was inherited by his brother Zack, who was a Confederate soldier and married a sister of the last Mrs. Lewis Parrent. Mrs. Zack Tureman was a Miss Kate H. Brown of Murfreesboro, Tennessee. After Mr. Tureman died, his widow and daughters left and sold this place to Thomas M. Tartt, the banker. Mr. Tartt built a house which burned, and then he built another.

To the east is where a family of McNortons lived. Some time after the Civil War it became the home of D.W. Mitchell, and after he died, it was the home of Marbry, a very popular man who was AGS Railroad station agent here. George Nichols of Columbia, Tennessee, lived here for a time. He was associated with a Mr. Mathers in the lumber business here. Mathers rented the Wetmore place after W.K. Smith moved. Then this became the home of James A. Mitchell, County Solicitor, who married Miss Alice Tartt. [This was the home of Miss Annie Bestor Mitchell until her death in 1996.]

Across to the east a Widow Inge once lived. Her daughter married Judge Ben Gaines. Then it was the home of David H. Trott, Sr., until he died. T.B. Smith acquired it and lived there many years, and then various families rented it. W.J. Hendley owned it and sold it to Dr. Brock of the Normal School.

South and across Monroe Street from the Mitchell Corner was the home of Dr. John H. Webb, who afterward lived at the Mason place. Then it was the home of Judge Ben Gaines, and then a McBride family, related to Judge Crews, lived there. William Beggs lived here a while and then it became the home of G.C. Gowdey. He was born in New Hampshire and came here when a very young man and married a Miss Miles, related to the Henagans. Among the children of Mr. and Mrs. Gowdey were Frank, Maud and Richard. Frank and Richard had children. The mother of Mrs. G.C. Gowdey was a Miss Henagan who married first Miles and then Moore. It is said that the Samuel H. Gowdey who gave the Bible to the St. James Church here was an uncle of G.C. Gowdey who had come south and married. He owned much property and soon a nephew came. This was Henry C. Gowdey, who served as a Confederate soldier. G. C. (George Clarence) Gowdey was a brother of Henry C., but was younger and came south after the war. G.C. Gowdey was for a long time one of the prominent and substantial men of Livingston, and at the time of his death he was President of the Bank of York. His sons, Frank and Richard, left descendants.

Mr. Gowdey sold his home here to R.L. King, who succeeded Marbry as station agent. Mr. King was married twice. His first wife left a son named Robert. The second wife was a Miss Yeatman, and she had a son named Yeatman King. When he left here, Mr. King sold this place to Mr. W.J. Hendley, who lived here some time, and then sold it to Joe Patton, the Tax Collector, and it is now his home. W.J. Hendley came here from Columbia, Tennessee, and married a daughter of R.W. Ennis. They had two children, Mrs. Rainey and Joseph. Joe Patton is a son of the late David Patton and a brother of W.W. Patton.

To the west of the last place is a house built by Wesley M. Sullivan, who married Miss Annie McLean. He sold it to Lewis McLean, Jr., and he now lives there. This Lewis McLean married a daughter of M. Luke (Miss Ruth), and they have two children, Louise and Lewis. [This son, Lewis, now occupies the home.]

South of this is a house built by the late B.W. Winslett, who came here from Epes and married Miss Kate, daughter of W.T. Wallace. The Winsletts had two daughters, Emily and Katherine. Emily married John W. Long of Jasper. After the death of Winslett the place was sold to C.H. Mason, who came here from Isney in Choctaw County. Mr. Mason married a Miss Clifford Mathis, and their children are Lita, Hugh, Aline, Mary and Lyman.

To the east of the last is a house built by the noted Bob Johnson, who lived in it. This became the town house of the Porter family, and it passed to the family of Mr. John Lawhon, who married Miss Annie Porter and, after her death, Miss Jessie Battle. A.M. McGehee bought this place and later on it was purchased by the late W.W. Williams.

Near the Depot a cotton warehouse was built in 1886. Previous to that time the cotton brought to town was piled in the streets around the courthouse square. Among those who kept this warehouse were J.P. Spratt, John L. Horn, Alex G. Horn, C.C. Seale and Clarence Larkin. About 1916 this warehouse blew down. A new warehouse was built about 1934.

South of this warehouse and its yard was the home of J.W. Harris (known to his friends as "Jack" Harris). He was a brother of H.H. Harris and married a Miss Helen Terrell. Among their children were Mrs. J. Eugene Cusack, Henry C. Harris, Mrs. Chiles of Chicago and Mason Harris. Henry C. Harris was killed in the Civil War. He was a member of the Barrett (originally Sengstak) Battery.

William Beggs bought this place. He was a native of Ireland and was left an orphan in this region when it was wild and abounding in Indians and game of all kinds. He talked interestingly of the early days. An old hunter, a Mr. Pace, once told him of a fight he had seen between a panther and a black bear, which the panther won. He also told of a Mrs. Fincher, a neighbor, who was left at home with the children when a pack of wolves appeared and began to jump over the fence surrounding the cabin. She ran in with the children and shut the door. The wolves tried to dig under, as it was nothing but a log hut with a dirt floor. It happened that she had a pot of hot water on the fire, and she went about scalding every nose that appeared until her husband returned and the wolves ran off.

Nowadays, it is questioned that wolves ever did attack human beings, as the present-day wolves have learned to thoroughly dread the very scent of man. The wolves of those days feared man but little, and were regarded as dangerous beasts. The wolves of this region were of the timber wolf (Lobo) kind, but were of a more tawny color than the northern and western wolves. An animal of this kind is about the size of a very large dog and is more than a match for several dogs.

William Beggs married Martha Alexander and two of their children survived to leave descendants. Emerson Beggs lived in Choctaw County and married a Miss Elizabeth Smith. They had a son, William B. Beggs. Mattie Beggs married James P. Spratt. [They were the parents of the author of this book.] Before her marriage she taught. Among those who attended her school were Colonel A.M. Garber, Dr. A.B. DeLoach, E.F. Allison, Crockeron K. Abrahams and others.

Mr. Beggs sold this place to Mrs. Thomas Lockard, who has been mentioned. The late Robert Seymour acquired the place and sold it to W.S. Nichols.

There is some low ground to the south, and then an elevation on which were a schoolhouse for boys, the old Methodist Church and the cemetery. The school and church have been mentioned and the cemetery will be mentioned later on. Mr. Johnston, the schoolmaster, once chased a runaway pupil into this low ground and became hopelessly mired up. He had on low shoes and white socks and it caused much amusement for the rest of the school.

To the west of the cemetery is an old place. H.W. Norville once lived here, and about the time of the Civil War it was the home of Mr. W.D. Battle, Sr. Later on it became the home of H.D. Fellows, who was blacksmith at the Houston shop. He was a good workman, a good citizen and served as a Confederate soldier. Among the children of Mr. and Mrs. Fellows were George B., John, Harry and Miss Zuleika. George B. Fellows married Miss Nellie Murdoch and moved away. They had a son, Hobart Fellows. Harry Fellows became a lawyer in Washington, D.C., and his widowed sister lived with him at last account. B.B. Rudulph of Lowndes County then lived here for several years, and after he left, it became the home of the widow of that William Beebe who formerly lived east of town. The old house burned in 1923, and Mrs. Beebe had a smaller house built.

To the west is the home of Leverett S. Fluker. He is a son of the late George M. Fluker and a grandson of Thomas Johnston of the Ben Ivy plantation. L.S. Fluker married Miss Elizabeth Cooper, and they have one child, a son named George. [George's widow, who was Martha Moon, lived in this home until her recent death in 1996.]

To the west is the house built in the 1890's by one Bowden. This is the home of Mrs. Sadie Reed, a niece of Mrs. L.S. Fluker. Mrs. Reed has one child, a son named Leverett Semmes Fluker Reed. [This house has now been divided into apartments.]

To the west is the old home of Josiah L. Scruggs, who went into the drug business in Livingston in 1837. Mr. Scruggs was twice married. His first wife was a daughter of General Joseph Arrington, and she was the mother of his children. His last wife was a Mrs. Gary. Mr. Scruggs was a pleasant-mannered man who was very neat in his personal appearance. He was quite bald and wore a curly brown wig. Once he was going home from his store and found the sidewalk crowded with Choctaw Indians. He took off his hat and then removed the wig, and the Indians scattered like they had seen the Evil One—they thought he had scalped himself. For a number of years, W.S. Chiles has lived at this place. This family of Chiles were mill people as far back as there is any record. W.S. Chiles spent the active years of his life operating sawmills. Mr. and Mrs. Chiles have two daughters, Mrs. Layfield and Mrs. Peacock, and both of these daughters have children. W.S. Chiles was killed by a "hit and run" driver on the night of December 3, 1929. [Mrs. Peacock made the old place her home for many years. After her death it was acquired by Hiram Patrenos.]

To the west is a road, built in 1924, which leads to York, Meridian, etc.

Just west is where J.C. Arrington had a cotton gin, and then Mr. Shulman built a small dwelling here which was acquired by the late M.W. Parrent, who married a daughter of the late Paul Gee. Parrent was named for the Methodist Bishop Marvin, his name being Marvin W. Parrent, but in his boyhood the other boys called him "Bishop" or "Bish." In more recent times, W.F. Cooper, related to Mrs. L.S. Fluker, has lived at this place. His sons Tom, B.B. and Guy Cooper were well known here.

To the west is a house that was moved from up the hill and was fixed up almost new by Roy B. Patton, who lived in it. He sold it to Dr. John P. Scales. Dr. Scales is a son of the late Thomas Scales and came here from Brewersville. His first wife was a daughter of I.W. Horn and was the mother of Myron and Curtis Scales. After her death Dr. Scales married a Nell Stallings of Tennessee, and she is the mother of Dick Scales. Myron Scales married Bessie Maud, daughter of W. Peter McLean. [This house and the preceding one are no longer standing. The Cooper house was on the lot where the Livingston Police Department is located, and the Scales house, which was removed only a few years ago, was next door.]

Farther up the hill, to the west, is where Mr. George Wilson lived at an early date. He was a Swedish sailor and became a baker and confectioner here. His name was something like Olsen in Swedish, but it sounded like Wilson, and so he became and remained George Wilson. He gave this Swedish name to one of his sons, but it was too much for the American tongue, and so this son became and remained "Alson" Wilson. Mr. Wilson was a staunch Mason and Methodist. He was a merry fellow and was very popular with the children to whom he sold sweets. He was married three times—to a Miss Jarvis, a Miss Anderson and a Miss Davis. The first wife was the mother of Alson, Alex, Hunter and Tom. The next wife had a daughter who married away from here. The last wife had two daughters, one of whom married Coyle, the first postal telegraph operator here. This last wife was an aunt of the late Paul Gee. Alson and Alex Wilson were Confederate soldiers. The Anderson family from whom Mr. Wilson's second wife came lived near the Lee place. Mr. Sherard is said to have moved their old house to the grove east of his own home.

William Lockard bought this place and rented it to various families, the Purdys, Bob Johnson, etc. Bob Johnson died suddenly at this place. This place was used as a schoolhouse by R.B. Callaway and then by G. Fred Mellen. Then Mr. J.B. Coleman rented it and lived there. Then it became the home of Mr. J.C. Arrington. After living in this house some years, Mr. Arrington had it moved down the hill to the east, and on the old site he built a larger house. This house was bought by Judge Jarman after Mr. Arrington's death, and it burned in 1924.

Across the street to the North of this last site is a house built about 1885 by the late J.O. Scruggs. He was a son of Josiah L. Scruggs and, like his father, he was a druggist. J.O. Scruggs married a daughter of Robert G. Houston, son of M.C. Houston. Among the children of J.O. Scruggs and his wife are Mrs. Dr. Dougherty, Mrs. Woodson L. Ennis, Houston, Joe, Mrs. Drever, Edward and James L. Mrs. Drever's first husband was Andrew Shelton. [This house has been divided into apartments.]

Scruggs (or Scroggs) is an old family of Bedfordshire, England. Josiah Leake Scruggs, Henry F. Scruggs and Dr. Samuel Oglesby Scruggs were brothers who settled here in early days. Josiah Leake Scruggs left descendants in Huntsville, Dr. Samuel O. left descendants in Louisiana. Josiah Leake Scruggs had a son, Dr. Sam Scruggs of Lauderdale, Mississippi, who married a sister of Thomas B. Smith. The name "Ludie" which occurs among the descendants of this Scruggs family is a corruption of Louisa.

To the north is the home of Mr. and Mrs. James B. Jackson. Mrs. Jackson was a daughter of Joseph W. Jenkins, and her first husband was Mitchell Eason. The children of Mr. and Mrs. Jackson are Mrs. Selby, Brockway and Jenkins Jackson. [In recent years, this was the home of Mrs. W.G. Story.]

To the north is the "new" Methodist Church, dedicated in 1892.

East of this church are some cabins and then a brick building once used as a jail, and now used as a dwelling by Frank Kruse. This jail was completed shortly before Steve Renfroe was lynched. Two legal executions took place within this jail yard, the executions of John Johnson and Steptoe. Steptoe was a Negro who killed an elderly Negro woman. He had enticed the old woman's daughter away from her and when the old woman denounced him, he got very angry and beat her to death. He buried her in what is still called "Steptoe's Hollow" about five miles north on the Gainesville road. He was hanged in 1893. John Johnson called Captain J.M. Winston's overseer to the door one night and shot and killed him. They never had any trouble and no motive was ever established. John was a bit simple-minded, and many thought that others hired John to do the killing. He was hanged in 1897. [The old jail was removed some years ago. It stood approximately on the site of the present-day BP service station at Lafayette and Madison.]

Across to the east was what was once called the "Parrent Block." Mr. Lewis Parrent, the blacksmith, owned it. He came from Tennessee in 1834 and was married at least three times. Some of his older sons were Confederate soldiers. One of them, James L. Parrent, was a member of Dent's Company and died at Pensacola of measles before seeing any active service—he was the first of this Company to die. The second Mrs. C.T. Roan was the next wife's child and she had no children herself. Mr. Parrent's last wife was a Miss Brown from Tennessee, related to Mrs. Zack Tureman and to the last Mrs. Paul Gee. This last wife was the mother of Mrs. G.B. Fellows, Marvin W. Parrent and the Reverend Walter B. Parrent.

Mr. Parrent lived at what was later the Turner house, on the northeast corner of this block. This is now the David White place. [This is presently the home of Mr. and Mrs. Gray Holycross.] Mrs. Roan lived at the northwest corner where J.C. Travis afterward lived. This last house was rented to various families from time to time. Mr. R.L. McCormick, the sheriff, who married Miss Irene Turk, lived here awhile, and after him, R.A. Barnes, who succeeded him as sheriff. Young Peteet also lived here in the early 1880's.

(Anyone knowing anything about one Council Randolph Wright who lived here in the early days, leaving in 1851, please make a note. He bought lots 58 and 59 from Jefferson A. McAlpine. Number 58 is where J.C. Travis resided at the time of his death. Number 59 is to the rear of 58.)

Back of and south of Mr. Parrent's house was an old house which was owned by Mr. Parrent. W.M. McRae lived there for some time. He was a Confederate soldier from Missouri who settled here and married a sister of William and Zack Tureman, Miss Angie. Mr. McRae served many times as Town Marshal. In his younger days he was in much demand as a fiddler at the dances. Mr. and Mrs. McRae had one son, Charles H. McRae, who lived in Birmingham until his death in 1928. Mr. George B. Fellows afterward lived here, and then J.M. Branch bought the lot and built a new house about 1904. [The Branch house is owned by William B. Stuart.]

South of this [at the corner of Jefferson and South Streets] John W. Moore bought a lot and built a house, where he lived until he moved to Florida about 1907. The widow of G.B. Fellows was living here when she died. Then it was acquired by J.A. Johnson, agent at the railroad station here. [This house is now divided into apartments.]

Across the street, to the east, is the Methodist parsonage. A number of Methodist pastors who have been stationed here became connected in one way and another with the history of the town. The Reverend E.J. Hamill of long ago was the father of the schoolmaster, Newton J. Hamill. Since Civil War days the children of the Reverend Mr. Boland married in the county. Two sons of the Reverend J. Bancroft married in the county. The Reverend F.A. Rogers married a sister of Philip Willingham, a prominent man of North Sumter. Mr. Rogers has served here longer than any other pastor in the history of the Methodist Church in Livingston. A daughter of Mr. Rogers married Mitchell C. Jarman. The Reverend H.V. Hudson married Miss Bessie, the daughter of W.S. Gulley.

The Reverend J. Bancroft was here in the early 1890's. One of his sons, Dr. J.D. Bancroft, practiced medicine at Sumterville and at Livingston and then removed to Birmingham. He married Miss Julia Brown, and after her death married Miss Isla Brown. These ladies were daughters of W.H. Brown of Sumterville, and both had children. Another son of the Reverend Mr. Bancroft was Frank H., who married Miss Louise Cox.

The present parsonage was built about twenty-five years ago. [This former parsonage was sold by the Methodists some years ago when they built a new parsonage on Spring Street. The former parsonage is now the home of Mrs. Doris Watkins.] It occupies the site of the old "Parson's Study" that stood in a corner of the old lot. The old parsonage stood to the north a piece and was remodeled and used as a dwelling by G.B. Fellows after the new parsonage was decided upon. [This house is now divided into apartments.]

The old parsonage was originally a private residence. It was at an early time the home of the Widow Brooks. She was a Miss Elizabeth Wiche Watson, who married William Middleton Brooks of Virginia, and their son was the noted Judge William McLin Brooks. Mrs. Brooks also had a daughter who married Wheeler and then married Fluker. Her Wheeler daughter married Travis King Miller, while her Fluker son was the late George M. Fluker who has been mentioned. Travis K. Miller was a druggist who once lived here and removed to Texas, where he met with success and died at the age of ninety-six years. A number of parsons lived in the old parsonage. Then, as stated, G.B. Fellows acquired it and fixed it up. Then it became the home of Paul Gee, who died there. His widow sold the place to a Mr. Headley. This last Mr. Gee married a Holder.

To the north is a house built by J.W. Killian when he was first married. He sold it to G.W. Brock and he rented it to various families. R.A. Pinkerton rents it now. [This house burned some years ago, and a new one was built on the site, which is presently the home of Mr. and Mrs. Carey Moore.]

To the north is where Samuel Campbell once lived. Samuel H. Chiles, a brother of Mrs. Short, once lived here. Mr. Chiles had been born in Petersburg, Virginia. He died in 1866. Then it was the home of H. Otto Voss. He was a brother of the late W.H.A. Voss and was a very powerful man physically. He married Bettie, daughter of Jim Mason, and they died leaving no children. Many families rented this place until it was acquired by the late M.D. Gould, who altered the house considerably and died there. It is said Major Cobbs also lived at this place. [This house is now divided into apartments.]

Across the street to the north was once the home of W.D. Battle, Sr., and he sold it to Judge Preston G. Nash. Judge Nash married a Miss Lampedo Whitfield, and among their children were Reverend Preston, Miss Eva, Dr. J.T., Gus, Dr. D.A., Price and Miss Juanita. The Reverend Preston Nash was, at the time of his death, a clergyman of the Episcopal Church and for years had been Rector of a church at Richmond, Virginia. Miss Eva is said by those of her day to have been the most beautiful woman they ever saw. She was the second wife of A.W. Cockrell and died leaving a son, Preston D. (P.D.) Cockrell. Gus Nash had a daughter named Hazel, who married William H. Arrington and died leaving two daughters. Dr. D.A. (Bunny) Nash was a dentist, and was Mayor of Biloxi, Mississippi, at the time of his death. Miss Juanita married J.K. Edmundson. Dr. Joe T. Nash continued to reside here after the death of his parents. He married a Miss McLemore (or McGowan?) and they had a son named Preston, who lives in Meridian. Various families have rented this place since Dr. Joe Nash died in 1909. Among these was O.F. Adams, a popular young man who seemed in perfect health, but died of a suddenly developed aneurysm of the aorta.

To the north is a small dwelling built by Steve S. Renfroe. He is said to have been too young to serve in the Confederate Army, and he came here from around Huntsville soon after the Civil War. He was married two or three times and became noted as a Ku Klux in the Reconstruction period. He was popular and pleasant-mannered and was elected Sheriff. After a time it developed that he was hopelessly bad. He mistreated his family, terrorized the Negroes, stole from everyone he dared steal from and is said to have threatened to reveal the secrets of the Ku Klux to a still vengeful Government. Every effort was made to induce him to change his ways. Money was given him to enable him to go elsewhere and make a new start, but he continued to hang around and plague everybody. One night he was hanged to a tree near the old covered bridge. His body was cut down, taken to the courthouse and then buried east of the cemetery just across the railroad on a sort of mound. Those who hanged him never said a word and no one ever found out anything about it. This happened in the summer of 1886, and for years afterward children were told that if they would go to Renfroe's grave and say, "Renfroe, what did they hang you for?" he would say, "Nothing at all." Renfroe was married three times and his last two wives are buried at Old Side Church near Sumterville.

Renfroe's last wife was a Miss Cherry Reynolds, a half sister of Colonel W.M. Stone, and they had a son who changed his name to Thomas Reynolds after this terrible affair. Tom Reynolds grew up in Livingston and was well thought of. He and Walter (Kit) Parrent worked under Captain Herr on the old *Livingston Journal*. Tom moved away and married. He and his wife died leaving no children. Many families rented this place, and then it was acquired by Jodie Battle, who married a Miss Holstun and lived there some years. [This place was, for many years, the home of the Clarence Hunter family and is now the home of Mrs. Clarice Hunter Hillman.]

To the north is a house built by Charles H. Allen of the *Sumter Sun*. Mr. Allen died here. [This house was removed some years ago and a new brick house built on the site, which is the home of Mrs. Billye McElroy.]

Across the street, to the west is what is called the "Tankersley Corner." Charles R. Gibbs, Bob Johnson, Mrs. Chiles, William Beggs and others lived here. Mrs. Chiles had formerly kept the Planters Hotel and was the mother of Mrs. M.C. Short. It became the town house of Mrs. G.G. Tankersley, and after she died, it passed to her granddaughter, Mrs. Henry Arrington, who lived there awhile. Then W. Tureman Wallace bought it and his son, W. Raymond Wallace, lived in it some years. W.T. Wallace was a son of Josephus Wallace, a prominent man of South Sumter. W.T. Wallace married a Miss Ward and their children were W. Raymond Wallace and Mrs. B.W. Winslett. For some time Mrs. N.J. Sutliff, a widow, has lived here. She is a native of Perry County and related to the Taylor family. Her son, Harry S., married Miss Lucile Searcy and their children are Harry, Travis and Lucile. This house is owned by the writer.

South of this is a small house said to have been built by Mrs. Tankersley for her widowed daughter, Mrs. Dr. Coleman. Various families rented this place and then W.T. Wallace bought it and lived there. He sold it to G.W. Brock and he sold it to the brother-in-law of G.H. Mason, Mr. Mathis, and it is now occupied by Mr. Mason's mother-in-law, Mrs. Mathis.

To the south was once a vacant lot belonging to the county. G.W. Brock bought it and sold it to a barber named Malone. Malone gave it up and Dr. Brock then sold it to the writer.

Next to the Wallace lot is a dwelling made out of the old W.K. Smith office. It was put up here in 1927. A.M. Smith rented it, then C.J. Jordan, then Mrs. James R. Jackson, then R.G. Ennis, who died there in 1935.

[All the original buildings in this block, on the west side of Jefferson Street between East Main and Madison, have disappeared except for the one on the south end of the block. It served for some years as the Presbyterian manse.]

Around the corner is a small house built very largely out of material from the old light plant.

To the west of this last is the county jail, and north of this is where H.W. Norville had a wagon factory in early days. Later on Mr. Parrent had his shop here, and after him, G.B. Fellows, Gus Koppius and a colored man named John Williams had shops there. Gus started the electric lights in this shop.

The town bought Gus's plant and sold it to the Alabama Power Company. The old building was torn down.

To the north of the light plant there was once a Masonic Lodge. In the early 1880's a Mrs. Hill lived in this house and kept the post office. She had two daughters, Annie and Flossie, and moved to Florida. She was living in Fort Myers at last account. Her husband was related to the late Ben Hill of York. This house burned and was succeeded by a cabin where Austin Coleman, the noted hotel porter, lived. This cabin burned and the lot was vacant for many years. Then in 1926 a garage was built and rented to the Livingston Motor Company, handling Chevrolet cars.

To the north is where the *Sumter Democrat* was printed. Phil Strother is said to have been editor. Later, Thomas and James Cobbs used the building as a law office, and then Major W.G. Little had it as an office. After Major Little's death it was used by his son, James H. Little, and when he moved to Birmingham, it became a millinery shop conducted by Miss Gertrude Lockard. This place has been used for years as a law office by W.W. Patton.

To the east is what was once Henry Rogers' Market. It stood back of the present Shamburger Mercantile Company's store and was moved to its present location about 1901. Dr. H.B. Smith has used it as a dental office for many years.

East of the last is an office built by one Creasman, a contractor. Both this and the Dr. Smith office are on the original vacant part of the Little office lot. This office built by Creasman has been used as a law office for many years by T.F. Seale.

To the east is where the town once had an ice house. Then it became a schoolroom. Miss Nellie Gibbs is said to have taught there. Then it was a law office. S.H. Sprott and J.J. Altman had their offices in this place. Young Peteet bought it and enlarged it into a small dwelling. He sold it to William Beggs and so it passed to his heirs. It has been rented by Mrs. Gould, the Misses Lockard, A.A. Cleveland, and Mrs. Crumpton.

To the east is the last home of George Wilson, the "candy man," who has been mentioned. It was the largest small house ever seen in this region. Mr. Wilson had a reasonably good-sized family and he took roomers, and frequently the jury on a difficult case would spend the night here. J.P. Spratt bought this place after Mr. Wilson's death. Judge George B. Saunders is said to have lived here before Wilson.

To the east is the Tankersley corner already mentioned.

Across north of the W.W. Patton office there was once a stable in connection with the Planters Hotel. Bob Johnson ran this stable at an early day. Later on the Artesian Hotel occupied this corner [where West Alabama Bank and Trust is now located] and had a stable on the corner to the east.

This Artesian Hotel was built soon after the Civil War by a number of citizens, including T.M. Tartt, A.W. Caldwell, E.W. Smith, W.R. DeLoach, W.G. Little, R. Chapman, and R.W. Ennis. In time, R.W. Ennis came to own it. It was torn down about 1919. I. James Lee, Hudson, Weisinger, W.D. Battle, Jr., Jim McDonald, Tisdale, William Shelby, S.B. Turk, W.T. Wallace, Sanders, Lewis McLean, Sr., J.O. Phillips and perhaps others managed this place from time to time. It was some three stories high, and it was a large, rambling frame structure. In early days there was a large bell on a post which summoned people to meals. This was succeeded by a large Chinese gong and old Aus Coleman's performance on this gong was worth seeing and hearing.

The writer has been in the dining room when a boy and remembers it as an immense room with long tables and numerous colored waiters hurrying around with trays of food. There was a long contraption running the length of the room and attached to the ceiling. This was decorated with strips of paper and was worked by a Negro pulling a rope and was for the purpose of keeping off flies, for that was a day when screens were almost unknown.

To the north were three small wooden offices used by various persons, among them Dr. Nash, Dr. Sledge, Alex Posey (the barber), Dr. Scales, Miss Lockard, Mrs. Lawrence (as postmistress), Roy B. Patton, H.A. Haralson, etc. W.D. Battle, Sr., who preceded Mrs. M.F. Hill as postmaster, also had the post office in one of these.

The Planters Hotel stood about where the Ennis store afterwards stood, and had a row of brick "offices" running to the north corner of the block. In one of these rooms the body of James L. Hainsworth lay after he was killed by Thomas Scales as previously recounted. In another a man named McLeod killed a man named Harris. Francis Foard, Jefferson C. McAlpine and others were early owners. John C. Gillespie, Robert Howie, Reuben Thom, Mrs. Chiles, Bennett Bell, and possibly others, kept this hotel.

One of Bennett Bell's daughters married W.R. (Dick) Arrington, and another was the second wife of Andrew J. Arrington. One of A.J. Arrington's daughters married the late William Mills of Epes, and Mr. and Mrs. Mills had a daughter who married O.M. Cathey. Mr. Bell also had two sons, John and Dave, who lived in Livingston at various times. Dr. Blake Little, who is buried in our cemetery, was the father of Mrs. Bennett Bell.

The Planters Hotel was a frame affair built in the very early days of the town. It was torn down before the writer's recollections of the town begin, and on its site was built a frame store that was used for many years by the late R.W. Ennis. This store building was torn down and so were all the other old buildings on this block to make room for a new hotel, which was opened for use in March, 1924, under the management of one Cameron Glover. This hotel was given the name Alabama Inn. Glover was succeeded by Mrs. Lillybeck Chapman Cobb, and she was succeeded by Mr. Washburn of Meridian. The Alabama Inn burned February 22, 1929.

Chapter 5
Business District

Franklin Street

We now come to the Franklin Street business houses.

Across from the Alabama Inn to the west, on the corner now occupied by the Sherrill Oil place, was the store of George Wilson, who baked bread and made pies, cakes, candies, etc. His store burned the same night as the *Eliza Battle* disaster, and the citizens built him another. It had burned previous to this and the citizens had built another for him then, too. After the Civil War Samuel Brown did business here, then S. & A. Brown, then Brown Brothers. Since their time various others did business here, but met with no great success, and the old building was torn down a few years ago and succeeded by the present Sherrill Oil building.

To the west is a brick store built, owned and occupied by H.H. Harris after the fire of 1857, which had destroyed his frame store here. It has been used by H.H. Harris; Levy; H. Otto Voss & Company; Voss & Gowdey; Voss, Lawhon & Gowdey; V.H.A.Voss, Brown Brothers; Tannenbaum Brothers; L.S. Fluker; M. Shulman; W.G. Little Company; and B.B. Cooper's Pool Room.

The Harris and Wilson stores were not destroyed by the great fire of 1901. The Webb Building, a thick brick affair, kept the fire from them, but was itself destroyed.

To the west was a small office occupied at one time by Alex M. Pickett, a lawyer who was related to the historian Albert James Pickett.

Then farther to the west was the store of Shearer & Lake, which was not rebuilt by them after the fire of 1857. Captain B.B. Little and Dr. R.D. Webb acquired the lot and built a brick office building. This was a two-story affair. On the right, going in, were two lower-floor rooms used by Dr. Webb, and later by Dr. Sledge, Dr. Brockway, and Dr. McCain. In front was a stairway and to the left were two rooms similar to the others which were used by many renters. Along in the early 1880's T.A. Clark from Vaiden, Mississippi, had a watch and clock repairing business here, and after that, Brown Brothers established the first bank here. This bank was succeeded by McMillan & Company. Upstairs, various lawyers had offices, among them David Patton, J.J. Altman, C.J. Brockway, S.C.M. Amason and Tom Curry. Now and then, when some family was unable to rent a house, this upstairs or a part of it would be used for light housekeeping purposes.

After Captain Little's death Dr. Webb acquired the whole building. After the fire of 1901, Captain Ben L. Brockway put up a two-story building here. Upstairs in the new building were a Masonic Lodge, some offices and the telephone exchange. Downstairs were a small store and a large store. The small place was variously used. The first picture show was started here about 1916 by one Mendler. This smaller place is now used as a barber shop and clothes cleaning establishment. The larger place was used by A.J. Grove, Ed Rosenbush, Frank Harris, Stinson & Mitchell, C.H. Mason, Pee Dee Cash Store, George Price, B.B. Cooper's Pool Room, and Pop Dance.

West of the old Shearer & Lake store was a vacant lot where the boys played at an early form of baseball, and traveling shows would pitch their tents here. The Bayley Troupe, which has been mentioned, held shows here in a tent.

It is said that, soon after the Civil War, Norville and Beggs built a frame building here. There was a small office next to the Webb Building, then a larger place, and then another small room. The first was generally used as a grocery store and numerous people rented it. The larger was used by J. Zimmern, W.H.A. Voss, Arrington & Gowdey, Spratt & Gowdey, etc. G.W. Dainwood was here when it burned in 1901, and Killian was in business at the smaller place. The small room to the west side was used as a millinery shop, a barber shop, a jewelry shop, etc. Its last use was as a postal telegraph office, with J.W. Killian as operator. The post office and J.M. Branch's store cover this old site.

To the west was a store not destroyed by the fire of 1857—the vacant lot just mentioned stopped this fire. It is said that J.C. Cusack built this store. There was a firm of Cusack & Thompson in those days, and Mr. Cusack built a brick store. After Mr. Cusack died, Brownrigg & Tartt—said to have been uncles of the elder Thomas M. Tartt—did business here. Then this became the store of M.C. and P.F. Houston, who did a big business before the Civil War. This business lingered on as Houston & Stone, J.C. Houston & Company, etc. For some years J. Hafter did business here. Courson Brothers were here in the early 1880's. Then it was used by Mellen & Hart, McMillan & Parker, Scruggs (J.O.) & Horn (P.N.), Scruggs (J.O.) & Parker, and then it burned in 1901. R.D. "Bob" Hart lived in Livingston several years and then went to Uniontown. G.H. Grant's Store is on this old site.

To the west was once an old shack used as a bookstore, etc. It was acquired by the Houstons, who put up a brick store building similar to the one they had, and used it in connection with their business. This place was used by B.M. Emanuel, W.K. Smith, McMillan (Douglas) & Sims, H.E. Little, T.B. Smith, Henry Arrington, Jesse Jackson and possibly others. McLean & Gulley (Peter and Zeke) were here when it burned. These two Houston stores were rebuilt after the fire of 1901. G.W. Dainwood, W.T. Wallace and G.H. Grant have occupied the new store on the original Houston store site. The other new store has been occupied for many years by H.L. Mellen & Company.

To the west was the Barker Carriage Factory, where a big business was once done. Ike Habor, T.B. Stone, T.E. Lockard, G.W. Dainwood, John R. Smith, and John W. Moore did business in the old place. A new store was built here after the fire, and has been used by Will H. Arrington, Moore &

(Solon) Arrington, Wade H. Coleman, Miss C. Langhammer, Mrs. Boyd, Mrs. Shulman, and Miss Janie Patton. The old carriage factory was brick, but from there on to the corner west, the buildings were frame.

Next to the west was a large frame building that was used in connection with the carriage factory. A part of it seems to have been used by H.D. Gibbons, a tinner. His family lived in this building. Gibbons went to war with Stone's Company, although a man of middle age. Some say he was killed and some say not. Dr. M.C. Kinnard had a drug store here. Others who did business here were J.C. Arrington, J.L. Scruggs, and W.S. Gulley, who was there when it burned. This place is now taken up by M.E. McConnell's store. McConnell bought the lot and built soon after the fire. The firm was first McConnell & Turner (Marcus and Travis). Turner sold out and later Lewis McLean, Jr., became a partner of McConnell.

The great fire of 1901 started in the store on this site then occupied by W.S. Gulley. This fire burned everything on this business street except the old Harris store and the old Wilson corner store. The old frame courthouse built in 1839 was burned at the same time.

To the west was a silversmith's shop where B.G. Cook and, later, Jim Ustick did business. On the corner was the printing shop of D.H. Trott, who once printed the *Voice of Sumter*, and later on had a paper called the *Sumter Whig*. The Whig Party was very strong in this region before the Civil War, but the horrors of Reconstruction drove the vast majority of them into the Democratic Party.

It is said that the two places just mentioned were acquired by Hawes & Levy, who had a large two-story frame building put up there. This was acquired by the elder T.M. Tartt, and he did business here for a long time. He was for some years associated with R.W. Ennis as Tartt & Ennis. Then Ennis went into business for himself, and two younger men became associated with Mr. Tartt as Tartt & Company. These men were A.C. McMillan and Stephen Smith. After Mr. Tartt died, the firm was McMillan and Smith, and then Mr. McMillan withdrew to enter the banking business, and the firm became Smith & Pickens, and so remained until the great fire destroyed the store in 1901. Mr. Ed L. Mitchell came here to work for Mr. Tartt in 1880 and was with Smith & Pickens when the fire came.

Mrs. A.M. Tartt had a two-story brick building erected after the fire, about 1902. One part is for the bank of McMillan & Company, and another part is for a drug store which has been operated by Scruggs & Parker, and then by James L. Parker. Then there are offices and a hall in this building.

Washington Street and Vicinity

Mr. J. Eugene Cusack said that the business houses along Washington Street were older than those along Franklin Street.

On what is now the Shamburger (formerly Spratt Hardware) Corner there was a rambling frame house, a sort of double affair where a family could reside as well as conduct a business. One Nicholas Burns lived here at an early day and had a bakery. [This was on the southwest corner of the intersection of Washington and Monroe, where Sumter Hardware was located for many years.] Then for years it was the home and place of business of Michael O'Connor, the Irish bootmaker. He had a number of children, including a son by the name of John, who was a bad boy and a worse man. This John killed George McDaniel on the street soon after the Civil War. They had some little trouble before, and O'Connor went off and borrowed a rifle from the "Yankee" soldiers encamped in the Square. He then shot McDaniel. Old Mike and his son John both served as Confederate soldiers. Then Captain E.W. Smith lived here until his death in 1874. Dr. J.C. Houston (pronounced "Howston") used this place for awhile. Then it became the home of M.B. Rosenbush, who moved out shortly before the fire of 1889 which destroyed all the business houses on the block.

This lot was vacant until 1901, when the writer's great-uncle, the late Samuel A. Barnett, built a two-story brick store here, which was inherited by the writer's father. Spratt & Gowdey used it, then the Y.M.C.A., then Travis Turner, then the Spratt Hardware Company. Then Woodson Ennis bought it and had a hardware store there. He then rented it to the Sumter Farm and Stock Company and, later on, established the Ormond Mercantile Company here, now A.E. Shamburger's store. Samuel A. Barnett was a retired commission merchant of Mobile. He spent much of his time in Livingston and is buried in our cemetery.

In connection with this store an office had been built just south for Drs. D.S. Brockway and W.J. McCain. When Ennis bought the building, Dr. McCain bought the office.

South of the Dr. McCain office was a sort of office used by W.T. McKnight. After the fire W.K. Smith built a law office here, and this was used by his firm—Smith, Vandergraaf & Travis. This became a doctor's office and was used by Dr. Joe D. Bancroft. Then W.S. Gulley acquired it and used it until his death. The first hot dog stand in Livingston was established here by one Patterson who lived in this office. This place was bought by L.B. Spratt and the old building torn down and made into a dwelling in another part of town. On the old site a cement block store building was put up and rented to the Sumter Farm and Stock Company. This was in 1927. [This store was located on the site now occupied by the arcade leading from Washington Street to the downtown parking lot.]

To the south were two places. One was Squire Hale's office, and the other was used as a silversmith's shop by Cook and afterward by H. W. Norville. After the Civil War, a Negro named Warren Edwards, an uncle of the Warren killed by Brenner some twenty years ago, had a saloon in the old Hale office. H.W. Norville seems to have acquired both offices, and both were being used by his son, John H. Norville, when the fire of 1889 destroyed them. John H. Norville then built a brick store on the site and did business here until his death. Then it was used for some time as a picture show place and is now used as a ware room.

To the south was once a large two-story frame affair with a platform extending out across the sidewalk and steps going up from the edge of the sidewalk. One John Smith had a saloon here in early days and fell off the platform, crippling himself. Then it was the tailor shop of N.D. Stockley, and his journeyman lived upstairs. Then Bill Kirkland had a saloon here. I. James Lee and Captain James Monette had a store here at a later time, and then Major Levy had a grocery business here.

Major Levy's wife was a Miss Metzger, who could play fine dance music on the piano. The Major was good-natured and was an enormous eater. It was said that he started off each day by taking a sort of appetizer soon in the morning. This appetizer consisted of six raw eggs in a glass which was then filled with whiskey. Once the ladies had some sort of play, and among other things there was a scene showing a plump little child with a bow and arrow, representing Cupid. The boys burlesqued this show and the burlesque was well-attended. When the Cupid part of the show was reached, the curtain rose revealing the portly form, bald head, and benevolent countenance of Major Levy, who was adorned with little wings, was smoking his meerschaum, and was armed with a shotgun.

Levy left Livingston and came back several years later to do business at another stand. He was succeeded here by H.E. Little, who has been mentioned. The store then burned, and sometime afterward a smaller brick building was put up and was occupied by J.W. Moore; H.L. Mellen; John R. Smith; Branch & Horn; Branch, Coleman & McConnell; Curry Brothers; Arthur Hall; and, then, Scruggs for Drugs. Branch (J.M.) & Horn (Preston N.) did a big grocery business here until Horn died in 1904.

South of this was a large double office of frame construction. At an early date it was occupied by Captain Little, John McDaniel and Mr. Davidson, a dentist. A.W. Cockrell bought it and had his office here. He sold it to A.G. Smith, who used one office while R. Chapman used the other. It was burned in 1889 and a number of years later Mr. Stephen Smith built a two-story brick store here. This was occupied by Gregory (D.J.) & Mitchell (Ed L.), then by Wade H. Coleman, then by L.S. Fluker, then by the Ennis Motor Company and then by the Ennis Hardware Company. W.W. Patton once had his law office upstairs.

To the south were two small offices belonging to Dr. Joseph A. Smith, who used one and rented the other. Various people rented these offices, among them Colonel T.B. Wetmore, Major J.G. Harris, G. Minor Quarles, Dr. A.M. Garber and possibly others. Dr. Smith was unmarried and lived at his office, where he died rather suddenly.

Just to the south was a small place used as a barber shop. Among the noted Negro barbers who used this little place were Ed Whitehead and Prince Robinson. Prince was a Democrat in politics and finally secured some position in Washington city during the first presidential term of Grover Cleveland. He went back to barbering and became a noted character around the capital.

After the fire of 1889 the site of these three offices was covered by an office put up by Mr. A.G. Smith, who used it for awhile, and then it was used by various lawyers. Then Stephen Smith altered it considerably. He had an office in this place that was known as "Steve Smith's Den," where he transacted much business with his colored customers. The widow of Mr. Smith sold this place to J.P. Spratt, who used part of it as his office, and the other parts were variously used. W.P. Spratt slept in one room. Dr. Brockway, and afterward Dr. Scales, had part of it for office purposes. The back part was used for storage. In 1926 it was converted into a store by L.B. Spratt and was rented by Fred Sims and then by R. Garrett Ennis, both of whom had hardware stores. The building is now used by George Price.

Next, to the south, was a two-story frame building known as the Geiger tailor shop. Geiger did business here during and after the Civil War. Then a family named Phillips lived here. Mr. Phillips had been a silversmith and his widow and children lived in Livingston for some time after his death. I think he was Adam Phillips.

To the south was the old drug store of Josiah L. Scruggs. He bought out the remaining stock of Dalton & McCants, the first druggists, in 1837, and some of the family and of the name have been in the drug business here ever since. His son, J.O. Scruggs, was a druggist for many years, and J. O.'s sons, Edward and Joe, now carry on a prosperous drug business. R.W. Ennis, Travis K. Miller, John Godfrey, John Jenkins, Charles DuBose, J.O. Scruggs, James L. Parker, John L. Parker and perhaps others learned the business under J.L. Scruggs. The first soda fountain brought here was installed in this old store about 1884. This fountain was burned in the fire of 1901. [A further historical note: Scruggs for Drugs/Scruggs Drugs, Inc., continued with the Scruggs name until 1994, when it was merged into The Drug Store—a total of 157 years.]

After the fire of 1889 there was some confusion as to the lots, and some time in the early '90's J.O. Scruggs put up a two-story brick building on the Geiger tailor shop lot, thinking it was his father's lot. This place was used by J.O. Scruggs as a drug store. There were offices for lawyers upstairs and the Knights of Pythias had their meeting room there. Nothing was said about the organization of the Knights here until they organized. Nearly all the men of the town joined and stayed so late their wives got very uneasy. Many young boys were sent out in search of their fathers. The writer was one of these boys searching all over the dimly lighted town of that day. The mystery was not explained until we heard singing by men's voices in the upper part of this building about 2:00 a.m., and soon our fathers came down and explained, and then did more explaining when they got home. It was the talk of the town for a week or more afterward.

J.O. Scruggs went into business with Pres Horn on the other street and was later in business there with J.L. Parker, and various people rented the place under discussion. It was used by I.D. Hoit, Travis Turner and Edwin Rosenbush. One Lancaster had a restaurant here when it burned along with the old Bank of Sumter in 1925. The Honorable Reuben Chapman had his law office in the upper part of this building and died there suddenly in 1902. The lot was acquired by J.W. Killian, who put up a building there in 1926. Fuller, a barber, did business in part of it and the Singer Sewing Machine Company used part of it. It is now used by L.S. Fluker, the Sumter County Farm Bureau agent, and Jenkins Jackson, attorney.

After the old J.L. Scruggs drug store burned in 1889, John J. Altman put up a sheet iron store that was used by Killian and later on was moved to the farm of W.T. Wallace east of town and was made into a barn. Then the Bank of Sumter was built here about 1905. About the same time banks were organized at York, Cuba and Epes in Sumter County. The Bank of Sumter was organized in 1905, with W.W. Patton as President, B. Tannenbaum and W.H. Arrington, Vice Presidents, and Hardin L. Jones, Cashier. Directors were W.W. Patton, P.B. Jarman, J.H. Norville, W.S. Nichols, B. Tannenbaum, H.L. Jones and W.H. Arrington. After a time Messrs. Jones and Arrington were succeeded by J.W. Killian and J.H. Pinson, and Mr. W.S. Nichols became cashier. This bank building burned in 1925 and was rebuilt the next year. This bank closed its doors in September, 1930. [The building now houses the Sumter Insurance Agency.]

South of the J.L. Scruggs lot was a building that was used by many people until it burned in 1889. Dick Parrish once had a saloon here, and then Mack Little had one. Branch & Battle, Dick Arrington, Jack Clark, and others did business here. J.C. Arrington and J.M. Branch had a business here when it burned. J.W. Killian built a brick store here that has been used by J.W. Killian, Wade H. Coleman, W.G. Little, O.F. Adams, R.A. Pinkerton, W.R. Stinson, Jr., and possibly others.

To the south was once a vacant lot. After the fire a brick store was built here and occupied by various persons doing business. Among them were G.C. Gowdey, Miss Lizzie Bradshaw, D.L. Kirkland, Sam Stein and possibly others. For many years it has been used in Wade H. Coleman's business.

On the corner the preacher and teacher, C.E. Brame, had a store at an early time and H.H. Harris moved there after the fire of 1857 destroyed his first place of business on the other business street. Mr. Harris was here when the Hainsworth and Scales duel occurred. Hainsworth fell dead in the doorway of the old store—it had steps up from the sidewalk.

Elnathan Tartt & Son did business here, and later on it was the place of business of Fred Evans. Arrington (W.R.) & Gowdey (G.C.) were here some time. D.L. Kirkland did business here when it burned. This was the first lot to be rebuilt on after the fire of 1889. A small brick store was put here and used by D.L. Kirkland, then by W.T. Wallace & Son and then by Wade H. Coleman. [This was on the present site of the Ruby Pickens Tartt Public Library.]

This Elnathan Tartt is said to have married a Miss Eason and she had a son named John who had a son named Elnathan. After the death of his wife, the elder Elnathan married again, and his second wife had a son named Elnathan who was born about the time this elder Elnathan died. It is this son Elnathan who became superintendent of the Confederate Veterans Home at Beauvoir, near Biloxi, Mississippi.

Across the street south of the old Probate Office—the library in 1928— was where the Choctaw Tavern stood. [This was on the corner of Washington and Marshall Streets, on the site of the present post office building.] This was a large frame building, larger and more rambling in design than the Artesian Hotel. Its first owner seems to have been W.B. Ogletree, who was also connected with the *Voice of Sumter*. Afterward Squire Bob Arrington and many others owned this place. In the late '90's it is said that Smith & Pickens owned it and had it torn down. A Negro man named William Larkin built a house out of the old material on land now owned by Killian.

A skating rink was built on the old site, and this then became a "Holy Roller" Tabernacle for awhile. This sect never obtained a real foothold here, and most of those who took part in the services were from other places. Some of the believers would roll on the floor and speak in unknown tongues. The people here attended the services and took much interest in these proceedings.

Then this place was converted into the town's first garage and automobile repair shop, which was under the management of the talented but reckless Ben Thompson. This man Thompson came from North Carolina and had been a railroad engineer, a conductor on a freight, a motorcycle racer and many other things. He had this place about 1915. At last account he was working on a steamship in the Oriental trade.

Among those who managed the old Choctaw Tavern were Squire Arrington, Stephen W. Murley, Jim Tucker, William Lockard, E.W. Hooks, W.D. Battle, Jr., Mr. Hudson, Mr. Cowin, Mr. Reynolds, Dr. Randall, Mr. Loftin, Dave Bell and perhaps others.

The Choctaw Tavern was torn down in 1930. Some of the small "office" rooms that belonged to this old tavern are still standing. In one of them died Dr. Fletcher, the brother-in-law of Daniel Webster. Captain Herr's printing office was here for years, and when Mr. Lawrence first came, his printing office was here. About 1890 one Schuneman, a German working man who lived in one of these rooms, was found dead in the alley between it and the stable to the east. [The only section still standing was moved some years ago to Madison Street, where it has been used recently as an office for the Livingston United Methodist Church.]

Mrs. Lawrence now owns the Tavern lot, and when the Thompson garage was torn down, she had a smaller place built, which is now used by the Alabama Power Company.

To the east of the Choctaw Tavern was a stable originally connected with the hotel. Bill Kirkland kept this in early days, and others who kept it at a later time were E.W. Hooks, J.W. Tisdale, Vice Tutt and Ben Winslett. The stable with its lots was purchased by the Ennis Motor Company and this concern put up a very substantial building here about 1924. Later the W.G. Little Motor Company had this place.

Chapter 6
Livingston and the Various Wars

The American Revolution

It is not known that any veteran of the War of the Revolution is even buried here, but the place was largely settled by descendants of those who took part in this struggle, on the American side.

The War of 1812

The town was settled long after the War of 1812 and nothing has been found to show that any early settler of Livingston took part in that war, although a Mr. R.D. Shackleford of Coatopa and a Mr. Herrod of Epes were veterans.

Richard Dunford Shackleford lived near Coatopa at what is now the Coleman place. He and his wife are buried near the old house site. He died November 6, 1866. His sister was the wife of General Nathan G. Whitfield of Demopolis, and his daughter married Dr. W.H. Coleman, grandfather of W.H. and Percy G. Coleman of Coatopa and Demopolis.

A Mr. Herrod, a great-grandfather of Ed L. Mitchell who is buried at Epes, was also a veteran of the War of 1812.

The Indian Wars

It is possible that some of the young men of the time went to the Seminole War, which was waged about the time the town was settled.

The Mexican War

A number from the County were in the Mexican War. Seth B. Thornton, a Captain of Dragoons, was killed in battle and his body buried here. He was a brother of H.R. Thornton, Sr.

John Jackson (afterward a lieutenant in Stone's Company, C.S.A.) was in the Mexican War. So were Ed Lockard, William Beggs and Marcus Parker. Whether any of them ever saw active service is not known to the writer.

William Beggs was the writer's grandfather, and he never saw active service in this war. He volunteered and joined a regiment commanded by Colonel Jones M. Withers of Mobile, and he spent some time on the Gulf Coast in training, but this regiment was never sent to the front.

The Civil War

From the time of the first settlement, some sort of militia organization was maintained up to and through the time of the Civil War.

At the outbreak of this war there was an infantry company commanded by Captain E.W. Smith, which was taken over by Captain John H. Dent and became known as Company G, 5th Alabama. It went to Virginia at the beginning and fought through the war, losing many men.

Stone's Company included many from in or near Livingston. This was a cavalry unit known as Company D, Jeff Davis Legion of Cavalry. When first organized, it was called the Sumter Mounted Rifles.

Older men disposed of their business affairs and joined other organizations from the county or from other sections. Younger men coming to a suitable age did the same. So we find that many from the town served with organizations from other places. Some became dissatisfied with one organization and joined another, and some went to distant parts seeking adventure.

After the Civil War a number of those who lived in border states and fought for the Confederacy found it unpleasant to go home, so they remained in the lower South. So many of these were from the state of Missouri that they were all known under the general name of "Missouri Soldiers." Jack Clark, B.C. Hunter, W.B. McRae, S.B. Turk, J.B. Francis, Captain Herr, David C. White, Nathan Copeland and others were of this group.

All through the 1890's the Confederate Veterans of Sumter County held annual reunions at Livingston, camping in the open for a few nights and having barbecue dinners. They usually camped in the pine grove in front of the old Dr. Garber place, near the noted spring. At least one such encampment was held on Captain Herr's place west of town and there was a pontoon bridge put across the Sukanoochi. The veterans gradually passed on, until there was but one left, so far as known, who went from the town of Livingston. This was T.E. Lockard, who went in the latter part of the war. He died November 26, 1929.

There has long been in existence a fairly complete list of the members of the Stone Company, but it seems impossible to find a complete list of the Dent Company, but the following is as complete as I can make it.

A Partial List of Dent's Company
(Company G, 5th Alabama)

Captain: John H. Dent, succeeded by N.R.E. Ferguson, who was killed, and then J. Holmes.

Lieutenants: Steve Potts, J.W. "Dick" Bryant, James Crews.

Chaplain: Reverend J.H. Harmon

Tom Alexander
Will Alexander
J.C. Arrington
Dick Billups
"Doc" Billups
William Carter
Quintus Cockrell
John Craig
Hugh Davis
W.R. DeLoach
George Dent
Frank Dill
_____ Dolman
Charles DuBose
Mason Dunn
N.R.E. Ferguson
Tom Fitzpatrick
N.W.[*or* N.S.] Franklin
W.H. Green
Warren Hale
J.T. Hawkins
John Hoard
Marion Hodges
Newt Hodges
Jim Holmes
John Howie
_____ Hughes
J.J. Hutchinson
A.H. Hutton
John Jackson
Albert Jenkins

Bill Jenkins
Dr. John Jenkins
Oliver Jenkins
Bill Kirkland
John Kirkland
Ben B. Little
Pembroke S. Lockard
Gus Mallard
Thad May
Asbury McDaniel
John McDaniel
_____ Mills
Jim Nichols
John Nichols
John O'Connor
Dr. Robert Park
Jim Parrent
Dan Ratigan
C.A. Reed
Solon Sherard
Nolan Stewart
Felix Tankersley
James Tankersley
Jim Taylor
J.M. Thomas
Zac Tureman
Lilbern Ustick
W.H. Walker
John Williams
Joe Zerney

Will and Tom Alexander, cousins of the writer's mother, worked for H.H. Harris. William Carter was an uncle of B.S. Barker. John Hoard was a brother of Billy Hoard and was related to Joseph W. Jenkins. Ben B. Little became the captain of another company and was killed. Mills is said to have carried the flag. Jim and John Nichols were related to W.S. Nichols. Jim Parrent died of measles at Pensacola before seeing any active warfare. He was a son of Lewis Parrent. Nolan Stewart was related to the Reverend Mr. Harmon. Jim Taylor was related to the Barkers. J.J. Hutchinson was an uncle of Mrs. Fred H. Jones.

LIVINGSTON, ALABAMA

A List of Stone's Company
"The Sumter Mounted Rifles"
Later known as Company D, Jeff Davis Legion

Captains: W.M. Stone, succeeded by A.K. Ramsey.

Lieutenants: I. James Lee, John Jackson and A.W. Cockrell. J. Clint Houston, Andrew Armstrong, J.L. Brown, R.S. Mason, Eph Henagan and W.W. Hopkins were lieutenants at one time or another.

Robert Allison
Andrew Armstrong
Dr. Sam Arrington
Leonard Binns
John Brewer
J.L. Brown
W.H. Brown
Perry Canterberry
S.L. Carroll
Fayette Cole
J.M. "Doc" Cook
R.S. Curry
Charles Dillard
James Donaldson
Joe Dubose
James Duncan
Joe Elliott
John Elliott
Sam Eskridge
Tom Eskridge
Robert Estes
Paul Evans
Charles Farmer
John Flowers
John Furwell
_____ Furwell
Samuel Gary
John Gaskie
H.D. Gibbons
Dr. John Godfrey
John Haigler
J.J. Harrison
John Hartnett
Willie Harwell
William H. Hawkins
Eph Henagan
J.J. Hillman
Billy Hoard
Evan Hodges
Henry Hodges
William E. Holloway
W.W. Hopkins
Dr. J.C. Houston
J. Clint Houston
Robert Howard

John Howell
Tom Hunter
John Jackson "Mexican John"
Cunningham Jones
_____ Johnston
Tom Jordan
Henry C. Knight
Ed Mason
George Mason
R.S. Mason
John May
Robert C. May
George McDaniel
Hugh McMillan
William McPherson
W.S. Moon
A.J. Mount
Dr. Jack Phillips
Thomas W. Powe
Billy Pruitt
A.K. Ramsey
Ben Rayfield
M.A. Rhodes
James Riley
_____ Rittenger
William Robinson
Bugler Roden
John Scarborough
Tom Scott
Cap Shepard
James Shirley
Joe Sledge
Otway Smith
Powhatan Smith
_____ Speers
James P. Spratt
Thomas B. Stone
Lee Summerlin
Dick Torrey
Nath Tureman
J.E. Walls
Dave Whiteside
James Wilson
Jesse Wimberley
Henry Wyatt

Robert Allison was a half-brother of Mrs. S.B. Turk. J.L. and W.H. Brown were sons of Lewis S. Brown. Leonard Binns lived near the crossroads on the Gainesville road and was murdered after the war. While clerking in a store there for A.J. Arrington, he was killed by a robber. The alleged robber, a Negro, was then hanged by the Ku Klux Klan. Canterberry was related to those of Linden. J.M. Cook, called "Doc," was a son of B.G. Cook, the silversmith. Robert Estes lived at Epes and died there in recent years. John Gaskie kept a saloon in Livingston.

The name Houston is pronounced "Hewston" by one family and "Howston" by another. J. Clint Houston, son of Robert F., was of the "Hewstons," while Dr. J.C. Houston was of the "Howstons" of Warsaw. Dr. Houston practiced awhile in Livingston and spent the latter part of his life at Belmont. His daughter married "Little Bob" Flowers.

Eph Henagan was a brother of Major Charles Henagan, Captain James M. Henagan, etc. He was slightly ill on the retreat from Yorktown and got on a steamboat to go to Richmond. He was never heard of again. He had a son named Eph Henagan. The Henagans were from South Carolina. There were four brothers and four sisters—Major Charles, Dr. Darby, Eph, Captain James M., Mrs. Dr. Moore, Mrs. William H. Brown, and two unmarried sisters.

Billy Hoard was related to Joseph W. Jenkins. It is said that he went out as a spy and got into the good graces of General George Custer—later killed by the Sioux. He was entertained by Custer, and when it was time to go, he took Custer's saddle horse. This horse was ridden to Livingston by R.S. Mason, who turned it over to his father, and it was long known around here as "Old Custer."

The writer's father related that he was in prison at Camp Douglas, Illinois, with one of the Austills of Mobile, a descendant of old Jeremiah Austill of "Canoe Fight" fame. One day Austill told him that he had a lady friend in Chicago who would conceal him if he could secure citizen's clothing, but he had no money. The writer's father had $50 concealed on his person, and he let Austill have this. Austill obtained citizen's clothing, slipped out and was concealed by this woman until the search for him subsided. Long after the War, he related his subsequent adventures. It seems that he reached New York City, where his family had old business connections. These former friends were afraid to do anything for him, and he almost starved to death. One day a parade passed, carrying signs calling for volunteers to join the Union Army. He joined the Union Army and shortly afterward was sent South on a ship to take part in an assault on some Southern port. His force was landed during a heavy fog. Austill managed to get away and kept going until he was able to rejoin the Confederate army.

The late John McInnis, who was born near Epes, who was related to the Whites and Henagans, and who spent the latter part of his life in Meridian, was one of those taking part in the famous St. Albans Raid. It seems that a number of Confederate prisoners had escaped to Canada. Under the leadership of Bennett H. Young of Kentucky, they swooped down upon the town of St. Albans, Vermont, and looted a bank. This almost produced international complications, and for a long time the United States Government seemed determined to capture them and treat them as though they were ordinary hold-up men. After the War these men took refuge in the West Indies and various parts of Central and South America. Then, when the bitterness between the sections began to subside, the Government was induced to leave them alone, provided they refunded some or all of the money taken from the bank. This was done and the matter was dropped.

John Jackson ("Mexican John") served also in the Mexican War, as has been mentioned.

Dr. Jack Phillips' people lived at what is now the Thomas M. Nelson place near Epes. It is said that A.J. Arrington's first wife was the doctor's sister and that this Phillips family was related to the Godfreys.

A Ramsey family lived near the present Emelle and a Ramsay family lived near Sumterville. A.K. Ramsey was of the Emelle family, who gave the name to old Ramsey Station.

Lee Summerlin is said to have been related to the Cedar Creek Brewers. Joe Sledge was a son of Albert Sledge.

Powhatan ("Pop") Smith was the first to die. He was thrown from his horse and killed as they were passing through Montgomery on their way to the front. He and Otway Smith were uncles of T.L. Smith.

Dick Torrey was of the Brewersville family. Nath Tureman is said to have been a brother of William and Zac. Jesse Wimberley was of the Wimberley family of this county.

Many men in this company came from other counties, especially from Tuscaloosa, the home county of Colonel Stone.

The other cavalry company of the Jeff Davis Legion was mainly from Marengo County and was commanded by Captain Ivy Lewis.

Stone's Company went to Virginia and served through the War. Its first active service was in the retreat from Yorktown, and it took part in a cavalry charge at the Battle of Williamsburg. In 1862, A.W. Cockrell and J.P. Spratt from Stone's Company came home, along with John McDaniel and James Crews from the Dent Company. The four decided to join General John H. Morgan, the noted cavalry leader of Kentucky, and they rode to Cynthiana and joined Morgan's force. They at first belonged to Company A, 2nd Kentucky Cavalry, commanded by Colonel Basil Duke, and later on were transferred to Company D, 14th Kentucky, commanded by Dick Morgan.

A number of men from Livingston went with the Williams, Vandegraff and Winston Companies from North Sumter. Among these were E.W. Hooks, Ed Lockard, H.T. Lide, R.W. Ennis, Dr. H.B. Leverett, and Mike O'Connor.

Reconstruction Times

After the Civil War there was much poverty and great confusion. The recently freed and enfranchised Negroes were inclined to take things quietly and peaceably, but they were kept in a turmoil by politicians. Most of these were from the North and were known as "carpetbaggers." It was said they carried their worldly possessions in the traveling bag of that day known as a "carpet bag." Some resident white people joined with these and were known as "scalawags." Such people cared absolutely nothing for the real good of the South. They wanted to use the Negro vote to get themselves into office so they could assist in the wholesale looting of the State then going on. It suited their purposes to stir up the Negroes against the whites, and so conditions at times were very bad indeed, but not so bad in Livingston as in many other places.

In those days many well-meaning and influential people of the North knew very little about the Negro people. They were inclined to idealize the Negroes. They honestly desired to help them, but usually had to do things through such agents as these carpetbag and scalawag politicians who were utterly corrupt, and so the whole thing was a mess. The white men of the South organized the Ku Klux Klan in an effort to combat the evils of the carpetbagger and scalawag regime.

For several years, many Negroes did not work, but roamed about expecting the Government to care for them forever. Now and then they were incited to deeds of violence, but, as a general thing, they behaved very well, indeed, with the conditions as they were. In the course of time the better element of the North learned more about the true conditions, and soon such changes were made in the treatment of the late Confederacy so as to bring about a much better state of affairs.

At one time during this disorderly period a mob of Negroes marched down the Gainesville Road with the intention of taking Livingston. Some of the younger white men met them a few miles north of the town and scattered them to the four winds. Dr. Sledge reported that he met them as he was going home.

In 1869 one Dr. Chateau came to Livingston. He lived in the "Smith Flat" and soon made himself a person of importance among the Negroes. Threats were made against him, so he hired a German tanner named Coblenz to guard him. One night some men went to his house and knocked. There was no response and the house was dark, so someone kicked in a panel of the door and one of the men, Dr. Bailey Browning of Sumterville, stuck his head through the broken door and struck a match. Coblenz was there and he shot the doctor, scattering his brains all over the floor. Those with Dr. Browning killed Coblenz, but could not find Dr. Chateau. Browning's body was taken to near Moscow and buried. Those who carried it were trailed by the blood that dripped along the road. After disposing of the body, they crossed the river at Moscow and all trace of them was lost.

Chateau hid in a space under the roof and was not found until the next day. Then Mayor E.W. Smith put him on a train and he never returned. The writer has been told that he went to Meridian and the men there, having been told about him, tried to get him, but he jumped from the second story of his hotel and disappeared. It is said that Dr. Browning was especially bitter against him because he had been Browning's preceptor in earlier days and they were then good friends.

Two other disturbers were Rolfe and Hayes, who worked for Barker and got themselves elected to the Legislature. They never came back here.

Along in those times Demsy Winn was elected to the Legislature and Dick Harris was elected Sheriff. They were both Negroes. Dick was the father of John and of Manny the "Wizard."

Then one W.P. Billings came to this county and lived near old Ramsey Station. He was a fine-looking man and of considerable ability. Said to be a native of Elmira, New York, he was a Northern lawyer who spent much time haranguing the Negroes. It seems that he belonged to a law firm of Billings, Greata & Wells, and came here intending to get elected to the State Senate. It seems that he intended to get control of the State's mineral lands and have them sold at a ridiculously low price to a Northern syndicate. It may be that he belonged to this syndicate, or was merely hired to do the work. It was a great scheme and, had it gone through, would have made millions upon millions for those who got the land.

While he was addressing a large crowd of Negroes at the old Parker place near McCainville, he was handed a note to the effect that his wife was ill and he was needed at home. He borrowed a horse from John W. Moore and rode toward his house. When he got to what is called the Billings field, near the Grindstone Prairie, a man stepped out and took a shot at him, but the horse threw up its head and was killed. The next shot killed Billings, and he and the dead horse lay there until the next day.

J.P. Spratt, J.L. Brown and J.E. Cusack were members of the Coroner's Jury in this case, and the writer has heard them tell about it—the dead man and the dead horse lying there in the hot sunshine with a thousand or more people standing around. Greata is said to have been living with Billings and to have walked to Livingston the night of the killing. Wells and Greata both left this section immediately.

Robert Reed, a Negro who was a friend and co-worker of Billings, was killed also about the same time. [A letter to Robert Reed from Billings appears in Appendix C.]

Tom Ivy was a mulatto who was reared in or near Livingston, and about this time he was serving as a railway mail clerk. He was considered troublesome because he made "incendiary" speeches, so his removal was determined upon. One day someone flagged the train near what is now Hixon. Ivy looked out to see what it was all about and met a load of buckshot.

Billings was killed on the first Saturday in August, 1874, and Ivy was killed on the last Saturday in August, 1874. After this there was little real trouble. Billings, Ivy, etc. were considered great disturbers, and, in the minds of the majority of the white people, killing them was the only thing that could be done under the circumstances. These "disturbers" were not slain by hired killers, but by men who were of high standing in the community.

Of course, there was much "to-do" after this, and a detective was sent here to find out about these affairs. He came here in a covered wagon, posing as a North Carolinian who had been forced to leave his state on account of his Ku Klux activities. He camped on the edge of town and dispensed various kinds of ancient North Carolina cheer—corn whiskey, hard cider, etc.—hoping to get some of the boys to talking.

The result of this was that Colonel T.B. Wetmore, Stephen Smith and an old Negro named John Little were arrested and taken to Mobile. The marshal taking them to Mobile kept them all in one room while waiting for a train, and Mr. Smith slept in bed with John rather than sleep in the same bed with the officer. They were held some time. One of the officers was unnecessarily insulting, and Mr. Smith promised him a beating if they ever met. Some fifteen years later Mr. Smith met this officer on the streets of some city and gave him a sound thrashing.

Many others were sought for but could not be found, and gradually the efforts to find them were abandoned, so that some came back home and others, having made new homes in other places, never returned. Colonel A.M. Garber says that his brothers, Messrs. Joseph B. and Buckner L. Garber, remained concealed in the woods for a long time on account of being sought for. There they were fed, not by ravens as Elijah was, but by their old family Negroes.

Federal soldiers looking for Mark Sledge surrounded the courthouse where Mark was present at some sort of an assembly. In some way he managed to slip through and left the county.

As a result of such conditions, all through the South, some of the wilder and more lawless Ku Klux members or imitators kept up disturbances. We had such a condition here in the doings of Steve S. Renfroe, which did not cease until he was taken out and hanged.

The Spanish-American War

There was no very great interest here in the Spanish-American War. People felt that Spain was over-matched and that our country was in no danger.

Among those who went to this war from Livingston and its immediate vicinity were Bob Mason, son of R.S. Mason; John P. (Pete) Jackson; Forrest Roan; W. Claude McCain; Oscar Riley, son of the Reverend B.F. Riley; Solly

Levi, a nephew of Mrs. M. Tannenbaum; Dr. R.E. Hale; B.C. Hunter, Jr.; and W.T. Alexander. Dr. J.S. Hough served in this war, but came here long after. Burlin R. Starnes volunteered in this war, but he had already left Livingston by then, as was true of Solly Levi.

Mason, Jackson and Roan never got farther than Miami, Florida. McCain served several years in the Philippines, and years afterward was a commissioned officer in the World War. Dr. Hale also served in the Philippines. Hunter and Alexander joined a cavalry company and spent their time in some western state.

The World War

During the World War the people of Livingston, with very few exceptions did their full duty. Men, white and black, went and did their best and returned to their work when it was over.

Among the white men from Livingston and its immediate vicinity who served overseas during the World War were W. Claude McCain, Joseph A. McConnell, Peterson B. Jarman, William P. Spratt, Carl W. McMahon, Donald McMahon, Edward P. Scruggs, Winston White, Robert W. Peacock, Jeff Battle, Dan Battle, Ernest Godfrey, Turner McLean and Jack Gregory. Lieutenant Spratt was killed in battle. Captains Carl McMahon and Joseph McConnell died soon after the war.

Among those who were in the Army service, but did not get across the sea were William O. McMahon, Dr. J.P. Scales, Joe Scruggs and M.B. Gould. Gould was discharged on account of ill health. Irving Mundy was sent to the Pacific coast on his way to Russia, but never got across.

Among those who served in the Navy were Russell Phillips, Fred Sims and Lewis McLean. Captain Ben L. Brockway of the Coast Guard worked with the Navy during this war. Harold Smith, a graduate of Annapolis, reentered the Navy as an officer and served during this war. He died suddenly soon after the war ended. Frank Sims was serving in the Merchant Marine, and Goldsby Lee, son of J.H. Lee, was serving in the Navy when the war came on.

Many who were former residents served with the Army or the Navy in this war.

Some men, on account of special fitness or delicate physique or for other reasons, were assigned to work of special nature, and among these were Tom A. Phillips, Crawford A. Battle, Harry Davidson, Harold Makin and possibly others. Crawford A. Battle died as a result of exposure.

A man named Brown, a former sergeant in the Army, was working at the heading mill when this war came on. He volunteered, but what became of him is not known.

Some of the very young men of that day were in training at what was called R.O.T.C.—Reserve Officers' Training Corps. Among such were James

A. Mitchell, Jr., Tartt Mellen, John E. Harris, Jr., Ralph Boyd, Charles J. Brockway, Jr., and Dru McDonald. Harris died during the war.

A number of men have settled here since this war who saw service, including Sid B. Jones, C.H. Scott, W.T. Scales, Adolphus Ormond, O.Y. Kemp, and Charles Gamblin.

Many who were born here and had moved away, or who had lived here formerly, served in either Army or Navy in this war. Among such were Harold Smith, Sid Smith, W. Blanks Everitt, Sterling R. Coleman, B.L. Brockway and Clarence Clanahan. Coleman died during the war and Harold Smith died soon after it was over. Clanahan died in France.

Negroes from the Livingston area who served in France during the World War included:

> Ike Clark, son of Jesse
> Manuel Edwards
> John O. Jackson, son of Martha—died
> David May, known as "Pistol." He contracted tuberculosis.
> Felix May, son of Esau
> Abe Moore, son of Abe and grandson of Tol
> Alex Morris
> Ernest Pratt
> Will Tartt, known as "Shine"
> Tom Tartt, son of Eli—died
> Leonard, son of Amos Brown. Went from a
> northern state and was killed.

In 1919 an American Legion Post was organized here by Peterson Jarman, Russell Phillips and others, but it did not function at that time. Russell died in 1938. There was a reorganization of the Post in 1923. It was named the William Polk Spratt Post, and Edward P. Scruggs served as President. Among the members were E.P. Scruggs, Dr. J.S. Hough, Sid B. Jones, Lewis McLean, L.A. Ormond, Charles Gamblin and Joe Scruggs. In 1927 there were fifty-five members.

In September, 1927, the Legion made a pilgrimage to France, said to have been the largest peacetime movement of people in the history of the world. Some twenty thousand went from the United States. Among those going from Sumter County were Edward P. Scruggs, Peterson B. Jarman, and Roland Adams of York.

On February 8, 1928, a Ladies' Auxiliary was formed, consisting of wives, mothers, and sisters of the Legionaires. On March 3, 1928, an application for a charter was sent in to Department Headquarters with the following names as charter members:

> Janie M. Hough (Mrs. Dr. J.S.), President
> Sadie F. Reed (Mrs. I.N.), Secretary and Treasurer

Tempie S. Ennis (Mrs. W.L.)
Mary C. Handley (Mrs. M.C.)
Hunter C. Jarman (Mrs. Judge P.B.)
Ella Gaines P. Jones (Mrs. Sid B., Jr.)
Lillian S. Kemp (Mrs. O.Y.)
Lillie H. Lowe (Mrs. L.A.)
Ruth L. McLean (Mrs. L.A.)
Flora S. Ormond (Mrs. L.A.)
Eddie Floyd V. Phillips (Mrs. T.A.)
Nelle S. Scales (Mrs. Dr. J.P.)

All the charter members were listed from Livingston, except Mrs. Lowe, who was identified as being from York.

Chapter 7

The Livingston Cemetery

According to Lewis Parrent, the first burial in the Livingston Cemetery [now known as Myrtlewood Cemetery] took place in 1834. The oldest stone to be found is that of John Perkins, a native of Lincoln County, North Carolina, who died September 27, 1834, aged thirty years. Near the Perkins grave is that of James Savage, a member of the Commission which laid off the lots in the town and sold them.

During and after the Civil War, when there was much confusion and distress, many were buried here and the graves not marked, and it is now impossible to identify a number of such graves.

There are some stones here to people that no one remembers. Some of these were strangers staying here temporarily. Others had friends and families, but these died or moved away long ago and all trace of who they were has been lost. Among such stones are those to:

Mrs. Tincy Swann

Thomas J. Blackwell of Trenton, N.J., who died in 1847.

John D. Smith of Goram, Maine, (editor of the *Gazette*), who died in 1836.

James N. Stillings, (a lawyer) who died in 1848, born 1821.

Thomas O. Henderson and his wife Mary.

John H. Stevens and his wife Penelope.

Others about whom a little is known are:

Samuel Monette, who died in 1854. He is said to have been an uncle of Captain Jim Monette.

Chauncy Coon of Utica, New York, who died in 1853. It is said that he was coming up from Mobile on a steamboat and had yellow fever. He died and was buried here.

Thomas O. Henderson, who owned lands in the region of the crossroads (9 miles north) and sold some to Jerry H. Brown.

Mrs. M.H. Goodloe, a teacher who died in 1882. Her grave is marked by an angle iron near the Otto Voss grave.

Leonidas W. Butler. His inscription reads: "In memory of Leonidas W. Butler, a native of North Carolina who died August 30, 1847, after a lingering illness contracted in Mexico while engaged in his country's war. This stone is erected by the citizens of Sumter in commemoration of his patriotism and virtue." He is said to have been a prominent man from another section and was passing through. His brother, Colonel Anthony Butler, was Minister to Mexico before the Mexican War. Mrs. J.A. Johnson of Livingston is related to this Butler family through her mother, Mrs. McLaurin.

Seth B. Thornton, brother of H.R. Thornton, Sr. He was killed at Chapultepec in 1847.

Peter Burk, an Irishman who served as a Confederate soldier.

Mrs. L.A. Adams, sister of Mrs. Theodosia Mooring.

The Reverend John E. Faust, a former Methodist pastor. His last wife was a Miss Dandridge of Gainesville. He went to his kitchen to stop some disturbance in which the servants were engaged and dropped dead. He preceded the Reverend Hermon Humphreys.

Just south of Mr. Faust's grave are the unmarked graves of the two Wagners who were drowned in Sukanachi some twenty years ago.

John F. Vary, Jr., son of a noted lawyer of Marengo of that name.

Elbert H. Vary, brother of John F. Vary, Sr.

Samuel H. Chiles, brother of Mrs. Mary C. Short.

Walton G. Kersh, a young Methodist preacher who was doing some study at the Normal School. His people lived at Clinton in Greene County.

Lieutenant Alex C. Maury, U.S.N., a member of the noted Maury family of Virginia and related to our Thornton family. He resided a few miles south of town and died there. His widow is said to have married the Reverend J.J. Scott, a former Rector of St. James Episcopal Church and afterward Archdeacon at Milton, Florida.

E.A. Powell, son-in-law of I. James Lee.

People named Hull, Wright and Verell, who were related, so it is said. Frank Hull, a dancing instructor, married a Miss Adah Wright. These were her people. It is not thought that they ever owned a home in the town.

Mrs. Mary Crockett. The inscription states that she was a daughter of General Davie. One W.R. Davie was a general in the Revolution and later was Governor of North Carolina, and it is likely that she was his daughter, Mary Haynes Davie. The writer's grandfather was named for this same man Davie, the writer's grandfather's grandfather having served under Davie in the Revolution. She was born in Halifax, North Carolina, in 1790, and died in 1849.

Ruth Pearson, daughter of a former Methodist pastor. She was killed by a train at the crossing near the cemetery. She was in a buggy with Mr. W.T. Wallace when a train struck them. Mr. Wallace was badly injured and Ruth killed.

Frank Newman, said to have been the son of a former Methodist pastor.

Frank S. Lee, brother of I. James Lee.

Mrs. G.W. Boggs, the wife of a former Presbyterian pastor.

John G. Brown, who lived near the old Sumter Lumber Company and was known as "Hell Roaring Brown." He was related to Mrs. D.H. Trott, to Mrs. Dr. Hal Arrington and to the Mims people.

Mrs. Maria Sobering Dotti and child, members of the family of a former music teacher at the Normal School.

Mrs. Sadie N. Parkman, mother-in-law of Hugh L. Allison, who was music teacher at the Normal School before Dotti.

R. Melville McHelm, a crippled man related to the Parkers.

Mrs. May B.Y. Graham, mother of a music teacher at the Normal School.

Dewitt A. Pruitt, a man who lived at the Walter Sims place a short time and died. His widow was for a long time connected with the Normal School.

Mrs. Lucy A. Cleveland, wife of "Marse" Tony (A.A.) Cleveland.

Middleton Praytor, who was killed by a fall from a railway bridge. Near him is buried his brother, W.J. (Jabe) in an unmarked grave. Mid Praytor's son Ad is buried in another part of the cemetery.

Lt. Col. James K. Norwood, who is said to have been a brother of Mrs. Daniel White.

Dr. Blake Little, who was related to the family of Bennett Bell. (Mrs. Bell was his daughter.)

E.R. Reed, James McDonald and Charles McDonald, who are said to have worked for the Sumter Lumber Company.

Mrs. W.W. Bell, wife of a postal telegraph man who lived here for awhile. The Bells also have a child buried here.

Mrs. Wimbish and Miss Lucy Petty, sisters of the last Mrs. D.L. Kirkland. (The Kirklands are buried in a Meridian, Mississippi, cemetery.)

The first physician to die in Livingston was Dr. J.L. McCants, 33, native of South Carolina, who died April, 1837.)

Confederate veterans buried in the Livingston cemetery include:

Edward Arrington	Lietuenant John Bradshaw
James C. Arrington	Lietuenant John Lewis Brown
W.R. Arrington	Charles H. Bullock
The Reverend Josiah Bancroft	Peter Burke
Benjamin S. Barker	Capt. Reuben Chapman
Samuel A. Barnett	Jack Clark
William D. Battle, Jr.	Capt. James Cobbs
William Beggs	Major Thomas Cobbs

Leonidas A. Cockrell
Jesse B. Coleman
J.M. (Doc) Cook
Nathan Copeland (or Coplin)
Tully R. Cunningham
The Reverend W. G. Curry
Hugh Davis
W.R. DeLoach
R. W. Ennis
Paul E. Evans
H.D. Fellows
A.D. Fortner
T.F. Gill
Henry C. Harris
Park M. Harris
Dr. Berryman Hawkins (dentist)
Capt. James M. Henagan
Capt. Ben F. Herr
I.D. Hoit
Zane Hoit
Erasmus W. Hooks
Lt. W.W. Hopkins
Lt. J. Clint Houston
Boanerges C. Hunter
Lt. John Jackson (Mexican John)
John Jackson
Capt. W.A.C. Jones
Nat Kennard
Lt. John Lawhorn
Frank S. Lee
Dr. H.B. Leverett
Hugh H. Lide

Capt. Ben S. Little
T.E. Lockard
George Mason
Lt. Robert S. Mason
James McDonald
Malcolm Boyd McDonald
William T. McKnight
W.B. McRae
Dr. A.E. Moore
Wellington A. Murley
P.M. Nelson
Lt. Col. James K. Norwood
Garrett Minor Quarles
Alfred Reynolds
Clement T. Roan
Walter Scott
Solon Sherard
E.W. Smith
John T. Smith
James P. Spratt
Capt. Samuel H. Sprott
W.S. Trigg
John J. Trott
Zac Tureman
Samuel B. Turk
H. Otto Voss
W.H. August Voss
Daniel O. White
George W. Williams
Alex Wilson
Richard D. Wilson

E.W. Smith was a Captain of Militia before the Civil War. During this War he organized another company, which could not be equipped, so he served under Captain W.A.C. Jones in the 40th Alabama.

T.F. Gill was badly wounded in battle and never recovered, finally dying as a result of this old injury.

Captain B.B. Little, Henry C. Harris and Wellington Murley were killed in battle and their bodies were brought here.

In addition to those mentioned, James L. Parrent and Robert B. Spratt joined the Confederate Army, but they both died of disease before seeing any real warfare.

Also, M.D. Gould, L.D. Norville and J.O. Scruggs set out for the front in the latter part of war, but all was over before they arrived.

T.E. Lockard (December 8, 1845-November 26, 1929) of Phelaria Battery, C.S.A., was the last surviving Civil War veteran of those who went to the War from Livingston and who were buried in the Livingston cemetery.

Joseph Hodges, who was a veteran from Livingston, died in Texas in 1933, aged about 90. He was an uncle of Dr. McCain. Mr. Ed Mason, who had been a member of Stone's Company, was living in Louisiana in 1933 and died soon afterward.

A.B. Chapman and Andrew Glasselle were here somewhere near the same time. They went to California.

Another Glasselle (David) is buried at the north end of the Colonel C.R. Gibbs lot in the cemetery. In this lot are buried Colonel Gibbs, his last wife, Judge Sannchers and his last wife. David Glasselle was a naval officer in the Confederate service.

Most of the early settlers died at rather early ages, but since the middle 1890's a good many have lived to be over eighty. Among the oldest persons buried in the Livingston Cemetery are the following, listed with their ages at death:

Women—

      Mrs. Isabella Morris (née Blakeney), 90

      Mrs. James A. Abrahams, 89

      Mrs. S.B. Turk (Henrietta Allison), 89

      Mrs. W.R. DeLoach (Susan Gibbs), 88

      Mrs. Wallis McRae, 88

      Mrs. Dr. A.E. Moore (née Henagan), 87

      Mrs. Sallie A. Houston (née Henagan), 87

      Mrs. A.M. Tartt (née Jones), 87

      Mrs. John T. Smith (née Houston), 86

      Miss Mattie Lancaster, 86

      Miss Ann Ward, 84

      Mrs. Sarah Tankersley, 84

      Mrs. M.G. Eason, 84

      Mrs. Virginia R. Hutchinson, 84

      Mrs. Rosa K. Brown, 82

      Mrs. Theodosia A. Mooring, 81

      Mrs. W.K. Pickens, 81

Men—

      Reverend A.C. Davidson, 91

      J. Eugene Cusack, 89

      Devereux Hopkins, 87

      Lemuel F. Whitehead, 86

P.M. Nelson, 85
Robert Mason, 84
Robert S. Mason, 83
Leonidas A. Cockrell, 82
W.A.C. Jones, 82
George A. Brown, 82
Sam B. Turk, 81
B.C. Hunter, 80

Mr. J. Montgomery Mitchell, who lived here in his last days, was buried at Epes. He was within a few days of his ninety-sixth birthday when he died. At present the oldest white woman buried here that we know of is Mrs. Isabella Blakeney Morris, widow of George Morris and a sister to the late Mrs. John Jackson and the late Jack Blakeney. Mr. J.E. Cusack, who was born here, died at the age of eighty-nine years and eleven months.

In the burying ground for Negroes that adjoins that of the white people, there are several who reached advanced ages. Marcellus Speight, the black-smith, lived to be ninety. Susan Kennard was possibly one hundred when she died in 1924, and it is quite likely that Hannah Lewis was in the neighborhood of one hundred. Both of these women were elderly when the writer was a very small boy. Hannah died in 1930 and her oldest child, if living, would have been 81. A singular thing is that she suffered with asthma all her life. George Young is now 98 (in 1930) if the 1880 census is correct.

Chapter 8

A Few Notes on Livingston's Colored People*

In early times most of the Negroes lived on the plantations. A few, house-men, carriage drivers, maids, nurses, cooks, etc., lived in town and many of them resided in houses near their work, frequently in a servant's house in the yard.

With the abolition of slavery, they began drifting to town, and in time there were considerable settlements known as "quarters." We have had Little's quarter, Coleman's quarter, Hopkins quarter, Gulley's quarter, Factory quarter, etc.

Little's quarter is one of the oldest and is possibly the largest. It grew up on what was once the "Smith Flat" and stretches from the premises of Mrs. E.C. Vaughan east to the railroad and then north to Mrs. James L. Parker's property. A crooked and forked alley known as "Tincup Alley" runs through it.

Once the Jowers family occupied a house here and behind it was Captain Jones' mill. With freedom, some of the more ambitious Negroes bought lots and built houses. Among those were Alex Houston, Minter Dodson, Dick Harris, Henry Posey, Tom Myers, Lewis Morris, Amos Cobbs, Ebenezer Bivins, Sam Matthews, Martha Christian, Carter Gibson, and various others who lived in this region. Major W.G. Little acquired the old mill property, and the whole region became known as Little's quarter. He built cabins and rented them to various Negro families.

Other noted colored persons of these earlier times were Tol Moore, Marcellus Speight, Bob Lucas, John Tolliver (he always said Taliaferro was the way to spell it), Ned Tankersley, Jim Dawson, Martin Brownrigg, Bill Clark, Jesse Kimball, Jim Kennard, Amzi Kennard, Pleasant Witt, Si Gillespie, Allen Arrington, Jake and Esau Thompson, Jim Edwards, Reuben Samuel, Alfred Epps, Venture Lee, Tess McMillan, Jim Gale, William Dale ("Slick"), Ben Gunn, Dick Gowdey, John Parker, Bob Witt, Tom Wright, Donum Jones, Solomon Larkin, Greene Lowe, Lawrence Hall, Andy Moore, Perry Moore, Charles Smith, John Patton, Jim Cunningham, Bill Pickett, Gabe Harris, Alf Harris, Bob Williams, Jack Coleman, Isaiah Coleman, Lewis Moore, Alex Lattimore, Dan Powell, Bill Pitman, Dennis Bates, et al.

Many of the women were quite noted either for general goodness, for excellent cookery, for being good nurses, for skill with needle or maybe for

* In the interest of preserving the historical tone of this work, the editor has chosen to retain the phrase "colored people," which at the time of Spratt's writing carried no negative connotations—unless, of course, the speaker's tone and words conveyed a slur. But the same can be said today of "African-American" or "white," for that matter.

just some personal peculiarities. Could any boy ever forget old Annie Mobile, who roamed around picking up cigar stumps and reciting some crazy-sounding poetry?

During slavery times, Negroes went by their masters' names, but after freedom they frequently took other names, usually taking the name of some family to whom they had formerly belonged. Thus, Reuben Samuel, Charles Tankersley, Paul Dawson, Paige Hicks, William Larkin, Alfred Epps, and Randall Glassco had all previously belonged to George G. Tankersley.

Gabe Harris, Paige Hicks, John Little and Walter Cook went to war with their young masters. Gabe brought home the body of his master, Henry C. Harris. Paige brought home the horse of his young master, John Tankersley, who was killed in Georgia. Walter went to war with William Godfrey, a brother of Dr. Jack and Lawrence D. Godfrey.

Marcellus Speight, Wes Norville, Walker Gibson, Daniel Moore and Major Williams were blacksmiths.

Sol Larkin, Donum Jones, Tom Wright, Z, Abraham May, Dempsey Eason, Amos Cobbs and Joe Lowe were carpenters.

Ned Tankersley, Ben Gunn and Jim Cunningham were well diggers.

Jesse Kimball, Ebenezer Bivins, Martin Brownrigg and Jim Kennard were sextons at the white churches.

John Little and "Little John" Watson were shoemakers.

Alex Houston, Matt Boling, Ike Chamney, and Bill David were yardmen and gardeners.

Joe Chapman for years handled the freight at the railroad station. Bob Witt, Big John Moore, Dick Gowdey, Bill Hicks, Lawrence Hall, and others were carters and dray men.

Dick Harris and Dennis Bates drove the town cart, kept the streets clean and looked after the old street lights.

Prince Robinson, Chap Brown and Ed Whitehead were barkers. Joe Griggs was the town's strong man.

Tom Myers and Allen Arrington were skilled woodworkers. Minter Dodson was a merchant. Alf Harris, Bill Clark and Charles Houston were livery stable drivers and to them may be added Jim Williams, about the last of these old-timers now living.

Iverson Dawson and Greene Lowe were noted preachers and were very able men. Of a later day is the Reverend Ike Champney, who was educated at Stillman and has for a long time lived in Montgomery.

Si Gillespie drove the college wagon, and his sister, Dallas, was the wife of Ben Gunn.

Isaiah Coleman was a mattress maker and could make more music on a mouth harp than any person I ever heard play one.

Eph Lewis, Henry Coleman and Andy Brewer cared for horses, kept stables in order, etc. Esau Thompson and his twin brother, Jake, were also great horsemen and drivers.

Henry Posey, Esau Thompson, Charles Houston, Ruffin Shelton, Alex Tarvin, Dave Jackson and Stuart Allison served at various times as courthouse janitor.

Austin Coleman and Alex Lattimore always worked at one of the hotels.

Jake Daley ran a grist mill south of town and prospered.

Peter Lewis and his wife, Minerva, were a most industrious couple.

Eli Tartt was able, energetic and honest. Other good men were Ed Gray, Jerry Porter, Bill Ivy, Addison Chapman, Armstead Chapman, and Josh Horn.

Venture Lee was quite unique. He is the one who made the statement that the Seale family is "a distinct nation."

In fact, in Livingston and in the farming regions around it there have been many worthwhile and interesting colored people. Many of them were quite intelligent and absolutely honest all the year, and during the Christmas season they came to town and enjoyed themselves to the limit.

Mary Campbell, Willis Watson and his noted wife Lizzie, Henry Coleman and Henry Witt's sons lived—and some of them still live—in the Hopkins quarter. [This was on the present-day Hopkins Street near the old Devereux Hopkins home now owned by the Thurns.] Pleas and Henry Witt were brothers and both had large families. Pleas married a daughter of Tol Moore, Mandy, and among their children were Bob, Sophie, Mack, John and Benjamin. Mandy's father, Tol Moore, was extraordinarily faithful to the family of his master, Josiah Moore, who died in 1859. Tol had other children, and among them were Andrew, who had a barber shop for colored people on "Dog Street," and Abe, who is still living though now quite old. Henry Witt's wife was named Mourning (known as Monica), and among their children were Martin, Will and Cliff.

Bob Witt, who died a short time ago, had much influence among his people. Although he never learned to read or write, he handled much express and freight here for years, but he was never known to make a mistake in giving change and was never known to deliver the wrong package.

The first school for Negroes here was taught by W.H. (Bill) Green, a white man. Until such time as books could be provided he used an almanac in teaching them their letters. There was later on a school in connection with and near the Negro Methodist church and another one near their First Baptist Church. In more recent years, many Negro children have attended the school conducted by Professor Allen S. Plump about a mile and a half north on the Gainesville road.

As a rule, I find that our Negro people are kind and indulgent to children and that they are often patient and cheerful under conditions that would drive white people to suicide.

Some of them have reached advanced years. Anthony Lockhart, Tol Moore, Pleas Witt, Wilson Dawson, Ben Brown, Lewis Morris, Ebenezer Bivins, Reavis Hines, Israel Tolliver, Ned McConnico, Elijah Daley, Walter Cook, along with various others, lived to be over eighty. Anthony and Walter are still quite active. Elvert Lewis (son of Peter), Marcellus Speight and John Tolliver all lived to be over ninety. Hannah Lewis and Susan Kennard were both probably well past ninety-five at the time of death.

Some outstanding persons among the women were Louisa Dodson, a sister of Joe Chapman; Jemima Cunningham; Caroline Arrington, wife of Allen; Lizzie Gray, wife of Ed and sister of Walter Cook; Chaney Posey; Mary Lucas, wife of Bob; Jona Arrington, wife of Dred; Fanny "Jake" and Bettie "Esau." The last two were the wives of the twins Jake and Esau Thompson.

Panola Hendicks, who had belonged to the Winston family, and Sallie Houston (wife of Alex), who had belonged to the Hibbler family, were ladies' maids.

Betsy Godfrey and Lou Williams were "nurses" for white children. [That is, they performed much the same function as the British nanny.]

Susan Kennard, Sallie Williams, Sabra May, and Carrie Gaines were good practical bedside nurses.

Emma Larkin, Rachel Kennard, Lizzie Watson, Ann Myers and others did good laundry work. Ann was noted for her ability to do up stiff collars and so was Susie Kennard. Susan Kennard's step-granddaughter, Susie, could also play the piano well.

Emma Larkin was of Northern birth. She came here with some tourists and married Sol Larkin, the carpenter. Finally, she and Sol went to California.

Among the noted cooks were Gracie and Bettie Scott, Mary Campbell, Belle Griggs, Gracie Moore, Jacqueline Witt, Sophie Witt, Josephine Lattimore, Lou Porter, Sallie Brown, Pocahontas, Florry, Nancy Davis (daughter of the noted Austin "Guinea" Wright), Jane Pickett and Hannah Lewis. Hannah, by the way, was noted for the neat kitchen she kept. Her husband Pryor and her son Frank were yard men. Frank for many years kept the white cemetery in order and was succeeded by Wiley Clark. John (Jiner) Tartt, who died in 1936, then did this work. His father Hardy had belonged to John H. Sherard, Sr., but took the name Tartt after being freed.

Some of the men also were good cooks and excelled at barbecuing meat. Among those who might be mentioned are Bob Williams, Oliver Bell, Phil Larkin and Isaac Howard.

Chapter 9

Conclusion

Those who have lived in Livingston know what a splendid little town it is.

It was settled shortly before the Civil War and was for years practically a frontier town, so we do not find the large colonial houses, etc., of towns that were settled long before the Indians left what is now Sumter County. Nevertheless, the town is reasonably clean, is well laid out, has good schools and good people, so what more could any sensible person want?

Judging from old records, etc., the early settlers here were people of a good type and, in spite of the fact that many of the older families have moved away, it would be very difficult to find better people to live among than the present inhabitants.

The writer got this up from various sources:

Old letters and papers belonging in the Cusack family.

Notes on the early settlement by the late Professor L.A. Cockrell.

Notes left on various matters connected with the town's history by M.C. Houston, Dr. R.D. Webb, G.C. Gowdey, J.P. Spratt and perhaps others.

Personal recollections of the writer and the results of inquiries made by him.

The writer wishes to acknowledge the assistance he has received from the following: Mrs. Julia Stewart, Mrs. A.M. Tartt, Mrs. W.K. Pickens, Mrs. S.B. Turk, Mrs. J.O. Scruggs, Mrs. Mary Phifer Smith, Mrs. Mary H. Jones, Mrs. James. L. Parker, Mrs. Bettie Cockrell, Mrs. J.M. Branch, Mrs. Sadie Reed, Miss Mattie Lancaster, Mrs. James B. Jackson, Miss Willie McRae, Miss Hettie Jones, Dr. D.S. Brockway, Dr. W.J. McCain, Dr. J.P. Scales, Dr. J.S. Hough, Dr. E.A. Young, Dr. Carl Hill, Dr. G. Fred Mellen, Judge P.B. Jarman, Mr. J. Montgomery Mitchell, Mr. William Winslett, Mr. Thad E. Lockard, Mr. Addison G. Smith, Mr. Thomas B. Smith, Mr. D.T. Battle, Mr. John H. Sherard, Mr. H.R. Thornton, Mr. J.C. Travis, Colonel A.M. Garber, Mr. John L. Horn, Mr. H.L. Mellen, Mr. W.S. Nichols, Mr. Ed L. Mitchell, Mr. W.H. Scarborough, Mr. W.T. Mitchell, Mr. James A. Mitchell, Mr. J.M. Branch, Mr. John E. Harris, Mr. T.M. Tartt, Mr. W.G. Little, Mr. Robert Foss, Mr. W.H. Coleman, Mr. J.A. Shelby, Mr. J.H. Hoit, Mr. W.W. Patton, Mr. T.F. Seale, Mr. James D. Browder, Mr. H.S. Sutliff, Mr. Jenkins Jackson, and Mr. W.M. Sullivan.

Although there are bound to be errors and omissions in this, from it may be gathered something of the history of the first hundred years of this town.

It is astonishing how many interesting events and how many once prominent people can be completely forgotten within that length of time even among a civilized people who keep records and have newspapers.

PRESENTED TO THE LIVINGSTON LIBRARY

August 15, 1928

A HISTORY OF

APPENDICES

A HISTORY OF

Appendix A

Letter Relating to the Horn Family

[Just prior to the 1974 publication of this history, the Sumter County Historical Society received this letter.]

Ralph A. Stilwell
Consultant
434 N. Laurel Ave.
Los Angeles, Calif. 90048

March 29, 1974

Historical Society
Sumter Co., Alabama

In your unpublished draft of "A History of Livingston Alabama" by Robert D. Spratt, M.D., 1923 [*sic*], on page 187, there is a sketch on a Jacob Horn and descendants of Sumter Co.

The second paragraph tells about a Jacob Horn and Mary M. Vines of Gaston, and their children were:

Martha	Born 6-11-1830 Md. A.E. Brockway
Allie Ann Elizabeth	Born 1-2-1834
John Henry	Born 12-28-1835
Mary Frances	Born 1-20-1838
Samuel Vines	Born 9-13-1839 Died as a child
Tempey Ann	Born 8-18-1840 Died as a baby
Margaret Amand	Born 12-17-1843 Md. R.P. Wyley
	Md. Dr. John N. Gilmore
Jacob Josiah	Born 10-15-1845 Died as a child
William Robert	Born 9-21-1847 Md. M.L. Donavan

Jacob died 4-20-1864, and Mary died 3-15-1886.

The renowned Hugh Johnston, Jr., of Wilson, N.C., gives the following progenitors of Jacob Horn. His father was Jacob Horn of Edgecombe Co., N.C. His grandparents were Isaac and Edith Richardson Horn of Nash Co., N.C. His gr. grandparents were Henry and Ann Pursell Horn of Nansemond Co., Va. and Wayne Co., N.C. He believes Henry's father to have been William Horn.

There was an Isaac Horn, brother of Jacob, who came to Alabama with him around 1835 and first settled at Jamestown. This is a different Isaac from Isaac W., who was son of Harrison Horn.

Respectfully submitted,

Ralph A. Stilwell.

Credit for much of the research on this family belongs to Mrs. Elizabeth B. Stegall of Emelle, Alabama.

Appendix B

Mrs. W. H. Coleman's Poem About the Baldwin Hill Ghost

[Note: The references in the poem are to Pratt Tartt and his wife, Ruby Pickens Tartt, who lived at Baldwin Hill for a number of years.]

Dere's A Ghost On Baldwin Hill

Git up roun' me closer, chillun.
Liza hush, now Wash be still.
Listen whut yo mammy tells yo.
Dere's a Ghost on Baldwin Hill.

Yas, Miss Ruby said she heerd him.
Miss Blanche said he pushed de swing,
Dat hit skimmied back and forth
And skeered her like everything.

Lawd, hit comes and shakes de winders.
Hit knocks right on de do'.
Kinder sof' and natchel lak,
Lak hit bin dere befo'.

Yo-all needn' think I'm jokin'.
Whut de white folks says is true.
I'd a done lit out fum here,
Chillun, ef hit wa'nt fer you.

Mr. Pratt, he ain't said nuthin'.
He's jest watchin', skeered and still.
Bet he's gwine ter mek hit hot
Fer dat Ghost on Baldwin Hill.

Jes' three uv em livin' yonder
But dem three's a right brave set.
Ef dat Ghost ain't mighty keerful,
Dem white folks'll git him yet.

So git up roun' me closer, chillun.
Liza hush, now Wash be still.
Listen whut yo mammy tells yo,
And stay 'way fum Baldwin Hill.

Appendix C

Letter Written by W.P. Billings to Robert Reed About Reconstruction Politics

[The Taylor mentioned was another Negro.]

Ramsey, Alabama
June 17th, 1874.

Hon. Robert Reed,
Belmont, Alabama

Dear Sir:

Capt. Wells and myself have been expecting to call upon you and Mr. Taylor before this but have been unable to do so. When the canvass gets further advanced we will cheerfully address the pro-republicans in your locality and trust you and Mr. Taylor will visit those of the party in this section.

I am just in receipt of letters from Judge Saffold of the Supreme Court and Mr. Hays. They both write in a hopeful strain the indications are very cheering that the Republicans will carry this election by a largely increased majority this fall.

Republicans in this part of the county are fully organized and alive to the issues and I doubt not that Sumter will give at least 1500 majority this fall.

I am in favor of placing as many good colored men on the ticket as we can to keep strength in the party. We must be as liberal as they are in Mississippi. As Mr. Hays' letter interests you I enclose it for your perusal. I see from Washington dispatch that Mr. Reynolds, Collector at Mobile, has been appointed Minister to Bolivia and it is rumored that Senator Goodloe will succeed Reynolds.

Capt. Wells of whom Mr. Greata mentioned to you, is an old army officer, a personal friend of Gen'l Grant's, was in ten years active service in the Union Army and has since the latter part of April taken up his residence and made some investments in this part of the country. My regards to Mr. Taylor.

Truly yours,

(Signed) W.P. Billings

Appendix D

Livingston Lawyers and Legislators in 1845

In Garrett's *Public Men of Alabama* are listed a number of lawyers and legislators said to be from Livingston in 1845.

Some of them were from the town, some from the county, and some have been completely forgotten. These are:

Montgomery Carlton
William S. Chapman
D. Wallace Fields
Gideon B. Frierson—(County Judge, went to Texas)
Alexander R. Gates
Philip R. Glover—(related to the Glovers of Greene County)
James T. Hill—(brother of Mrs. Colonel Wetmore)
Moses F. Hoit
Alexander G. Horn—(first cousin of Isaac W. Horn)
Robert S. Inge
Albert G. Loftin
Lawrence D. Phillips—(said to have been the father of Dr.
       Jack Phillips)
George B. Saunders—(son-in-law of Colonel Gibbs)
Henry F. Scruggs—(brother of Josiah Leake Scruggs)
Stephen U. Smith—(the Reverend Stephen Uriah Smith)
Charles E.B. Strode
Philip S.C. Strother—(editor of the *Sumter Democrat*)
Bennett B. Thomas
Elbert H. Vary—(brother of John F. Vary)

Index

Breitling, R.O. 87
Breitling, Robert O. 61, 67
Brenner 104
Brevard County 28
Brewer, Amanda 19, 29
Brewer, Amanda F. 19
Brewer, Andy 129
Brewer, Ann 19
Brewer, "Cedar Creek Bill" 32
Brewer, "Holihta Bill" 32
Brewer, John 113
Brewer, Margaret 29, 40
Brewer, Matthew 32
Brewer, Miriam 32
Brewer, Pinckney 86
Brewer, Robert 32, 48
Brewer, William 19, 32
Brewer, Willis 32
Brewersville
   26, 32, 34, 47, 51, 52, 80, 83, 84, 86, 87, 93, 115
Brice, Mrs. Judge C.R. 77
British Honduras 53
Brock, Dr. 68, 90
Brock, Dr. G.W. 14, 80
Brock, G.W. 61, 96, 98
Brock, John E. 67
Brock, Mildred 80
Brock, Mrs. John E. 44
Brockway, A.E. 8, 27
Brockway, B.L. 120
Brockway, Ben L. 27, 101, 119
Brockway, C.J. 101
Brockway, Carrie L. 17
Brockway, Charles 27
Brockway, Charles J. 27, 82, 120
Brockway, D.S. 19
Brockway, Dr. 9, 101, 106
Brockway, Dr. Augustus E. 27
Brockway, Dr. D.S. 27, 52, 65, 132
Brockway, Dr. S. Dudley 27
Brockway, Helen 27
Brockway, James 27
Brockway, Martha Horn 27
Brockway, Mary Stansel 18
Brockway, Miss Leonora 27
Brockway, Mrs. 27

Brockway, Mrs. C.J. 18
Brockway, Mrs. Charles J. 31
Brockway, Mrs. Martha 8
Brockway, Mrs. W.G. 88
Brockway, W.G. 27
Brooks, Judge William McLin 96
Brooks, Susan 32
Brooks, Widow 96
Brooks, William Middleton 96
Browder, James Chapron 72
Browder, James D. 72, 132
Browder, Joe 72
Browder, Miss 72
Brown Brothers 43, 101
Brown, Adolph 43, 61
Brown, Amos 120
Brown, Ben 130
Brown, Bestor 12, 45
Brown, Bestor P. 88
Brown, Captain 44
Brown, Chap 129
Brown, Clara 46
Brown, Colonel I. Chap 44
Brown, Colonel Isaiah Chapman 44
Brown, Ed 47
Brown, Emil 12
Brown, George A. 44, 50, 127
Brown, "Hell Roaring" 71, 124
Brown, Hugo 43
Brown, I.C. 14, 21, 26
Brown, Isla 96
Brown, J.L. 113, 117
Brown, Jerry H. 24, 46, 55, 65, 122
Brown, John 45, 46, 47
Brown, John E. 44, 46, 54, 88
Brown, John G. 71, 124
Brown, John Lewis 12, 34, 46, 68, 124
Brown, Julia 96
Brown, Kate 50
Brown, Leo 43
Brown, Lewis S. 35, 46, 114
Brown, Mary 26
Brown, Miss 95
Brown, Miss Kate H. 90
Brown, Mr. 68
Brown, Mrs. 37, 68, 71

149

H

157

Jowers, Joe 66

K

Kelley, Mr. 15
Kembrell, A.A. 13
Kemp, Lillian S. 121
Kemp, O.Y. 120
Kennard place 8, 87
Kennard, Amzi 128
Kennard, Ben 45
Kennard, Chestleigh 74
Kennard, James 74, 80, 81, 86
Kennard, James Pinckney 74
Kennard, Jim 128, 129
Kennard, John 37
Kennard, Miss 56
Kennard, Nat 8, 9, 37, 74, 78, 87, 125
Kennard, Oglesby Smith 74
Kennard, Rachel 131
Kennard, Susan 87, 127, 131
Kennard, Susie 131
Kennedy, John 34
Kennedy, Nath 38
Kennedy, Tom 34
Kent, James 7
Kentucky 27, 39, 47, 59, 115
Kern, Mrs. W.M. 34
Kersh, Walton G. 123
Ketchum, Dr. George A. 13
Ketchum, George A. 13
Kewanee, Mississippi 42
Key, Mr. Parks O. 35
Key, P.O. 35
Killian, Douglas 26
Killian, H.W. 46
Killian, J.W. 71, 96, 107
Killian, Joseph W. 26, 77
Killian, Mrs. Harris W. 36
Kilpatrick, Mrs. H.C. 44
Kimball, Jesse 82, 128, 129
Kimball, John 82
Kincey, Mrs. 27
King, R.L. 91
King, William Rufus 65
Kinnard, Dr. M.C. 56, 66, 103
Kinnard, Dr. Michael C. 75

Kinnard, Judge James P. 75
Kinnard, M.C. 19
Kinnard, Mrs. Dr. 86
Kinnard, Mrs. Dr. M.C. 74
Kirkland, Bill 49, 50, 105, 109
Kirkland, Bob 58
Kirkland, D.L.
    21, 30, 47, 50, 66, 107, 108
Kirkland, John 112
Kirkland, Mrs. 40
Kirkland, Mrs. D.L. 124
Kirkland, William 69
Klondike 74
Knight, Henry C. 113
Knights of Pythias 106
Knowles, Mrs. 37
Knox, Dr. J.C. 30
Knox, Rosa 46
Koppius, Gus 52, 65, 98
Kornegay, Alonzo 60, 71
Kornegay, George 70, 72
Kornegay, Mollie 58
Kruse, Frank 52, 94
Ku Klux 39, 97, 114, 116, 118
Kubiack, Mrs. Sam 39
Kynerd, Miss 62

L

LaGrange School 13
Lake family 79
Lake, Harden 31, 82
Lake, J.G. 12
Lake, John 38, 78
Lake, Joseph 27, 44, 78
Lake, Mrs. 42, 78
Lake, Mrs. Harden 42
Lake, T. Harden 70, 78
Lancaster, Albert 25, 68
Lancaster, Lewis 25
Lancaster, Mattie 126, 132
Lancaster, Mrs. Elizabeth 68
Land, Mrs. Kelly 61
Langhammer, Miss C. 103
Lanham, Mrs. 78
Lanphier, Charles H. 36
Laporte, Mrs. 18

McDonald, Cliff 86
McDonald, Dru 78, 81, 120
McDonald, James 124, 125
McDonald, Jim 100
McDonald, M. Boyd 86
McDonald, Moses 78
McElroy, Mrs. Billye 98
McGaha, Reverend A.H. 21
McGahey, Mr. and Mrs. James 68
McGee, Mrs. J.S. 39
McGehee, A.M. 68, 88, 91
McGowan, Mr. 16
McGrew boys 60
McHelm, R. Melville 124
McInnis, John 114
McIntosh, John P. 7
McKay, Mrs. 58
McKinley, John 85
McKnight, F.H. 24
McKnight, Mary 21
McKnight, Mr. W.T. 48
McKnight, Mrs. W.T. 27
McKnight, Robert 28
McKnight, Thomas H. 28
McKnight, W.T. 12, 24, 27, 75, 104
McKnight, William T. 125
McLaurin, Mrs. 123
McLean Place 86
McLean, Annie 91
McLean, J.D. 20
McLean, Lewis
    22, 77, 85, 86, 91, 100, 103, 119, 120
McLean, Mrs. Lewis 70
McLean, Ruth L. 121
McLean, Turner 77, 119
McLemore, Miss 97
McLean, W. Peter 77, 85, 87, 93
McLeod 100
McMahon place 54
McMahon, Captain Carl W. 54
McMahon, Carl W. 119
McMahon, Donald 54, 119
McMahon, Lilah 18
McMahon, Mrs. 54
McMahon, Mrs. C.W. 18, 48, 53, 54
McMahon, William O. 54, 119

McMahon, Winston 18, 54
McMillan & Co., Bankers 37, 51
McMillan & Company 43, 101, 103
McMillan & Parker 102
McMillan, A.C. 37, 39, 47, 51, 52,
    53, 103
McMillan, Alice 71
McMillan, Allen Clifton 51
McMillan, Drury 51
McMillan, Felix G. 52, 83, 85
McMillan, Hugh 113
McMillan, Mr. G. Felix 51
McMillan, Mrs. 27
McMillan, Mrs. Douglas 28
McMillan, Robert 52
McMillan, Tess 128
McNeal, Angus 19
McNeal, Susannah 19
McNider, Mr. and Mrs. Greg 61
McPherson, William 113
McQueen, John 12, 76
McRae, Charles H. 95
McRae, Mrs. Dr. W.P. 42
McRae, Mrs. Wallis 126
McRae, W.B. 111, 125
McRae, W.M. 95
McRae, Willie 42, 132
McRea, Dr. W.P. 28
McRea, Miss Willie 28
McRea, Widow 28
McShaw, Mrs. 13
Mellen & Hart 102
Mellen, Charles H. 16
Mellen, Dr. 16, 88
Mellen, Dr. Fred G. 16, 132
Mellen, Dr. Seth S. 16
Mellen, G. Fred 16, 94
Mellen, H.L. 17, 18, 21, 33, 37,
    102, 105, 132
Mellen, Henry L. 16, 21
Mellen, Henry L., Jr. 37
Mellen, J.L. 12
Mellen, Maude 37
Mellen, Mr. and Mrs. Tartt 90
Mellen, Mrs. 16
Mellen, Mrs. H.L. 37

165

Moore, Odis 6
Moore, Perry 128
Moore, Tol 128, 130
Moore, Widow 39
Mooring, "Bully" 45
Mooring, Captain James 60
Mooring, Janie 53
Mooring, Mrs. Theodosia 123
Mooring, Mrs. Theodosia A. 126
Morgan, Dick 115
Morgan, General John H. 80, 115
Morris, Alex 120
Morris, George 127
Morris, Isabella 126
Morris, Lewis 128, 130
Morris, Mrs. 88
Morrow, Dr. 29
Morrow, Mrs. Dr. 29
Morrow, R.P. 18
Morton, Mrs. 54
Moscow 5
Moulder, Professor 81
Mount Moriah Academy 38
Mount, A.J. 113
Mt. Hebron 53
Mt. Moriah School 34
Mt. Sterling 16, 33, 46
Muckleroy, M. 12
Mudd, W.S. 85
Mundy, Irving 119
Murdoch, Miss Nellie 92
Murley place 90
Murley, S.W. 87
Murley, Stephen W. 81, 108
Murley, Wellington 58, 125
Murley, Wellington A. 81, 125
Murleys 22
Murray family 70
Murray, Mrs. Lewis 63
Muskhogean 3
Myers, Ann 131
Myers, Tom 80, 128, 129
Myrtlewood Cemetery 122

N

Naheola 64

Nall, R. 19
Narkeeta 4
Nash County, North Carolina 33
Nash, Dr. 100
Nash, Dr. D. A. (Bunny) 97
Nash, Dr. J.T. 65
Nash, Dr. Joe T. 97
Nash, Gus 89, 97
Nash, Judge 53, 67, 97
Nash, Judge P.G. 25, 33
Nash, P.G. 14
Nash, Preston 97
Nash, Preston G. 21, 97
Nashville 53, 65
National Cemetery 36
Naval Academy 43
Neeley, Miss 85
Neilson, Mrs. John 34
Neilson, Mrs. Robert 54
Neilson, Nellie 87
Nelson, Mr. 72
Nelson, P.M. 58, 125, 127
Nelson, Thomas M. 19, 115
Nettles, Mrs. 46
Neville, Sam 38
New England 40
New Hampshire 83, 90
New Mexico 77
New Prospect 76
New York 1, 7, 39, 114, 117, 122
New York *Tribune* 73
Newman, Frank 124
Newman, Mrs. Judge J.B. 30
Newspaper
    8, 11, 19, 33, 40, 63, 83, 132
Newton, Louise 37
Nichols, George 90
Nichols, Jim 112
Nichols, John 112
Nichols, Miss Jessie 64
Nichols, Mrs. W.J. 64
Nichols, Mrs. W.S. 58
Nichols, W.J. 64, 65, 66
Nichols, W.S.
    6, 21, 54, 65, 65, 79, 87, 92, 107, 112, 132
Nichols, William S. 62, 64

168

Shelton, Andrew 85, 94
Shelton, J.K. 61, 75
Shelton, Miss 28
Shelton, Robert 61
Shelton, Ruffin 130
Shepard, Cap 113
Sherard estate 87
Sherard place 84, 87
Sherard, Chris 84
Sherard, John H.
    39, 56, 61, 83, 84, 88, 131, 132
Sherard, Mat 35
Sherard, Mr. 94
Sherard, Mrs. John H. 57
Sherard, Napoleon 60, 72, 84
Sherard, Solon 84, 112, 125
Sherrill Oil 101
Shirley, James 113
Short lot 78
Short, Jordan 78
Short, Mary C. 14, 16, 66, 123
Short, Mrs. 78, 96
Short, Mrs. M.C. 98
Shower bath 41
Shulman, M. 61, 101
Shulman, Mr. 93
Shulman, Mrs. 103
Shumulla 5
Silliman, A.F. 19
Silliman, Dr. 64
Silversmith 48, 76, 103, 104, 106, 114
Simmons, Minnie 17
Sims, Asenath 7
Sims, Frank 28, 119
Sims, Fred 106, 119
Sims, John 7
Sims, Mary 8
Sims, Mr. 28
Sims, Mrs. 20, 40, 66
Sims, Mrs. W.A. 28
Sims, Shelton 28
Sims, Thomas 28
Sims, Thomas W. 43
Sims, W.A. 39, 67
Sims, Walter 28, 124
Sims, Walter A. 28

Singer Sewing Machine Company 107
Skating rink 108
Slaughter, Sophia 58, 68
Sledge, Albert 7, 39, 115
Sledge, Dr. 100, 101, 116
Sledge, Dr. Edward S. 35, 52
Sledge, Dr. W.H. 52
Sledge, Dr. William H. 35
Sledge, E.S. 35
Sledge, Forrest 35
Sledge, Joe 113, 115
Sledge, Joshua 35
Sledge, Mark 35, 118
Sledge, Mrs. Albert 36
Sledge, Mrs. Joshua 35
Smith Flat 80, 82, 116, 128
Smith, A.G. 12, 51, 63, 105, 106
Smith, A.M. 98
Smith, Addison G. 132
Smith, Alexander 19
Smith, Ann 54
Smith, C. Brooks 71
Smith, Charles 128
Smith, Chess 70
Smith, Dr. H.B. 87, 99
Smith, E.W.
    12, 42, 43, 51, 54, 63, 71, 73, 79, 99, 104,
    111, 117, 125
Smith, Edward 42
Smith, Edward D. 51
Smith, Elizabeth 92
Smith, Hadden 70
Smith, Hadden B. 71
Smith, Harold 43, 119, 120
Smith, Helen 59
Smith, James R. 70, 73
Smith, John 105
Smith, John D. 122
Smith, John Little 11
Smith, John R. 89, 102, 105
Smith, John T. 70, 71, 73, 125
Smith, Joseph A. 11, 73, 105
Smith, Luther A. 85
Smith, Maggie 36
Smith, Mary B. 18
Smith, Mary Phifer 132

Winston, Mr. Charles 48
Winston, Mrs. Charles 48
Winston, Olive 18
Winston, William O. 6, 7, 48
Withers, Jones M. 110
Witt, Bob 66, 128, 129, 130
Witt, Henry 130
Witt, Jacqueline 131
Witt, Pleas 130
Witt, Pleasant 128
Witt, Sophie 131
Wolfe, W.G. 20
Wolves 92
Womack, Mrs. Jesse 45
Woodford 57
Woods, Miss 84
Woodson, Miss 84
Woodson, Reavis 27
Wooten, Joe Dick 84
World War 1, 29, 34, 36, 43,
    50, 51, 52, 55, 58, 62, 75, 119, 120
Wrenn, Ed 75
Wrenn, George 75
Wrenn, Joe 33, 75
Wrenn, Mabel Randall Clare 18
Wrenn, Mrs. 33
Wrenn, William 33
Wright 123
Wright, Captain J.W.A. 15, 16, 28, 40
Wright, Council Randolph 95
Wright, Dr. Ruffin A. 15, 16
Wright, Henry T. 15, 16
Wright, J.C. 21
Wright, James W.A. 14
Wright, Julius T. 15, 16
Wright, Lucien B. 23
Wright, Miss Adah 123
Wright, Oliver 68
Wright, Patience Ann, 57
Wright, Reverend Allen 6
Wright, Reverend L.B. 13
Wright, Tom 73, 128, 129
Wyatt, Henry 113
Wyeth, Charles A. 13
Wylie, Oliver 16, 48

Y

Yancey, William L. 82
Yantley 42
Yeatman 91
Yellow Creek 71, 72, 74
Yellow fever 28, 49, 62, 122
York 1, 20, 29, 32, 40, 58, 70, 71, 73,
    91, 93, 99, 107, 114, 115, 120, 121
Young, Agnes 84
Young, Bennett H. 115
Young, Dr. 83, 84
Young, Dr. Elisha A. 83
Young, E.A. 15, 132
Young, George 127
Young, Joseph 83
Young, Mrs. Dr. A.E. 29
Young, Nan 29
Young, William Clarke Crawford 84

Z

Zeigler, Dr. W.H. 81
Zerney, Joe 112
Ziegler, W.H. 18, 20
Zimmern, J. 50, 102